Being Single
on Noah's Ark

Being Single on Noah's Ark

Leonard Cargan

ROWMAN & LITTLEFIELD PUBLISHERS, INC.
Lanham • Boulder • New York • Toronto • Plymouth, UK

ROWMAN & LITTLEFIELD PUBLISHERS, INC.

Published in the United States of America
by Rowman & Littlefield Publishers, Inc.
A wholly owned subsidary of The Rowman & Littlefield Publishing Group, Inc.
4501 Forbes Boulevard, Suite 200, Lanham, Maryland 20706
www.rowmanlittlefield.com

Estover Road
Plymouth PL6 7PY
United Kingdom

British Library Cataloguing in Publication Information Available

Library of Congress Cataloging-in-Publication Data:

Cargan, Leonard.
  Being single on Noah's ark / Leonard Cargan.
    p. cm.
  Includes bibliographical references and index.
  ISBN-13: 978-0-7425-5958-5 (cloth : alk. paper)
  ISBN-10: 0-7425-5958-0 (cloth : alk. paper)
  ISBN-13: 978-0-7425-5959-2 (pbk. : alk. paper)
  ISBN-10: 0-7425-5959-9 (pbk. : alk. paper)
  1. Single people—United States. 2. Single people—United States—Public opinion.
  3. Stereotypes (Social psychology)—United States. I. Title.
  HQ800.4.U6C36 2007
  306.81'50973—dc22   2007008424

Printed in the United States of America

∞™ The paper used in this publication meets the minimum requirements of American
National Standard for Information Sciences—Permanence of Paper for Printed Library
Materials, ANSI/NISO Z39.48-1992.

Contents

List of Tables

Preface

According to the tale of Noah's Ark, humans as well as animals boarded the ark in pairs—two by two—and so it has been throughout history. We live in a world of couples and their families. To be single in a couples' world is to be out of step with the prevailing belief about what constitutes a full life.

Although the function of marriage has changed over time, it has always been the means by which social relationships are organized. The result is that most people will want to—and will, in fact—marry at some time in their lives. This is true despite the current statistics showing a slight majority of singles in the adult population due to delayed marriage. For this reason, those who are single—either by choice, by divorce, or by death of a spouse—are virtually ignored. Their only meaning, as people, is derived from their relationship to marriage: They are the unmarried. The twin factors of not being married and lack of knowledge of this type of behavior has led to stereotypes regarding what it is like being single as compared to being married. Not surprisingly, most of these stereotypes about singles are negative, since all societies believe that pairing off is the preferred relationship and that those not in such a relationship must be selfish or sick. However, like marriage, singlehood is a complex experience that is different in each stage in the human life cycle. The title of this book refers to this relationship: What is it really like to be single in the world of the married? As a means of answering this question, the author asked a random sample of four hundred married and single individuals, among other items, about such issues as their satisfaction with life, activities, happiness, health, feelings of loneliness, sexual endeavors, and relations with their parents. In addition, the singles were asked about efforts to meet others, why they would marry, and whether there were any pressures to marry. In short, the questions asked, and the resulting text, attempt to get to the bottom of the question: Are the stereotypes regarding singles myths or realities?

Part I

A BIT OF HISTORY

Chapter One

The Traditional Family

INTRODUCTION:
UNDERSTANDING BELIEFS ABOUT THE FAMILY

In order to understand the commonly held beliefs regarding what marriage and singlehood are supposed to be like today, it is first necessary to compare those beliefs with the facts surrounding the two conditions both before and after the 1950s. The 1950s was chosen as the comparison point because the common public beliefs about what marriage and single life are supposed to be like were developed at that time. This was also a period when marriage was so idealized that 96 percent of all adults were married: the highest figure in history.

EARLY HISTORY: BEFORE THE 1950s

The term "traditional family" is actually a catchall phrase referring to the typical style of family life during a particular time period. The idealized nuclear family of the 1950s is the current "traditional family" model, and it is believed that this system should be maintained. Changes that are believed to threaten this system are opposed, often by law, and stereotypes abound about the evils of the change. But in reality, the "traditional family" concept has changed throughout history, always referring to the family structure typical in different societies and cultures at different time periods.

A brief glance at the early history of this country reveals that our concept of the "traditional family" was derived from the ancient Greeks, Romans, Hebrews, and Christians. All these societies had strong patriarchal systems in which women had few rights but were treated with respect as long as they performed their wifely duties and retained their virtue. This power differential meant that women had no citizenship rights, and married women had no control over either their husbands' or their own inherited property. It also meant that, in societies where it was accepted, divorce was solely a male prerogative. Christians saw marriage as a sacred institution instituted for God's purpose, and so divorce was not allowed for either sex. Again except for the Christians, this power differential also meant that premarital and extramarital sex was acceptable for males but not for females. Christians saw sex as a necessary evil endured in order to fulfill the obligation of procreation, so sex was acceptable *only* within marriage and *only* for this purpose. This meant that any type of birth control and abortion were also prohibited for Christians. As can be seen, the major factor in the "traditional family" was the power differential between husbands and wives. Perhaps adding to this power differential was the gender differential: There were usually more spinsters and widows due to males' higher death rate, their service in the military, and their emigration.

This "traditional" type of family structure began to change with the fall of Rome. Without the orderly processes of protection and trade provided by the Roman armies, societies devolved into simpler systems based on agriculture. Now protection would be provided by the former soldiers, who eventually took over the lands and created a system of serfdom. Property and power became the main assets of society and a new "traditional family" emerged to accommodate this new system. Marriage became mainly a business contract to protect and improve family resources. In such a marriage system, the kin group determined by blood relations took precedence over the nuclear family of husband, wife, and children.

In the settlement of North America, the main industry was agriculture, and so the "traditional family" model used was borrowed from the agricultural societies of the Middle Ages. The importance of agriculture meant that the whole family was usually involved in the system of production, so population growth was important for both society and the individual family. Both society and the family unit benefited in their desire for more children by the absence of effective contraception.

Agriculture was so important that property transmission was the main basis for marriage. Passion and the frivolity of love were not considered viable reasons for marriage. In fact, love and passion were actually considered taboo in considering the ideal mate. More important in seeking a mate was his or her ability to do the work necessary to conquer the land, which included providing a large family. Large families in the past might have been the result of the absence of birth control methods, but with the settling of the North American continent came an emphasis on population growth, and those not marrying at an early age and contributing to the needs of the settlement were denigrated.

This emphasis on population growth meant that a widow with children became a desirable asset: She had proven her fertility and brought with her inherited assets from her late husband. With family farms nearby, the extended family was an important asset.

Major changes in the development of this new "traditional family" occurred in the colonies, encouraged by the colonists' distance from parents, relatives, and the "mother church," and the Protestant Reformation of the sixteenth century. Distance meant that a number of the concomitants of the then-"traditional" system of marriage—the parent-dominated extended family—were weakened. Free choice in marriage quickly became an American ideal and the nuclear family began to take precedence over the kin group, but the implication that such marriages were based on idiosyncrasies such as romantic love would be misleading. Love was believed to come *after* marriage, as a duty of the relationship. Also aiding this movement away from the "traditional family" of the time was the absence of a strongly organized clergy. Another major factor was the changes encouraged by a number of beliefs held by the Puritans as Protestants. Protestants had accepted the Hebrew belief that sex in marriage was a human need as well as a requirement for procreation. For the Puritans, this meant that sexual pleasure was "God's way" of encouraging a harmonious relationship between husband and wife. Protestants also did not see marriage as a sacrament, so divorce was considered acceptable for such reasons as abandonment, adultery, bigamy, cruelty, failure of the husband to provide sustenance, or impotency. In short, divorce was seen as unfortunate, but it was believed that it could lead to the making of a good marriage in the future.

The new "traditional family" at this time also dealt with the roles of women and children in the family hierarchy. A carryover from Europe, the power differential between the sexes remained. The idea of rights for women seemingly did not exist: Women were considered by law to be the property of their fathers and husbands. As late as the 1830s, women still had to cede their income and legal control of their inherited property to their husbands when they married. Legally, they could not enter into legal contracts—except their marriage vows, which they could not escape through divorce. Politically, they also were not allowed to vote or hold political office. Improvement through advanced education was denied them, since they could not enter college. The result is that women were limited to being responsible for family welfare and household chores. In this way women became adjuncts to men, and their dependence on men was perpetuated; furthermore, the acceptance of a sexual double standard ensured husbands that their "property" was actually theirs. Female sexuality recognized this dual aspect of ownership: The virtuous woman saved herself for her property owner—her husband; but, on the other hand, it was admirable for a man to be a libertine. The result was a woman's cultural image was defined by these factors: domesticity, subordination, and virtue.

In appearances, the image of the "traditional family" was changing slightly, but not with regard to the power differential between the sexes. However, this power differential began to change at a very early stage of colonial development, when women began to demand more rights—rights they felt were due them as a result of their growing affluence, their importance to the work required to build a new nation, and their role in population growth. At first these demands were difficult to achieve since there were few economic opportunities for women, and their lack of education meant that they qualified mainly for unskilled labor. By the mid-nineteenth century, rapid industrialization and the establishment of seminaries and colleges for women began to add emphasis to their demands.

The onrush of technological development and the decline of agriculture by mid-century also meant that husbands now worked in factories as the family "breadwinners," and since opportunities for women were still limited, the wives remained home as "housewives." For the first time in American history, the role of housewife and mother became part of the "traditional family" image—an image that really applied only to the upper classes. For the working classes, technological change only meant that wives, like their husbands, would work in factories rather than fields. Despite restrictive legislation designed to encourage married women to stay at home, their participation in the labor force grew rapidly with more that a quarter of them in the labor force by 1919. Except for the added ability to seek employment and participate in public service, the cultural status of wives remained mostly unchanged. No matter what her age, work, or position in the world, the female—married or unmarried—was seen as an adjunct to the family. Also unchanged, despite increasing reproductive control, was the double standard regarding sexuality. But however small the changes, they apparently signaled a lessened need for marriage, as the percentage of adult singles would reach a peak of 46 percent in 1900 that would not be surpassed until the twenty-first century.

In this early period of the nation's founding, the position of children was similar to that of women. What was important was the role children played in contributing to the common economic tasks of survival, and so parents' love of their children was a secondary factor in "traditional family" life. Change in regard to the treatment of children resulted from their lesser need in regard to survival needs. Family size declined because children were no longer considered economic assets. There was also a movement away from physical punishment—which was historically a common method of disciplining children—to a greater use of such psychological techniques as deprivation, isolation, and shame (Langman 1987). Despite this movement away from physical punishment, the idea of children's rights remained nonexistent. An example of this is seen with regard to child abuse: The first child abuse report was actually filed by the Society for the Protection of Small Animals.

As can be seen, the development of an industrial/urban society led to a changed image of what was considered a "traditional family" in four broad ways, outlined in table 1.1.

Further changes in the "traditional family" came about as a result of first a setback and then an acceleration in family development factors. The setback was the Great Depression of the 1930s, which caused many couples to delay getting married and resulted in family disintegration as husbands left their families to seek work as vagrants and parents placed their children in custodial institutions because they could no longer afford to take care of them. The acceleration came with the economic improvements brought about by World War II. With the men going off to war and a resulting need for labor, the taboo against middle-class wives and mothers working was seemingly ignored, and their participation in the labor force increased rapidly. There was also a rush to get married: Many couples compensated for the delays brought about by the Depression and started families in the hopes of avoiding the draft. This rush into marriage led, in turn, to a dramatic rise in broken marriages at the end of the war.

Although it started with the stock market crash of October 1929, the effects of the Great Depression really took hold in the 1930s. During that period, almost two-thirds of the population had incomes below the poverty line, and families were uprooted or torn apart by a large increase in informal separation as men traveled long distances looking for work. Domestic violence and violence generally both increased, with a large increase in the murder rate—there were more murders in 1933 than in the whole decade of the 1980s.

Table 1.1. Changes in the Traditional Family

Change	Effects
Individualism	Marriage choice was now based on affection and companionship
Choice	Carefully supervised get-togethers of individuals began to give way to a means for selection based on individual choice and dating as a means of interaction without commitment
Primary Role	Care of children and household maintenance were considered the wife's main functions
Parents' Efforts	Increasingly centered on the rearing of children
Children	Birth control methods plus the economic liability of children meant that the size of the average family decreased significantly

Table 1.2.   Adult Population Changes: 1900–2006

Year	% Married	% Single
1900	54	46
1920	58	42
1940	60	40
1960	67	33
1980	60	40
2000	60	40
2006	49.7	50.3

Although economic conditions improved with the war, the stability it provided was limited as the returning soldiers often came home to find that it was difficult to reestablish their domestic authority with wives and children grown used to their absence. The result was that by 1945, one in every three marriages ended in divorce. Couples remaining together faced the difficulties of an acute housing shortage that forced them to double up with their own parents, whose ideas on child training were often not similar to their own.

THE 1950s: A NEW "TRADITIONAL FAMILY" IMAGE ARISES

The image that is currently considered the "traditional family" in American society was in fact a late phase in family development in the 1950s. It was only in this period that Americans began to identify the nuclear family as the center of all personal happiness, the fount of virtue, and the main source of childhood socialization. The nuclear family seemed to be an oasis, a welcome refuge from worldly troubles. It was a system newly promoted by advertisers, family therapists, and the movies: Cut any ties with the old system of networks that might compete for your emotional attention to each other. This new attitude was the result of a number of improved economic changes at the end of World War II.

The demand for consumer products denied during the war meant an economic boom and the availability of work for most everyone—except women. The same women who had done their patriotic duty by becoming "Rosie the Riveter" were now forced to leave the workplace so that the jobs they filled would be available to men being released from military service. Now it was the women's patriotic duty to stay home, bear and rear the children, and bake the apple pies. In order for this change in roles to take place, the belief became that men should work to support the family while women attended to the home. In short, a family system that had developed earlier for the upper classes was now promoted as the ideal for all families.

Throughout American history, women had always been seen as the dependent partner in the marriage system. The emerging norms after the war encouraged and added to this dependency, as women's wages were intentionally kept so low they could not support themselves on their own. A means of resolving this problem seemed to be marriage, which was in demand by those who had earlier delayed it because of the Depression and wartime military service. They saw themselves as more mature and ready to take on the tasks associated with marriage, and work was readily available to support a family. Nonetheless, many women, who had tasted a new independence during World War II, were unhappy about being forced to give up their jobs. True, it was a time when men and women were more equal than they had ever been—both in fact and in law—but it was still difficult for women to obtain high-paying jobs or divorce without stigma.

Also aiding the push into marriage for both men and women were the restrictive sexual mores of this time period. The value of virginity for women but not men meant that a double standard with regard to sexual behavior still existed—women were supposed to save themselves for marriage and hold the line against men, who matured earlier and were though to be more naturally sexually aggressive.

Another factor supporting the belief that marriage was a normal developmental task associated with early adulthood was various psychological books published at this time. For example, psychologists indicated that the tasks involved during this time period included selecting a mate, learning to live with a partner, starting a family, rearing children, managing a home, getting started in an occupation, taking on civic responsibilities, and finding a congenial social group. The sitcoms of this period implied that these tasks were not difficult to accomplish. Television shows like *The Donna Reed Show*, *Father Knows Best*, *Leave It to Beaver*, and *The Adventures of Ozzie and Harriet* were aimed at young couples who had married at a young age. Although most people recognized these sitcoms as not true reflections of family life, they were watched as an idealized, impossible-to-attain image of family life; they perhaps provided something to strive for. Sitcoms reassured families that there were good, easy means to deal with family issues, that it was okay to relate to their spouses and children in this idealized manner, that it was okay to buy those new ranch homes in the suburbs and move away from parental family influences. In sum, marriage was seen as the best way of providing economic security, providing emotional security, and raising children responsibly.

These factors led to the idealization of marriage: It got women out of both the parental household and out of low-paying, uninteresting work, it resolved the issue of sexual demands, and it seemed to be, according to the media, the "thing" to do. The result was that in the 1950s, women became focused on marrying and raising children rather than having careers outside the home. This meant that they would abandon attempts to go to college in order to advance themselves. The abandonment of higher educational goals meant that for the first time in one hundred years, the educational gap between young middle-class women and men increased, and job segregation between working men and women peaked. These demographic changes increased the dependence of women on marriage, in a reversal of the opposite trend that had been the case since the early twentieth century. These changing conditions also meant that the family was no longer an economic contract and marriage could be based on the idea of romantic love.

Early marriage also meant that very few young people spent any extended time in a nonfamily setting. Young adults moved from their parents' households into their own family households after only a brief experience with independent living—if they lived on their own at all—and they started having children soon thereafter. The result of this was that family life and gender roles became much more orderly and settled than they had been twenty years earlier, or, for that matter, than they would be twenty years later. For the first time in a hundred years, the average age at which people married fell, the age of first parenthood fell, the number of women remaining childless fell, and the divorce rate dropped sharply. The result was a rapidly increasing birthrate: The population of the United States had grown more in the seven years between 1946 and 1953 than it had in the previous fifteen years, and by 1964, 76 million babies had been born in a generation that would become known as the "baby boomers."

In reality, the marriage and family trends of the 1950s were more a result of socioeconomic and political happenings than a concerted effort to change family forms and values. In fact, it would be the children of this era of family stability who would later be the innovators of a sharp break with this "traditional family" of the 1950s. Modern lamentations of the loss of this family style, with cries for a return to personal commitment to family life, ignore the fact that it was mostly brought about by improved economics—heavy postwar investments by corporations in plants and equipment due to delayed demand and the Marshall Plan, a great deal of government assistance in the form public works, student loans, housing subsidies, and veterans' benefits. Economic fluke or not, the "traditional family" of the 1950s is a reminder of what marriage and family can accomplish: stable marriages, devoted parenting, and personal and social security. In short, the "traditional marriage" of husband as breadwinner and wife as homemaker can work very well—if the couple is satisfied with these roles and perform these accepted roles competently. But for those who do not accept these roles, attempts to shake them off are difficult, because they have been deeply imbedded through socialization and are probably impossible to escape completely.

The result of these economic and political endeavors was that by 1957, 96 percent of adult Americans were married, and, as noted, they were marrying at younger and younger ages than previously. Considering the fact that the 4 percent not married included those prohibited from marrying due to religious beliefs—Catholic nuns and priests—homosexuals, and those in institutions, it is easy to claim that during this period of time Americans truly believed in marriage: They were marrying earlier, staying married longer, and remarrying after divorce more frequently (80 percent) and more rapidly than the people from most of the industrialized nations of the world. By 1960 only 28 percent of women aged twenty to twenty-four were still single, 90 percent of all households were families, 86 percent of all children lived in two-parent homes, and nearly 60 percent of these children were born into a male-breadwinner/female-homemaker household—an all-time high. With most of the adult population married and the beginnings of a baby boom under way, America had seemingly entered a golden age of marriage and family, celebrated in mass-circulation magazines and songs. Indeed, the 1950s was the heyday of the nuclear family.

A seeming obvious question to ask at this point is: Why this emphasis on marriage? If it can be assumed that human behavior is oriented toward gratification of needs, then it would appear that marriage at this time was viewed as a main source of need fulfillment. Besides the economic and sexual issues mentioned earlier, why was there such a strong orientation toward marriage? An important sociological term is "socialization," and in almost every way people are socialized into the acceptance of marriage for fulfilling their needs.

In addition, most societies have prescribed marriage and family as the natural pathway to what is productive and moral in human existence (Chudacoff 1999).

Marriage, then, was presented as the only healthy solution to the needs of life and as the social norm by one's family and society. Adding to this emphasis on marriage and family for need satisfaction were the changes brought about by the dependence on the automobile and the move to the suburbs, since it meant a movement away from parents, kin, and traditional extrafamilial networks that had been a major source of need satisfaction. Marriage had always been part of the "traditional family" image, but in this golden age of marriage it became a must.

Although the emphasis on early marriage had begun to change somewhat in the 1960s by the growing need for education and getting established in work, which made being single somewhat more acceptable up to what was considered a turning point in one's age development—the age of thirty—the social expectation was that one should be married. This expectation resulted in a societal push toward marriage and a backlash against those who were still single.

Table 1.3.   Marriage Emphasis

Reason	Explanation
Reared in a Family	Develop the belief that this style of life is normal
Children	Taught that adulthood consists of roles related to marriage and parenthood
Parents	Usually want their children to marry and establish families of their own since they want grandchildren
Future	Parents also believe that their children will have fewer future emotional and psychological difficulties if they marry, since marriage provides the giving and receiving of affection, companionship, a steady sex partner, and help with the chores of daily living—in short, there is security and stability in being married
Couple Oriented	Living in a world of couples meant that all things good have meaning only in relation to marriage (Stein 1976)

Pushes came from the fact that most social behavior is oriented toward couples—from party invitations to seats at a popular entertainment event and even good seating in restaurants. Economic incentives to marry are seen in discounted larger-sized items as family size increases, travel arrangements, discounts on insurance, and in obtaining credit. Other economic incentives are seen in the job market: Since the married are seen as more settled and responsible, it is often easier for married men to find work or secure promotions. This bias toward marriage is also reflected in the implication of a request for information: "What is your marital status?" A more neutral request would be phrased, "What is your civil status?"[1]

In addition to these cultural pushes toward marriage, personal needs that are especially important in a society are characterized by impersonal relations: The availability of a significant other provides companionship and emotional security and so gives one a sense of completeness. Thus, both cultural values and personal needs lead us to the belief that marriage is the normal, accepted mode of life. Thus, it is not surprising that in the 1950s a survey indicated that 93 percent of Americans rated having a happy marriage as an important objective, and in selecting their top two goals in life, having a happy marriage far outpaced such goals as having "a good family life" (36 percent) or "being in good health" (35 percent; Waite and Gallagher 2000).

On the other hand, there has always been curiosity and a stigma about singlehood as a seemingly permanent lifestyle. For example, psychologist Bernard Glueck wrote in a typical essay about bachelors at this time what could easily be applied to all singles. In "Why Are You Single?" (1949), he stated that emotional maturity and marriage were equivalent, and those not marrying suffered from some kind of psychological defect. Therefore, the bachelor represented immature and infantile modes of thinking." He identified three basic types of bachelors: the "sexually incomplete person," who lacked the ability to achieve emotional independence from his mother or sister; the "excessively narcissistic type," who thought only of himself but also exhibited sadistic tendencies and was thus not suitable for marriage; and the "impulse-ridden" person, who was so poorly socially adjusted that it was impossible to complete any responsible task and thereby attract a marriage partner. These types of bachelors could be just as easily applied as spinster types.

For Glueck, marriage represented progress and a healthy life: "[T]he permanent union between the sexes . . . offers . . . the most dependable opportunity for the fostering of the culturally indispensable enterprise for transmitting physiological hunger and biological pursuit into human values and human ideals." As has been seen, stereotypes were developed in order to understand and explain the deviant behavior of the unmarried. Thus, men and women who "failed" to marry were denigrated as maladjusted or neurotic. Obviously, men who were bachelors must suffer from "emotional immaturity and infantile fixations," and unmarried women were biological inferiors who should be discarded as not very good matrimonial prospects (Ehrenreich 1983). A woman "might be brilliant, famous, visibly pleased with herself, successful in every way—but the judgment hung over her that she was a failure as a woman" (Ehrenreich and English 1978). Surveys taken at the time confirmed this negative attitude regarding those who were unmarried—80 percent of Americans said that people who did not marry were "sick, neurotic, and immoral" (Coontz 1992). And this view was often accepted by singles: The norm for the day was marriage, a family, and a home—this was normalcy—so they must be flawed because they were not married. Those not conforming to this norm were relegated to the margins of society, and in order not to be considered as such, people often felt obligated to get married.

Despite the developing changes in the reality of the "traditional family" of the 1950s, it is still being used as the model of what a family should be. But in fact, the current behavior of modern young adults with regard to family life is completely in line with what was considered the "traditional family" in prior periods. It is actually the decade of the 1950s that is aberrant when comparing family lifestyles in both prior and later periods.

THE 1960s: CHANGES IN THE IMAGE

The conditions of the 1950s that created the golden age of marriage lasted about ten years. Since the 1950s there has been a dramatic and persuasive weakening of the seeming normative imperative to marry, to remain married, to have children, to restrict intimate relations to marriage, and to maintain separate roles for males and females. However, when roles change and women move toward working outside the home and having more authority, husbands usually become more dissatisfied because the shift means they are expected to help with housework. Surveys have shown that the more housework a husband thinks he is doing, the less happy he rates his marriage. People may marry for passionate love, but many men also marry to be the center of someone's attention and to be taken care of, while many women marry for security and because of limited alternatives. By the 1960s, the older long-term trends began to reassert themselves. The 1960s was a period of criticism and turbulent change—change that was magnified by the development of the public's fascination with television. A number of historical events unfolded in the 1960s that challenged the basic beliefs of American life: Civil rights marches confused the public, since what was being demanded was supposed to already be the law of the land; two beloved leaders—President John F. Kennedy and civil rights leader Martin Luther King Jr.—were assassinated; and the war in Vietnam, which few people understood, became larger in scope, with more people involved, maimed, and killed, resulting in an antiwar movement and a nation divided. The ethical challenges to the war led to the questioning of other areas of American life. Major ones were the moral structure of family life and the role of women, both in the family and in society at large. In a sense, the development of the "hippie" communes and the women's liberation movement were protests against what was considered to be the rigidity and isolation of the nuclear household.

As noted, the happenings of the 1950s underscored the rigid gender role structure of the past. This rigidity came under challenge and began to loosen with the publication of Betty Friedan's 1963 book *The Feminine Mystique*. Women forced into marriage by the gender roles of the 1950s recognized that they were being stifled and became disillusioned with the limitations imposed upon them by marriage. The women's liberation movement became a prominent force in the idea that it was marriage and family roles that destroyed people. The result was a return of women to the workforce in large numbers in the 1960s. Adding to this push was the recognition that two incomes were needed to keep up with the emerging consumer lifestyle. Women's improving financial position led to even more feminist ideas and more challenges to the gender system, to the theory of what it is to be a female, and to the "facts" of family life: "the immutable maternal instinct, the sanctity of 'vaginal orgasm' as representative of female emotional maturity, the child's need for exclusive mothering, all the shibboleths of mid-century psycho-medical theory showed in the light of feminist theory" (Ehrenreich and English 1978).

Interwoven with these challenges to gender concepts were ideas that would lead to what was referred to as the "sexual revolution." Thanks to the development and availability of new types of contraceptives and the challenges to parental authority, sexual activity outside of marriage became more widely acceptable. An unforeseen development of this increasing openness with regard to sexual behavior was a move toward more openness by the homosexual community. These changes in both gender relationships and sexual openness led to greater flexibility in family relationships—cohabitation, open relationships, and single-parent families.

These changes also meant that it became more common to criticize marriage, and as a result more adults would be spending more time being part of a singles community. This, in turn, meant a different set of problems for those who chose to remain single for a longer period of time. The conditions of the 1950s had led to a large decline in the numbers of singles, so there were few role models. It would be necessary to develop new norms for this "new" lifestyle. But despite these changes in attitude toward marriage and family, the idealized image of the 1950s remained, so all these changes were viewed by society as negatives. Since the married still constituted the dominant portion of society, singles were still seen as a deviant community and so continued to experience alienation, discrimination, and a confused struggle about their the new roles.

THE 1970s: THE CHANGES CONTINUE

By the 1970s marriage was declining, as it had a century earlier. It appeared that the single condition was being recognized as an acceptable adult lifestyle for anyone for the first time in human history. The factors that led to this reversal of the marriage boom are varied and many.

The 1970s brought a number of recessions, and the resulting economic instability placed additional pressures on the changing family structure. Despite the continuing belief that men should earn a living to support their families and that it was better for wives to remain at home with the children, it was no longer possible for most families to live on the income brought home by one wage earner. The result was a large influx of mothers into the labor force. Some 41 percent of all mothers entered the workforce during this period. With this movement into the workforce also came a resurgence of women obtaining college degrees, which meant that women could now get better jobs with better benefits. The necessity of a college education and a job meant a delay in marriage until these tasks could be accomplished. The average age of first marriage spiked, and thereby raised the population of singles. The delay in marriage also meant a delay in having children and a decrease in their number. The result was a record-low birth rate of 1.7 babies per family during this decade.

This movement of wives and mothers into college and the workforce also led to changing responsibilities for husbands and wives—changes that placed a great deal of pressure on the marital system. Since women could now obtain better jobs with higher incomes, a change occurred in their marital role—they were now expected to be also "breadwinners." This meant that wives were now saddled with tasks both outside and inside the home. Despite the fact that their wives were now working full-time outside the home, husbands still seemed to believe that housework was "women's work" and did not share fully in these efforts. On the other hand, the income now being contributed into their households by women gave them more power in their relationships with their husbands, as well as a profound sense of satisfaction. The result was pressure by the wives for more equal sharing of household tasks.

This disparity in the roles of husbands and wives led to the development of the idea that what was considered a marriage was, in reality, two marriages—his and hers (Bernard 1982). Although the men complained about it, on the whole marriage was a more satisfying experience for them than it was for women. The marital home provided a lair in which to relax after work; meals, clean clothes, and other amenities; steady sex; and limited responsibility for their children. All this was theirs with limited extra effort. The result was that married men fared much better with regard to measures of mental and physical health than single men. On the other hand, the women had suffered an abrupt lowering of status from their courtship days; they were expected to contribute income to the family, keep the home, and conform to their husband's demands. For married women, this meant marriage was of less benefit to them.

The changing role expectations and mixed benefits from marriage led to a new source for the growing singles population: the divorced. The divorce rate practically doubled in the 1970s. For these new singles, there were two major complications: the single-parent family and reentering the dating world. There were also few role models for these singles, and few organizations to help them through these trying times. A result was a rush into remarriage, but few were prepared for the problems they would encounter in this new venture and so many were divorced again in a short time.

Societal changes also affected changes in mate selection. Prior to the twentieth century, meeting the opposite sex was more difficult than it is today: After elementary school, boys and girls usually went to separate schools, although most young people met at public gatherings such as church socials; their introductions had to be arranged through young women's parents; and there was little leisure time for them to spend together since most of the time their time was occupied with work and family activities. With urbanization, a rise in manufacturing jobs, and public schools came greater opportunities for young people to meet, and with the development of automobiles came the possibility and widespread practice of people dating, alone, away from the supervision of the family—as well as increased opportunities for physical intimacy. By the 1930s and 1940s casual dating had become the initial relationship that led to steady dating and engagement. This seems to have had three major results: For the time, mate selection was close to being an open choice; first intercourse became common during this "going steady" period, rather than during the engagement; people began getting married at earlier and earlier ages, so that the average age for marriage during the 1950s was twenty-two for men and twenty for women—the youngest average age for marriage in the twentieth century. Since most people marry, it could be said that the dating system has been a successful system.

Until quite recently, males controlled the dating situation, since women were expected to wait for men to call and make the date, plan the evening, and pay for it. Since the 1980s, dating has become less formal: both females and males now initiate dates and often alternate or share costs. Along with these changing roles in the dating process has come a change in the focus of dating from finding a marital partner to a system of socialization and recreation. The seemingly more difficult situation for finding a date in a rapidly changing social system has also led to the rather recent innovation of finding dates via newspaper ads, dating services, and Internet matchmaking.

Despite these changes, the fear of AIDS tends to lead to more monogamous relationships and limit the number of dating partners to a few. Another seeming outcome of the return to steady dating is the rapid rise of cohabitation. Since the 1970s, there has been a 400 percent rise in the number of cohabitants. This rapid growth means at any one time, 14 percent of all singles are cohabiting with a partner of the opposite sex. Cohabitation has become the norm prior to marriage, with 54 percent of first marriages starting out in this fashion. One might expect that this would lead to greater marriage stability, since couples have already dealt with the initial difficulties of living together. However, the statistics imply that cohabitation is not related to marital stability, since 65 percent of those who first cohabit and then marry go on to divorce.

As can be seen, the social process of dating has been undergoing change since it began as a system in which people came together as couples. It has also become more complex as lifestyles have changed: More couples increasingly date for longer periods of time, since more are delaying marriage or not marrying at all, and more older people are dating because they have been divorced or widowed. These challenges to and changes in the roles of dating and marriage made this decade a difficult one to adjust to, but it was also a decade for the expansion of rights for various disfranchised groups, including singles. In sum, what was previously considered as normal was being redefined.

The earlier decade had begun with a great deal of enthusiasm for promoted reforms in marriage and family life. However, the happenings of 1970s led to a great deal of disillusionment, since it is always difficult to deal with rapid social change. The traditional ethic—the Protestant ethic of the value of hard work and striving for economic security—was seemingly traded in for an emphasis on the "me"—a turning inward and a new emphasis on immediate enjoyment. This emphasis on self-gratification led to a host of organizations to foster it: communes, weekend communal retreats, and self-help support groups.

The results of a 1977 poll illustrate this changing social emphasis. Important prior to this time was hard work, saving and financial security, religion, marriage and having a family, and the recognition that one had to be prepared to make sacrifices for the children. The poll revealed that there was now a rejection of many of these values—there was less emphasis on patriotism, religion, savings and thrift, and having a family. Having children was seen as an option, rather than a must, and there was a lower willingness to make sacrifices for them.

These changes in beliefs brought about a series of debates regarding the "death of the family." Using the image developed in the 1950s, the pro side—the people who believed it was happening—cited such facts as the lower marriage rate, the decline in average family size, the rapid increase in the divorce rate, and the increase in unmarried-couple households and one-parent households. Although their statistics were correct, the pro-"death of the family" debaters were using low-indicator statistics to claim major changes. The alternative facts revealed that at this time, 89 percent of the population was living in families, 75 percent of families were living in married households, and 81 percent of families with children under eighteen had both parents present. In fact, more families had two parents in the 1970s (81 percent) than in the country's colonial days (70 percent); what divorce was doing then to disrupt families, death did in those earlier times; and it is doubtful that the mothers of that period were able to spend more time with their children than late-twentieth-century working mothers since they had to do all the tasks of the household without modern labor-saving devices (Bane 1976). The con side noted that the death of the family was not happening; they pointed out that the overwhelming majority (90 percent) of people still married at least once, the percentage of Americans who say they want to marry had been a steady 96 percent for the previous thirty years, there was a very high rate of remarriage, and most people claimed that a good family life was a very important goal in life.

What both sides of the debate were ignoring is that marriage and the family is not an unchanging institution. The changes occurring during this time and the resultant growth of the singles population meant a greater recognition of their numbers and its implications. In 1977 *U.S. News & World Report* proclaimed that "an emerging lifestyle center around the activities of unmarried men and women is adding a new dimension to American cities and towns," and a pollster added, "[T]his is a trend with enormous implications for business, government, and everyone else in our society" (1977).

THE 1980s: A SINGLES BOOM

The changes in marriage during the 1970s would also impact the unmarried population. The 1980s brought second thoughts about the many alternatives presented in the 1970s—marriage choices, no-fault divorce, and working wives, to name a few—and their long-term consequences. The move toward a more conservative political atmosphere did not seem to spur a return to more conservative social endeavors; for example, there was no change in the "new" theories about what it was to be a woman, and the divorce rate continued to increase, with a resulting increase in the number of children living in single-parent households. Seeking a scapegoat, singles were blamed for this seeming deterioration of "traditional" American life. The result was a backlash against all singles: the never married, who were thought to have put their own pleasures before society's needs; the divorced, who were considered to be selfish parents who had put their own interests before those of their children; feminists, who were endangering marriage with their high expectations and demands; and gays, who would not conform to the norm or marriage between a man and a woman.

By the end of this period, it would be difficult to ignore the facts of family change: In one generation, the number or people marrying had halved—it was now the lowest recorded in this century; widespread cohabitation reemerged—around 70 percent of women cohabited with their future husbands; the number of couples divorcing peaked; and the number of children born outside of marriage—no longer just a situation involving unwed teenagers—increased fourfold, to about one in three of all births.

As can be seen, the American family is not a singular concept. There are a number of of American family styles: single-parent households, unmarried couples with and without children, remarriages that bring together children with unrelated backgrounds, married couples without children, families in which both parents work outside the home, and families in which parents have switched "traditional" household roles.

THE 1990s: ANOTHER SINGLES BOOM

Perhaps, as an adjustment to the many changes occurring since the 1950s, marriage and family life began to stabilize in the 1990s. Rates of abortion, cohabitation, divorce, premarital sex, and single parenthood were holding steady, but some of the demands for change continued. For example, women's demands for equality continued, with a a major impact on both marriage and family life. Over the course of the twentieth century, women achieved legal and political equality, the right to divorce, and increasing admittance to college, but were still limited in regard to graduate or professional endeavors. Despite this limitation, there were more jobs for educated and married women. This improvement in the condition of women can be seen in a number of firsts occurring in the last thirty years of the twentieth century:

- The first female rabbi in 1972
- The first female head of a major surgical department in 1977
- The first female driver in the Indianapolis 500 in 1977
- The first female justice of the Supreme Court in 1981
- The first female vice-presidential candidate in 1984
- The first American female astronaut in space in 1985
- Females outnumbered men enrolled in college by 1999
- Females outnumbered men in such traditional male fields as law and medicine by 1999

Despite all these strides, it should be noted that women still make up a small percentage of the occupations noted, and there remain many occupations in which such breakthroughs have not occurred.

At the end of the twentieth century, women enjoyed greater independence in controlling their person and property. They could chose whether or not to marry, or to divorce an unwanted mate. They could also seek and obtain managerial and professional positions as well as political office. Society had adopted many of the goals of affirmative action, with positive movement for women with regard to economic success and independence. But despite these gains, men were still considered to be the oppressors of women, even though women outnumbered men by almost 10 million in the United States, outlived men by six years on average, and were the aggressors in fatal instances of domestic violence as often as men.

The effect of these changes in women's rights with regard to marriage and family life is seen in the demands of women: They remained interested in marriage and having a career, but were beginning to see marriage as a partnership and were willing to sacrifice some of their career desires to fit the needs of their families. Since they depended less on their husbands to support them financially, they began to make more demands of their husbands, something most husbands seemed willing to accommodate by sharing housework and child rearing and by agreeing that a necessary component to a good marriage is mutual respect.

Beliefs about singles, on the other hand, continued from earlier periods. The economic problems of the 1990s once again required a scapegoat. Because they mostly lived in urban areas, a large and growing singles population was easily visible to take on this role. The result was the continued alienation of singles from the rest of society. Adding to this alienation was the time lag between the establishment of institutional structures to support this type of lifestyle and their depiction on television as undeveloped, unthoughtful people.

As is usual with an alienated group, singles tended to blame themselves rather than a society still organized around marriage and family. For example, work systems were focused on family life, with family Christmas parties and spousal support benefits. In addition, women's salaries continued to lag behind those of men, placing women in the position of needing to marry in order to raise their standard of living. Singles also faced difficulties in climbing the corporate ladder, since they were considered to be not as stable as the married. What was true in the work world was also true in other areas of life. Religious life is centered on marriage and the family, so little thought was given to the needs of singles in spite of their growing numbers. Even in the family singles faced an onslaught of negativism toward their lifestyle, since their parents had been socialized with the belief that the task of raising children is not complete until they are "safely married."

Supporting these attitudes were stereotypes about living the single life:

Swinging: Singles were more likely to satisfy their sexual needs by "swinging," or bed hopping from partner to partner.
Lonely/Unhappy: Despite having more time and money to do fun things, singles were lonelier and less happy.
Unhealthy: Living alone also meant more heath problems.

All of these negative messages from the outside world indicated to singles that their lives were incomplete and that they would be fulfilled only if they married. This may explain why most singles eventually marry. In the meantime, because of the obvious bias of the larger community, singles turned to their friends in the singles community for acceptance.

Interestingly, singles were no longer an invisible group. There had been, over the years, a complete turnaround in the early marriage trend. Whereas in the 1950s a minority of both men and women between the ages of twenty and twenty-four were unmarried, in the 1990s a vast majority of them were still single. Their large numbers led to their being seen as a separate consumer market, so they were increasingly depicted on television, in the movies, and especially in ads. They remained invisible, however, to the institutions of society. It is here that their needs were still not being met, and so it was necessary for singles to continue to work for the changes necessary to correct this situation—in their own community, in the half-and-half world of cohabitation, and in the larger community of the married.

CONCLUSIONS:
THE "TRADITIONAL FAMILY"—IMAGE AND REALITY

This brief look at the history of marriage and the family reveals that these institutions have changed more in the past forty years than in previous history. This vast change might be summed up in just one word: freedom. People today have unprecedented freedom about whether to marry, whom to marry, and when to marry. People are freer to make these decisions since the shackles of social and economic pressure that once kept them marching in lockstep have been mostly cast aside.

The details of this increased freedom may vary from society to society, but the same trends are visible almost everywhere in the Western industrialized world. Only about 7 percent of all families in the Western industrial world now live in a "traditional" 1950s-style family—both parents living together with their children of that marriage, where the father is the breadwinner and the mother is a full-time housewife.

Today, a majority of wives work, as do a majority of mothers with children. It appears that there are other benefits besides increased income for these women. Depending on family preference, employed wives have better physical health, better mental health, and higher overall levels of life satisfaction compared to full-time housewives. Nor do the children of working mothers suffer negative effects: These children are, on average, better organized, more independent, and no more prone to problems than are children whose mothers do not work outside the home.

In the "traditional family" of the 1950s, marriage signified that a couple had entered into a stable relationship, and the marriage itself may have actually have promoted the stability since it constituted a public declaration of commitment. In this type of family, the married couple was actually only a part—and often not the main part—of the family. Having children was an expectation of marriage rather than a distinct and specific decision guided by emotional and psychological needs. Ties with children and other relatives tended to be equally important, if not even more important, than the marital relationship in the day-to-day conduct of social life.

The idealization of the conditions of the 1950s-style family meant that changes in these conditions would be seen negatively—and usually falsely. Thus, a quiz about marriage given to college students in 1988 revealed that the following statements were believed to be true:

1. A husband's marital satisfaction is usually lower if the wife is employed full-time outside the home than if she is a full-time homemaker.
2. Marital satisfaction for the wife is usually lower if she is employed outside the home than if she is a full-time homemaker.
3. In a marriage in which the wife is employed full-time outside the home, the husband usually assumes an equal share of the housekeeping.
4. In most marriages, having a child improves marital satisfaction for the couple.
5. Maintaining romantic love is the key to marital happiness for most couples. (Larson 1988)

A glance through the preceding false beliefs about the family also indicates that many of these changes revolved around the role of women. Like these beliefs, they are turning out to be false. A major example is seen in the increasing age of those getting married. The increasingly early age of first marriage in the 1950s led to the belief that women who delayed marriage were condemning themselves to a lifetime of being single. As noted, the average age of marriage for women at that time was twenty, so it was easy to believe that if she was not married soon, her situation would become hopeless. Of course, this belief was proven false as more and more women went ahead to obtain more education or worked longer in order to build a nest egg before marrying. These factors meant a delay in marriage, but not its impossibility. Today, the average age at first marriage for women with a high school diploma is almost twenty-six; with a bachelor's degree it is over twenty-seven, and with degrees requiring more education it is thirty.

Another belief was that the pursuit of higher education and a successful career was factor that determined whether or not a woman got married. It was believed that men were reluctant to marry women who were educated and independent. This may have been true in the past, but statistics reveal that this is no longer the case. Actually, more educated women are more likely to marry than women with lower levels of education.

A third related belief about women getting married later is that they were like those marrying very young—more prone to divorce. Again, the statistics do not support this belief with older, educated women; actually, the divorce rate for those women has been declining, while it has increased for those without a college education.

The impact of change also revealed that there had been a pervasive weakening of the imperative to marry, to remain married, to have children, to restrict intimate relations to marriage, and to maintain separate roles for men and women.

In turn, these changes have also raised the question of the need for the family. As noted earlier, in the past the family performed a number of important functions for both the survival of society and the sustenance of the individual. However, as societies changed, so did the function of the family. Prior to industrialization the family performed important functions in economic survival, education, protection, recreation, and religion. With modernization, people have becoming increasingly dependent on the bureaucratized system to meet their primary needs for food and shelter, as well as their secondary needs for education, leisure, religion, social services, and work:

- Hospitals and nursing homes have taken over care of the sick and the aged.
- Protection has become a function of various government agencies.
- Recreation changes mean that leisure has become age-graded, with specialized commercial facilities serving the different groups of children and adults.
- Religious education is now provided by various institutions, from parochial schools to churches.
- With their future no longer simply a question of following in the parents' footsteps, schools have taken over the teaching of essential skills and good work habits to the children.
- Meals are often prepared by fast-food restaurants, and in the home parents can serve easy-to-prepare meals made from frozen foods.
- Clothes are bought already made and are made of easy-care fabrics, and laundry can be taken care of by laundromats or dry-cleaners.

The result is a rising belief that the family was becoming obsolete.

The declining marriage rate has led many to a fear that the family is a dying institution. For the believers, this belief is seemingly confirmed by the dramatic increases in divorce, in single-parent families, and in children born out of wedlock over the past thirty years. Since all of these factors are believed to leave people worse off—the women and the children become distressed, the one parent is likely to be overwhelmed by the enormous responsibility that taxes the efforts and energies of two parents, and children born out of wedlock are in most cases born into poverty—it is believed that people should marry and stay married. On the other hand, blaming our social ills on the breakdown of the family is a simplistic analysis that ignores the changing nature of what is believed to be a "traditional family."

Other factors believed to be signs of family destruction are, in reality, one-sided assertions:

- What divorce is doing to disrupt families today, death did in earlier times.
- Living in unhappy two-parent homes can be more dysfunctional for children than living in other family situations.
- It is doubtful that yesterday's mothers doing housework without labor saving devices were able to devote more time to their children than today's working mothers. (Bane 1976)

The current statistics on cohabitation, divorce, and remarriage actually reflect changes in the system of courtship and marriage that now place a higher value on democratization of family values and personal fulfillment. The desire by many to return to the idealized "traditional family" of the 1950s is actually a contradiction of the currently accepted rules of domestic life. For example, few would want to return to a household in which the husband's role was that of breadwinner and the wife's role was taking care of the house, and few women would wish to give up the gains they have made in education, in legal status, or at the workplace. Nor would very many want to return to segregated gender roles. The price of these gains is that marriage has become a more risky venture in the maintenance of the family bond. Actually, most people probably approve of the greater freedom allowed in setting up alternative family forms and reproductive arrangements, but, as is true with most change, people need time to adjust to the new rules.

This examination of the history of the "traditional family" reveals that there have existed several types of marriage and family arrangements within the "traditional" structure, and perhaps these should be recognized as such. In marriage, monogamy—each individual having one spouse, and having children only with that spouse—is considered to be "traditional," yet the high rate of divorce and remarriage means that people are now engaging in serial monogamy—one spouse at a time, but more than one over time. A similar situation is seen in the family structure. The nuclear family—husband, wife, and children—is considered the "traditional family," yet the high rate of divorce means a large growth in the number of single-parent families, the high rate of remarriage brings about an increase in blended families, increasing life spans mean that the extended family with grandparents and other relatives is a reality, and the extended period before a first marriage or between marriages means more people are living in a cohabitated family situation.

In sum, the desire to return to a "traditional family" exaggerates claims about the past as an enticement to return to what was perceived as a golden age of marriage and family. In reality, neither the rising age of first marriage nor the frequency of divorce is eliminating the desire of the vast majority of Americans to marry. The cries over the death of a supposed extended kinship network ignores the fact that, through modern conveniences and a longer life span, children actually have more and stronger contacts with their parents and grandparents.

Concentrating on a "traditional" past denies the benefits of the present and ignores the diversity of families throughout history. The death of the family is not a reality; the family is, as it always has, changing to meet new conditions. As usual, with major economic and political restructuring comes a belief that there is a crisis occurring that could be resolved by returning to "tradition." However, the family values and forms that coordinated family life with older economic and political systems are out of sync with the realities of modern society, and returning to those "traditions" would not avert the so-called crisis in family values. In fact, it is believed that the reduction in family functions has been a good development, because it allows the family to perform the functions it *does* better. The family remains an important priority for most people. As society has become more bureaucratic and impersonal, it is more necessary to create an intimate, protective space in which personal relations can grow and thrive. It is the family that continues to provide the continuity, intimacy, love, satisfaction, stability, and support that cannot be easily found elsewhere.

Perhaps this is why marriage remains popular, despite the increasing number of people living single. The United States is one of the most marrying nations in the world: 90 to 95 percent of its population will marry at least once, most of these marriages will be long-term, and most of those divorcing will remarry. Although Americans now value personal gratification more than they did in the past, the high marriage and remarriage rate indicates that this relatively new value is merely another commitment to marriage and family. What now seems to be part of the marriage mixture is the possibility of divorce. The United States has been aptly labeled a high-marriage, high-divorce society. However, with mortality rates declining and divorce rates leveling off, couples marrying today are more likely to celebrate their fortieth anniversary than were couples of a hundred years ago. Today, the couple, married or unmarried, is at the core of family life, as economics have been replaced by romantic love and sexual attachment as the basis for forming marriage ties.

Another factor contributing to the change of the marital relationship is the decline in fertility rates. In the past, high fertility rates were required to compensate for the high death rate. However, as survival conditions improved, birth rates declined until the boom period brought about by the conditions following World War II. Since that period, fertility rates have returned to their declining ways. In fact, in all of the developed nations of the world, fertility rates are already at below-replacement level. In this regard, however, the

United States is somewhat better off thanks to the absorption of immigrants. Those decrying the "death of the family" cite this decline in fertility rates in their calls for a return to the "traditional family" of the 1950s. Ignored in this assertion is the fact that before the 1950s, fertility rates were declining—as the postindustrial world required fewer but more-educated workers, as more adults continued their education in order to meet this demand for more educated workers, as there has been a real decline in male wages and employment security since the 1960s, and as both parents work as the costs involved in raising children are constantly increasing.

The return to smaller, closely planned families and the increase in average life span meant that a husband and wife can now expect to live together in an ever-lengthening empty-nest stage of married life. It appears that marriage and family have become shell institutions—they are called by the same name, but inside their basic character has changed. These changes in marriage and family relationships mean that the terms "coupling" and "uncoupling" would be more accurately used to describe personal life. Perhaps a better question to ask than "Are you married?" is "How is your relationship coming along?"

Instead of looking at the vision of 1950s as the "traditional" system of marriage—one to return to as the ideal—we should recognize that what is considered "traditional" and desirable has always changed with changing conditions. Nostalgia for the 1950s is real and should be recognized as such, but in reality few would want to return to the past. The 1950s was, after all, an aftereffect of the Great Depression of the 1930s and the anxieties of the war years.

The government's experience with the Depression and passage of New Deal legislation meant that federal assistance programs were generous and widespread, and were a major reason for social mobility at the time. The 1950s was also a time when there was a clear "moral order" in the community to serve as a reference point for family norms, a time of more predictability on how people formed and maintained families, and a time when there were fewer complicated choices for both parents and children to grapple with. A majority of families during this period could dream of creating a secure oasis for their family since real wages grew more each year than they did in the entire decade of the 1980s, a majority of the population were now in the middle-income range, and it was possible to buy a home on only 15 to 18 percent of the average salary. During this time, there was a large increase in nonmarital pregnancy, but more than 70 percent of couples married prior to the birth of the child.

The 1950s did provide a more family-friendly economic and social environment and it did provide a greater feeling of hope for the family's long-term future. Yet a 2000 study of one hundred spouses in self-described "happy" marriages revealed only five wanting a marriage like their parents'. The husbands surveyed "rejected the role models provided by their fathers and the wives said they could never be happy living as their mothers did" (Wallerstein 2000). The reasons for this rejection are associated with the long-held American ideal of individualism: The increased individualism in the choice of a marriage partner has resulted in greater responsibility. It is this factor that led to the need for alternative means to evaluating a potential marriage partner on the basis of more personal desires and the arrangement of such from the carefully supervised and committed forms to one of its opposite—dating. Similarly, greater sexual permissiveness may really only reflect the fact that both females and males are biologically ready for sex in their teens; a rising divorce rate could mean a rising requirement for compatibility among individualistic desires; a lower birth rate could be seen as a greater concern for the welfare of each individual child, as indicated by a large decrease in the number of children being raised by relatives, foster homes, and institutions; and the realization that the traditionally segregated husband-wife roles denied them individualistic goals and ways of relating to each other.

It is also apparent that these changes have not endangered the desire for marriage and family. Despite higher divorce rates, there are more intact families today because of high marriage rates, high remarriage rates, and falling death rates. The result is that for the first time in history, most of the parent-child relationship takes place after the child becomes an adult and that the average family now has more parents living than children.

Despite the growth in the singles, it appears that marriage as we have known it is not dead, and it does have a future. In fact, there are few human relationships with a more assured future. As noted, at the height of the marriage boom in the 1950s, 96 percent of the adult population married. During the current singles boom, 90 percent of baby boomers will have been married or will marry. Jessie Bernard (1982) backs this assertion by noting that people will continue to marry because

> men and women will continue to want intimacy, they will continue to want the thousand and one ways in which men and women share and reassure one another. They will continue to want to celebrate their mutuality, to experience the mystic unity that once led the church to consider marriage a sacrament.

As has been true throughout history, marriage will change but some form of commitment will continue, and the future will include both marital options and conflicts, since no form of marriage guarantees utopia. One of these options will be that of remaining unmarried or remaining unmarried for an extended period of time, which seems to be the most popular current option, since the number of those who are currently unmarried has reached a new peak. Some would claim we are approaching a postmarital culture. Whether this is so is an unknown factor at this time. What is known is that marriage has become a *choice*. This being the case, it is important to examine these choices to see in what ways they differ from each other, and what are the myths and realities that we hold of each.

THE PULLS AND PUSHES TOWARD MARRIAGE

The Pulls

Approval of parents
Desire for children and family
Example of peers
Job availability, wage structure, and promotions
Legitimization of sexual experiences
Love and emotional attachment
Physical attraction
Romanticization of marriage
Security, social status, social prestige
Socialization
Social policies favoring the married and the responses of social institutions

The Pushes

Cultural and social discrimination against singles
Desire to leave home
Fear of independence
Loneliness and isolation
No knowledge or perception of alternatives
Pressure from parents (Stein 1976)

NOTE

1. It seems strange that singleness is usually defined as a marital status. It seems contradictory to define the term "single" as a marital status. On the other hand, the use of the term "civil status" allows for singleness to stand on its own rather than in its relationship to marriage. For these reasons, the use of the term civil status rather than marital status will be used throughout this book.

Part II

BEING SINGLE
ON NOAH'S ARK

Chapter Two

The Growing Singles Population

INTRODUCTION: WHO ARE THE SINGLES?

The word "single" is a label for a large and diverse category of people as a means of treating them on the basis of their one common characteristic—their unmarried status. It is a term coming into wide use as a replacement for the pejorative terms "bachelor" and "spinster." At the same time, the term ignores the fact that there are several categories of unmarried people—the never-married, the divorced, and the widowed.

The fact that singles comprise several categories results in a failure of singles to identify with one another despite their common status as unmarried persons. This can lead to difficulties in attaining possible common goals, such as the dispelling of the stereotypes that are applied indiscriminately to all of them. Interestingly, the married are also composed of several categories—first marriage, second marriage, and so on—but they are nevertheless all identified as married people who have similar values. The disregard for different categories of people under the umbrella of "unmarried" also hides the fact that there are different reasons for their growth in overall numbers. Therefore, it is necessary to examine each of these categories separately.

THE NEVER-MARRIED

The percentage of the never-married in the overall population fell throughout the first half of the twentieth century, reaching its lowest percentage in a period seen as the golden age of marriage—the 1950s—when 96 percent of American adults were married. As noted in chapter 1, a number of social conditions came together to produce this rise in the marriage rate and the bestowing of the title "golden age." Those going against the grain had a number of conditions applied to explain their refusal to marry: They were selfish because of their refusal to marry; they were neurotic and sick; they were social misfits; they were physically or psychologically unacceptable; they were not heterosexually inclined. It appears that it was not considered possible that one might freely choose to remain single beyond the age of expected marriage.

Starting in the 1960s, these figures for both the married and singles steadily reversed direction. By 1973 *Newsweek* proclaimed that "within just eight years, single-hood has emerged as an intensely ritualized—and newly respectable—style of American life," proclaiming:

> The term "single" usually connotes a lonely heart, a temporary loser whose solitary status was simply a way station on the passage to matrimony. The lonely hearts may still bleed, but for millions of others under 35 . . . , single-hood has become a glittering end in itself—or at least a newly prolonged phase of post adolescence. (*Newsweek* 1973)

This new attitude, like the idealized marriage of the 1950s, was reflected in television programs that glorified single life, such as *Friends* and *Seinfeld*, and in such magazines as *Playboy*. Many national magazines included articles—mostly positive—on singles: "Teaching Poetry Writing to Singles," "Going It Alone," "Goodbye to Marriage," and "Unmarried Lifestyle." In addition, a number of positive books about single life appeared at this time: *First Person Singular, Flying Solo, For Singles Only, How to Be Single Creatively, Living Single Successively*, and *Single Blessedness*, to name just a few.

The result was that the trend continued and by 2000 the marriage rate reached its lowest point in history—64 percent would eventually marry—and the number of never-married singles had reached an all-time high—28 percent of the population, an increase from 22 percent in the last thirty years. The main reason for this trend seems to be the rising age at first marriage from an average the 1950s of 20.1 for women and 22.5 for men to an average of 25.2 for women and 27.1 for men in 2000. Another telling figure about the young age for women in the 1950s is the recognition that as an average, it indicated that many women getting married in the 1950s were teenagers; it also means that in 2000 many were marrying at much older ages. It had been expected that the jump in the never-married population among baby boomers in the 1980s would decline as these people, socialized with the values of marriage, entered the married ranks. That this did not occur was the result of unforeseen conditions that brought about an increasing age for a first marriage. Another unforeseen factor in this growth in the never-married was greater female independence and entrance into higher-education institutions.

Since the biggest increase in the number of singles is in the never-married segment, and that it is the result of an increasing delay in getting married, it would appear that a good question to ask at this point is: Why is there a growing delay in marriage, and, for that matter, remarriage? As noted, there are a number of factors that spur an individual toward marriage: parent and peer pressure, cultural pressure that idealizes marriage and family, and economic security. In short, most people marry for love, the desire for children, and mutual aid. Within the post–World War II period of rapid social change, factors emerged that made marriage less imperative in accomplishing these goals. The process of industrialization greatly reduced the number of people in farming occupations, and so fewer people were needed to take on farming occupations. This development also led to a movement to urban areas, where there was less room for families to expand. With improvements in medicine came a drop in infant mortality and an elimination of the need to have a large number of children to compensate for those who might die at an early age. This reduced the child-bearing functions of the family. Increasing urbanization, the development of national highway systems, and the concept of social welfare reduced the need for mutual aid from the immediate and extended families; this need is now more often taken on, for both married couples and singles, by an extended network of friendships. The development of effective means of contraception reduced the fear of unintended pregnancy and so allowed for greater sexual permissiveness without the blessings of marriage. In a sense, the usual reasons given for getting married largely disappeared, and a new question arose: With companionship, domestic comforts, and sex available elsewhere, why marry? As summed up by a single in a singles organization: "As the benefits one can expect from marriage decrease in value, the drive for it slackens."

This lessened dependence on the family structure led, in turn, to other changes that encouraged adults to remain single for longer periods of time. Most of the reasons for this delay in getting married revolve around need and technological change. With the continuing rapid technological change came a greater need for education, especially advanced education. This, in turn, aids the delay in committing oneself to marriage. For example, in order to get a job, especially a "good" job, one needs to be better educated, which usually means delaying marriage until that education is obtained. Lessened dependence on the family spurred greater independence for the individual, in thought as well as in action. This is especially true for minority groups that were not previously perceived as such: the handicapped, homosexuals, and women.

The lessened dependence on the family also meant individuals could practice their sexual orientations with greater ease and eventually openness. Another important reason for this delay in marital commitment is a change in sexual relationships from a prescribed relationship within marriage to an acceptance of both premarital and extramarital sexual relationships. One no longer has to get married in order to be involved in a sexual relationship. The gay rights movement was an outgrowth of this independence. World War II led to more job opportunities for women, and they proved that they could do these tasks. However, they were released from these jobs at the end of the war and were forced to return to a dependency on men. For many, this was a clarion call to the idea of "women's rights," especially in advanced education and hiring practices. As a result of the women's movement, modern women are able to obtain better occupations and higher income, and they no longer have to get married to improve their standard of living—a changing situation since the 1950s.

In fact, *Newsweek* magazine ran a cover story in 2006 asking: "Who Needs a Husband?" The article noted that of the 43 million single adult females, 60 percent owned their own homes, they are increasingly likely to have children on their own (birth rates among single women in their thirties has increased by 15 percent since the 1960s), and it is no longer necessary to marry in order to have children. The seeming acceptance of nonmarital births has led to a growing number of these births: It is now about 33 percent—an increase of more than 14 percent since 1980. The lessened need for women to marry may have also lessened the need for men to marry, since they are no longer considered irresponsible if they do not marry.

Various other developments that have emerged fortuitously have also aided the independence of individuals to choose whether to marry. Conveniences such as the easy availability of fast-food restaurants and frozen foods and the greater ease of maintaining one's appearance via Laundromats and easy-care clothes encourage the trend.

A major factor aiding the desire to remain single longer was the emergence of singles as a distinct commercial market. Various commercial endeavors have begun to recognize singles as a market with a large discretionary income, since they do not have the expense of feeding and educating children. The result was the emergence of apartments, bars, nightclubs, dances, and packaged vacations for singles, all designed to make it easier to meet other singles and enjoy the single lifestyle. There has also emerged marketing to counter the effects of what are considered the negatives of being single—the supposed insecurities and loneliness. Perhaps the best example of this is the emergence of online and video dating. It has been estimated that some 16 million people have used these means of meeting others. So vast is the market that numerous specialized sites have emerged. For example, there are now sites for what is known as "guerrilla dating"—dating numerous people at the same time. Other individual advantages enjoyed by singles are the opportunity to explore by taking classes, dating widely, and trying new roles. A special advantage is the ability to relate to others as an individual rather than as part of a couple. Thus, the availability of greater freedom, self-sufficiency, and a supportive community has served as an attractive alternative to being married and as an inducement to remain single.

Another factor aiding the growth of singles is the development of a number of national support organizations such as Divorce Anonymous and Parents Without Partners. There are also numerous local programs held at colleges, churches, synagogues, and such organizations as the YMCA or YWCA on such topics as "How to Be Single," How to Achieve Autonomy," and "How to Meet People." There were even regional expos "On Being Single."

There are, of course, a number of personal reasons for the growth in the never-married: They have freedom to do things married people do not, they can be in control and do as they wish, and they can engage in numerous activities and strive for personal achievements. However, the never-married also must deal with negative effects: the need to plan and organize in order to ensure social contact, the problem of being lonely, the expenses of living alone, exclusion from couples-oriented social situations, feelings of inadequacy because they have not formed a partnership, and the stigma attached of being a single (Gordon 1994). Thus, the never-married are considered social misfits who are selfish since they refuse to marry.

Often-overlooked reasons for the rise in the number of the never-married include a reluctance to commit to a marriage lifestyle that has been criticized by both the mass media and scholars for its problems; the rise of the women's movement that was supposed to benefit men also, but for some became a turnoff with its accompanying hostility and resentment; and the "marriage squeeze"—the unequal ratio of men to women in the adult marital age bracket. Prior to 1940, men had outnumbered women in this category, resulting in a shortage of women available to marry. Since that time, however, there has been a shortage of marriageable men.

There are at least two major reasons for the disappearance of men available to marry: an increasing openness regarding sexual orientation and a deliberate turning to bachelorhood. Prior to the sexual revolution of the 1960s, many homosexual men married. Now they are free to follow their desired sexual path, which removes a number of men from the potential marriage market. The increasing age of marriage also indicates that a number of men have decided to forgo this option all together. By the year 2000 the number of men between the ages of thirty-five and forty-four who were not married had doubled since the end of the 1960s.

In part because of social changes and in part because of demographic changes, people are not marrying as quickly or as readily as in the past. The result of these conditions is mostly a delay in going into a first marriage. In fact, the average age of first marriage may soon pass what had been considered the watershed age of thirty, the age at which the preliminary stage of adult life is over and the concerns of singles, both men and women, should turn to other aspects of their lives (see table 2.1). This belief meant that aging singles were even more out of sync with their married peers and led to a seemingly stepped-up effort by singles themselves, their families, and their married friends to get them married off in order to relieve this situation.

What are the results of the delay in getting married? Obviously, both partners will be older, which could lead to several problems: Older women often face greater risks in pregnancy and childbirth; the couple will probably have fewer children, and this, in turn, affects the industries that supply baby food and clothes plus school supplies; the age difference between the parents and

Table 2.1.   Stages of the Single Adult Life Cycle

Life Cycle Stage	Emotional Process
Not Yet Married	1. Shifting the relationship with the family; restructuring interaction with family from dependent to independent orientation 2. Taking a more autonomous role with regard to the world outside the family in the areas of work and friendship
The Thirties: Entering the "Twilight Zone"	1. Facing single status for the first time 2. Expanding life goals to include other possibilities in addition to marriage
Midlife (Forties to Mid-fifties)	1. Addressing the fantasy of the ideal American family 　a) Accepting the possibility of never marrying 　b) Accepting the possibility of not having own biological children 2. Defining the meaning of work, current and future 3. Defining an authentic life for oneself that can be accomplished within single status 4. Establishing adult role for oneself within one's family of origin
Later Life (Fifties to When Physical Health Fails)	1. Consolidating decisions about work life 2. Enjoying fruits of one's labor and the benefits of singlehood 3. Acknowledging the future diminishing of physical ones 4. Facing increasing disability and death of loved ones
Elderly (Between Failing Health and Death)	1. Confronting mortality 2. Accepting one's life as it has been lived (Schwartzberg et al. 1995)

their children will be greater and so adjustment may be more difficult; and because older adults tend to be more set in their ways, the compromises required in marriage are more difficult to adjust to. On the other hand, studies have shown that being older and more mature at marriage makes couples more willing to work toward a successful marriage. An alternative for the thirty-something single is to be open to marriage but to also think about other options. This will make the future seem less hazardless.

It also could be that that the decline in marriage rates is not what it seems, since cohabitation is basically marriage without the legalities. The rapid growth of cohabitation as a lifestyle implies that it is replacing marriage as a first experience in shared living together. Forty-five percent of those now married began their life together in this manner. By the beginning of the twenty-first century, the number of couples engaging in this forerunner to marriage was 3.8 million, a jump of almost 1 million couples in a mere ten years, although about half of such relationships dissolve within two years.

Another factor affecting both the marriage rate and the cohabitation rate is the growing number of gay and lesbian relationships. Since these relationships are still considered taboo by many, it is difficult to get an accurate estimate of their numbers, but a clue to their rapid growth is provided by the organizations that are popping up as their numbers are increasingly recognized as a market. Thus, in the medium-sized metropolitan area of Dayton, Ohio, in the past thirty years the number of organizations has increased from one to more than sixteen, and these are only those that advertise in a local news and culture paper. Their variety is indicated by a few names:

- Couples of Miami Valley
- Diversity Dayton
- Friends of the Italian Opera
- Interweave
- Lesbian Book Club
- Lesbian/Gay Support Group
- Parents, Families and Friends of Lesbians and Gays
- Transgender Support
- Youth Quest Dayton

Upon inquiry, the author was assured that these organizations are not tiny.

Asked the same questions as the study sample in regard to stereotypes, respondents gave the following replies:

- *Family Relations*: Over the time period of the two studies, relations with parents improved considerably as their lifestyle became more acceptable.

- *Sexual Relations*: Gay men are seen to be more interested in multiple affairs, while lesbian women prefer serial monogamy.
- *Happiness*: Many people do not believe that those involved in homosexual relationships are as happy as other singles since there are a number of difficulties involved and most desire an ongoing relationship.
- *Loneliness*: Gays and lesbians are seen as no different than other singles when it comes to loneliness.

An added concern is the problems gays and lesbians face at work—federal laws do not provide them with job protection and many employers do not provide them with domestic-partner benefits, and although singles can adopt children, they are not allowed this privilege in many states.

Just as there are developments aiding the growth of singles, there are also false beliefs about marriage that hinder the move to a single status.

THE PULLS AND PUSHES TOWARD SINGLEHOOD

The Pulls

Availability of sexual experiences
Career opportunities and development
Exciting lifestyle and freedom
Psychological and social autonomy, self-sufficiency
Support structures: friendships, gender support groups, etc.

The Pushes

Boredom, unhappiness, anger
Lack of friends, isolation, loneliness
Obstacles to self-development
Poor communication with mate
Restricted availability of new experiences
Sexual frustration
Suffocating relationship, feeling trapped (Stein 1976)

THE DIVORCED

Throughout most of history, marriage was considered a permanent pairing and divorce was rare. However, the idea of dissolution of marriage other than by death goes back to the ancient Hebrews, Greeks, and Romans. Since these were patriarchal societies, divorce was a male prerogative usually granted on the basis of some misdeed by the wife, such as adultery or barrenness. As noted earlier, Christianity considered marriage a sacrament and placed greater restrictions on the dissolution of marriage. The Protestant Reformation transferred the regulation of marriage to the state, which meant that the state recognized the fact that marriage could be dissolved for certain reasons, including adultery, cruelty, and desertion. Despite this lessening of the binds of marriage, divorce remained rare until the twentieth century because the family was the core for the essentials of family life, a basic necessity, and marriage was primarily an economic partnership—a means of pooling resources in order to survive. Getting married also implied a commitment on the part of the couple, the permanence of "until death do us part." The premise of permanence may have arisen in the past because marriage was a practical institution performing many personal and social functions not readily achieved by the single person; thus, permanence could be promised since marriages were held together by economic necessity, external pressures, and fear of social disapproval.

Like the numbers of the never-married, the rate of divorce has also been increasing. As noted, the divorce rate in the United States remained fairly steady until 1960, then it surged by 250 percent in the next twenty years to become the highest by far in the industrialized world. That this occurred between 1960 and 1980 provides clues as to the reasons for the seemingly sudden increase in divorce rates. These factors are seen in the cultural change occurring at that time regarding obligation to others. The fact is that marriage today is based more on the desire for companionship, the need for emotional support, and, of course, love, rather than practical needs. This change in function means that marriage is a more difficult endeavor today, since these more personal demands of marriage require greater interpersonal skills on the part of the married.

Also during this time, compared to earlier times, there developed a firmer belief in individualism—in personal choice and self-expression. Personal choice meant greater freedom in mate selection, which resulted in higher divorce rates since there are higher expectations regarding this intimate relationship. Individualism also meant that marriage was seen first and foremost as a means to achieve personal happiness, which meant that people were far less inclined to remain in an unhappy marriage "for the sake of the children." Finally, individualism led to the idea of women's rights. With the women's movement came a surge by women into the workforce and less dependency on men for financial support.

In 1969 California began the destigmatization of divorce with the passage of the first no-fault divorce law; by 1985 it had become standard in every state.

The result is that divorce became easier to obtain and less of negative application for the individual. But by moving away from the legal standard of fault,
the country was also moving away from the moral standard of responsibility.

Another factor leading to an increase in the divorce rate was the rapid pace
of social change, which brought with it, not unexpectedly, changes in values.
It is perhaps unrealistic to expect each partner to adapt to this change equally.
One such change was industrialization and urbanization. These twins of the
modern age meant there were fewer social restraints on personal behavior
imposed by relatives, friends, and neighbors. Rapid change also meant technological improvements, which added to the greater propensity to divorce by
bringing about changing gender roles—which may be ultimately liberating
but have been difficult to adjust to—and by enabling couples to limit family
size via improvements in contraception. Smaller families make it easier to
divorce because there are fewer impediments to leaving. Finally, by adding to
life expectancy, technology meant that people had to adapt to longer periods
of rapid social change.

What all these changes add up to is the fact that more is being asked of the
nuclear family. In the past, relationships were founded on large families, long-
time friendships, and close communities to whom people could turn for help
to when things were not going well at home. As noted earlier, things are much
different today, due in part to the demands of a changing working environment that requires higher mobility. This has resulted in greater isolation from
family, friends, and community, and means that modern marriages must cope
with the missing assistance that was once provided by those relationships.
Now the couple must not only be confidant and lover to each other, but also
family, friend, and community.

A final reason for the increased divorce rate might be the recognition that a
number of beliefs regarding the effects of divorce are false, as illustrated in
table 2.2.

All of these reasons for the increased divorce rate could easily be placed
under the broad heading "personal factors," but this ignores other conditions
that increase the propensity for divorce: young age at the time of marriage,
hasty marriages such as occurred at the end of the war, lower socioeconomic
status, an increasing number of interfaith and interracial marriages, marriages
that take place as a result of unintended pregnancy, and having been divorced
or coming from a divorced family.

These are not the personal reasons individuals cite when attempting to
explain their own particular divorce. Most divorcing couples cite such factors
as a breakdown in communication, general dissatisfaction, and sexual failure
in their marriage. Of course, individual reasons for a particular divorce are
related to the changing conditions noted earlier. For example, the number-one

Table 2.2. Myths of the Post-Marriage Culture

The Myths	Explanation
Divorce is usually the best answer for kids when a marriage becomes unhappy.	This does not make sense. If you are in an unhappy marriage, your children will probably be better off if you divorce.
Marriage is mostly about children. With no children it makes no matter what one's civil status is.	Staying in an unsatisfying marriage is a sacrifice unhappy adults should not make "for the sake of the children."
Marriage may be good for men but bad for women.	The latest scientific evidence tells us that "his" marriage is far better that "hers."
Promoting marriage and marital obligation puts women at risk for violence.	Domestic violence statistics do not support this contention. (Waite and Gallagher 2000)

area of disagreement for couples at six months, one year, and five years of marriage is household tasks (Bader 1981), but unhappiness with the division of household tasks is related to the growing tendency for married women to work outside the home.

It is these changing values that have reversed beliefs held during the heyday of marriage in the 1950s. At that time it was believed that women who delayed marriage were condemning themselves to lifelong singleness. Since the average age for marriage at that time was twenty, it was easy to believe that a woman not married by the end of her twenties would never marry. However, with more women now attending college the average age of first marriage is increasing, and lifelong singleness is no longer the sentence for delaying marriage. A related belief was that women who delayed marriage in order to pursue advanced degrees were less likely to marry, but in fact, women pursuing advanced degrees are more likely to marry than women with lower levels of education. A final belief was that people who marry earlier or later than average had a higher risk of divorce—these were the people who are less mature and those who were believed to be the least competitive in the marriage market. This belief regarding divorce is still true for those marrying earlier than average, but is rapidly changing for those at the other end of the spectrum. As noted, the women most likely to be among those marrying late are those that are more educated, and so are those who have both greater maturity and higher earnings. The result is a declining divorce rate for these women while it continues to increase for those without a college education (Coontz 2006).

Table 2.3. The Effects of Divorce

Belief	Reality
Divorce has only two outcomes: winners and losers.	Actually divorce is too complicated a process and so the adjustment to it is a process that changes over time.
The pathways following a divorce are fixed and unchanging.	Actually, the path is not destiny but one based on decisions made as one progresses in time.
The big winners in divorce are men.	Two factors confirm this belief as perhaps the biggest myth about divorce—two-thirds of marriages that end do so because the wife desired it, and women usually do better emotionally than men after the divorce.
Children lose out after a divorce.	In reality, this may be a self-fulfilling prophecy. Children are expected to be scarred after a divorce and so define themselves that way. In reality, most children of divorce adjust to the tasks of young adulthood and appear to be no different from children nondivorced families.
The absence of a father and consequent poverty are the two greatest post-divorce risks to children.	This myth is based on another myth one that says a child is automatically psychologically adjusted if he or she with a father. Rather, these traits have to be nurtured patiently by an active father. A psychologically absent father before a divorce and a competent custodial mother can overcome both these negative factors. (Hetherington and Kelly 2002)

The result of the changes noted previously has been a growing divorce rate since the mid-nineteenth century. However, since the 1970s, when the divorce rate reached its peak, it has since leveled off. Most will not be surprised to learn that the divorce rate is near an all-time high. What many people don't know is that it is less than half the figure—50 percent—reported in the media. This is due to a misinterpretation of the statistics. In any one year, there are about half the number of divorces as there are marriages. For example, in 2005 there were 2.6 million marriages and 1.3 million divorces. If all these divorces came only from the number of marriages in that year, than the divorce rate would indeed be 50 percent, but the divorces in any one year come from all of the *existing* marriages at the time, not just those from a single year. Thus, the correct figure would be the number of divorces per hundred existing marriages, which is 24 percent, a much lower figure than those decrying the allegedly high divorce rate like to acknowledge.

Although the rate of divorce is holding steady, it is a major contributor to the growing singles population because it applies to a constantly increasing population and because the time interval between divorce and remarriage has been increasing. The divorced now consist of about 10 percent of the population. The never-married proportion of the singles population seems to have reached a peak for the time being, so the divorced now make up more than 24 percent of the singles population—the second-largest segment.

Divorce has been labeled "the great disrupter of family life," whereas, in fact, the number of families being disrupted has remained the same for the past century. What has changed is the cause of the disruption: What death used to do, divorce now does. The result is that family permanence has continued at about the same level for the past century. The slow general increase in divorce rates since the turn of the century has been accompanied by a slowly declining death rate, and this pattern has held throughout the century except for the 1950s and early 1960s. The change from death to divorce as the more likely cause of marital disruption brings with it a different point of view regarding that disruption: The public accepts death as a natural act, whereas divorce is perceived as a failure, and so there is a lack of institutional support for people whose marriages end in divorce. On the other hand, defenders of the divorce system see it as an expression of our idealism regarding marriage—it is better to dissolve a difficult marriage than to try to keep it together against all odds. This belief translates into the idea that people will have better marriages and more fulfilling family lives because they no longer have to put up with the dissatisfaction of a marriage in name only. Divorce, then, is an expression of our freedom.

Still, the question remains: Is today's relatively high divorce rate a problem for society? The appeal of the anti-divorce movement lies in the incontrovertible truth that divorce has serious and even dire consequences. There are usually intrafamily conflicts and steep income losses prior to the divorce, and this usually continues after the divorce. It also appears to many that in moving away from fault to no-fault in divorce, America has also set aside the moral standard of responsibility, resulting in a number of serious negative effects on the children. The one million children involved in divorce each year have higher rates of depression and other psychological illnesses, resulting in more suicides; they have poorer school attendance and are less likely to finish high

Table 2.4.   A Marriage-Friendly America

Suggested Reform	Reason
Get the message out.	Discuss the ways that we support or undermine marriage as an institution.
Get the facts.	Know and understand the characteristics of the people marrying or divorcing.
Create a tax and welfare policy that is pro-marriage.	The tax code has become significantly less supportive of both marriage and family.
Change laws to strengthen marriage.	The legal code is directly at odds with the social purposes and the cultural meaning of the marriage vow.
Restore the special legal status of marriage.	The courts and legal system need to develop a new model of the rights and responsibilities that come with marriage.
Enlist community support.	This would require marriage preparation and community support for all marriages.
Scrutinize policies for unintended anti-marriage consequences.	Governments should consider the potential effect on unwed childbearing when drafting policies.
Discourage unmarried pregnancy and childbearing.	Schools, media, sports figures, magazines, and models should stop glorifying and supporting unmarried pregnancy and childbearing.
Rethink domestic partnership.	The state of social science research legislation. sheds little light on the question. The answer depends on the extent to which gender matters. (Waite and Gallagher 2000)

school or attend college, leading to more joblessness; they have higher crime rates; they are more likely to become pregnant as unmarried teens; and they are more likely also become divorced (Galston 1996).

Single-parent families have always existed, but until the 1970s they totaled an average of 10 percent of all families. Since then, that rate has climbed to more than 26 percent of all families because of the increased instance of divorce (42 percent), long-term separation (24 percent), and unmarried women becoming mothers (27 percent). The relatively high number of divorces means that the single-parent family, although usually transitory, was the fastest-growing type of family in the 1990s and is more common today than ever before. In a mere thirty years, single-parent families have grown from 12 percent to almost 28 percent of all families. Not surprisingly, 87 percent of the children involved are living with their mothers. However, the number of single-parent households being maintained by fathers is slowly increasing, which results in a better income position for the family. Obviously, single-parent households have more inherent problems than two-parent households. In practical terms alone, they lack the personnel to fill all of the normatively expected positions in the family—a working single parent simply cannot give a child the attention that two parents can. Other problems for single parents include finding satisfactory housing in a satisfactory neighborhood due to their reduced income; juggling such factors as work, child-care duties, and home maintenance means little time for other activities; and living with no other adult in the house may lead to feelings of emotional isolation, loneliness, and powerlessness. The result is that the custodial parent usually experiences responsibility overload, since there is little recognition or help from society's institutions; task overload, since employed parents have less time to spend on child care, household tasks, personal care, and, perhaps, volunteer efforts; and emotional overload, which speaks for itself. These factors have led to a number of stereotypes about single parents and their children. According to some of these stereotypes, single parents are failures, ineffective parents, immoral, irresponsible, unreliable, and unhappy. This leads to children who are, according to the stereotypes, undisciplined, spoiled, unsupervised, deprived, and, because they wander the streets, streetwise with regard to drugs (Nuta and Jacobs 1981).

A popular monthly column titled "Can This Marriage Be Saved?" is read by 5 million people, who apparently believe that most marriages can and should be saved. Of course, if the columnist or society at large were really interested in saving marriages, they would support programs that deal with the changes noted earlier, such as providing an effective marriage and family course for people of all ages, visits to trained marital counselors to provide help resolving difficulties, and low-cost child-care centers for working couples. What the column is really about is a fear on the part of the public that the family is disintegrating. What the columnist apparently believes is that the "traditional family" of the 1950s is a stable and relatively unchanging institution. In fact, as the discussion in chapter 1 about the history of the family shows, the perception of what is considered a "traditional family" has always been fluid. And it is important to remember that the relatively high remarriage rate indicates that divorce is a rejection of a particular mate, not of marriage in general. Only about 20 to 30 percent of those who divorce never remarry, a figure that should decline with the increasing number of divorced people and thus more potential partners. Currently, about 50 percent of all marriages involve at least one person who was formerly married.

Since marriage is the main cultural belief of society, there is a column on how to save it, but no advice on adapting to divorce—a condition currently affecting 24 percent of all existing marriages. Such a column would therefore be helpful for individuals dealing with the effects of divorce, who have just gone through a rather severe blow to their self-esteem and now must reenter the world of the single—to relearn dating and how to relate to the opposite sex. This can be an even scarier situation for the long-time married than for the teenage beginning dater. Many times this leads to an initial outburst of sexual experiments, since it makes the person feel loved and cared for, and being sexually desired can be a boost to one's self-esteem. Of course, the benefits of sexual experiments may lead to the newly divorced being exploited, requiring care and awareness of this factor. Another problem for the divorced is the presence of children, who can complicate dating and courting. But in fact, adapting to being divorced may be easier than one would think, since there is a large population of divorced people out there to help ease the transition. Having experienced divorce, these people can and do respond with empathy. The readily available supply of people to meet, to interact with, and to date can add a boost to one's feelings—especially helping ease the feelings of rejection and failure.

Despite the seemingly high odds against having a successful marriage, marriage is still the "in" thing for most adults in America. Surveys indicate that 96 percent of men and women in this country say they want to marry, and 90 percent will eventually marry. Most of these people—three-quarters—still believe that marriage is a lifetime commitment that should not be terminated except under extreme circumstances. In fact, it is possible that the main reason for the rising divorce rates is the high expectations placed on marriage. This belief in marriage is supported by the remarriage of the 67 percent of women and 75 percent of men who have had failed marriages but go on to remarry. In fact, 20 percent of all marriages are actually remarriages.

THE WIDOWED

A third group must be considered in order to understand the magnitude of the growth of the single population: the widowed. An increase in longevity has resulted in an increase in this limited addition to the singles population, making up less than 14 percent of singles.

The death of a spouse is one the most major crises one faces, requiring an adjustment to both the emotional act of bereavement and its aftermath. Initially there is shock, numbness, denial, and disbelief; this is followed by pining, yearning, and depression. The third stage in the process begins a stage of recovery, with emancipation from the loved one and readjustment to the new environment. This is followed by identity reconstruction (Parkes 1972). As can be seen, over the long term there is generally a need for total restructuring of one's life. This is especially the case for the widow, who may find herself much poorer, socially isolated, and left without a meaningful life pattern. Widowhood is best perceived as a "roleless role," since widows continue to define themselves primarily as wives and mothers. Remarriage is usually not a way out of this dilemma, since there is only about one widower for every five widows. Since women have a longer life expectancy than men, as baby boomers reach old age it is expected that the widowed population will grow. These factors suggest that there a need to explore what mix of private and public efforts can fill in for these problems of widowhood and forge relations with social service programs (Hiltz 1981). In a sense, the growth in numbers of widows and widowers is also the result of changing values, as people take better care of their health and thus live longer lives.

THE COHABITING

Technically, those in a cohabiting relationship should be included in the singles category since they are, after all, not married, but in this study they will not be since their lifestyle is more similar to that of those who are married. Cohabitation is actually the fastest-growing type of relationship in America. About 10 percent of first marriages begin in this manner, as do one-third of second marriages. Not counting gay relationships, there are currently about 4 million couples in cohabiting relationships. This is eight times the number of couples who cohabited in 1970, and this figure is probably low since living together requires no license from the state.

Cohabitation usually follows a steady sexual dating relationship that drifts into a cohabited home for practical reasons, and many think of it as a trial marriage. The idea of a trial marriage as the main reason for cohabiting is especially true if one or both partners has been previously divorced and is fearful of making the same mistake again. A final reason given for cohabiting lies in the difficulties related to divorce and a philosophical belief that it is better to not be legally entrapped. Thus, it attracts those who are less traditional minded and therefore less bound by rules. In fact, not too long ago cohabiting relationships were referred to as "common law" marriages. The result of these beliefs is that a majority of cohabiting couples either break up or marry within two years.

Although those who cohabit generally have a liberated view of marriage, they usually have not thrown off the shackles of the traditional gender roles. Men tend to list sex as their major reason for cohabiting, and men who cohabit are more likely to be unemployed than are married men. Since cohabiting women are much more likely to be employed than married women, this may imply that some men see cohabiting as a means of economical benefit as well as a situation that ensures steady sex. On the other hand, women in cohabiting relationships may be as overburdened with tasks as working wives are.

CONCLUSIONS

Changing Values

During the past forty-five years, marriage has seemingly become less an expectation, and as a result, the number of singles has increased. The result is that the trio of the never-married, the divorced, and the widowed now makes up more than 50 percent of the adult population, versus a mere 4 percent at the end of the 1950s. An examination of the reasons for this trend indicates that it can be safely said that the decrease in the numbers of the married is mostly the result of changing values rather than population growth—a change from the large growth in the singles population in the 1980s, which was due to the baby boomers becoming of adult age. Now it appears that singlehood is largely due to an increasing delay in the age of first marriage. This delay in first marriage commitment is the result of a number of changing values.

As a specialized group within the singles category, the divorced benefited from many of the factors that affected all singles, but several value changes related particularly to them.

Marriage Still the "In" Thing

This chapter has discussed the reasons for the large growth in the singles population. Table 2.6 illustrates these reasons by presenting personal reasons given by the study sample as to why they are not married. The reason cited most reiterates the fact that marriage is still the "in" thing: 40 percent implied that they are looking for but have not found the "right one." The next two reasons are related to supposed benefits of being single: loving their freedom/independence (22 percent) and having too much fun (11 percent)—reasons far more likely to

Table 2.5. Changes Affecting the Divorce Rate

Factor	Effects
Acceptance	Divorce has become a reasonable alternative to an unhappy marriage.
Reform	Laws have changed to make divorce less difficult to obtain.
Secularization	The influence of religion in restricting divorce has declined.
Fertility	Fertility rates have declined.
Women's Role	Changes in the role of women make it easier for women to participate in the labor market and be economically independent.

The result of all these factors is that there has been an increase in divorce for the past century. However, divorces are not fatal—people tend to remarry at about the same rate that they marry for the first time, but are delaying this recommitment longer.

Table 2.6. Why Aren't You Married? (Three Choices)

	Current Study Never Married	Divorced	Combined
Love My Freedom (Independence)	23%	19%	22%
Having Too Much Fun	14	3	11
Lost the Right One	8	13	9
Never Found the Right One	42	38	40
Marrying Would Be a Wrong Decision	5	7	6
Other (Combined Replies)	7	19	12

be given by the never-married than by the divorced (14 percent versus 3 percent). Not surprisingly, the divorced were more likely than the never-married to claim they have lost the right one (13 percent versus 8 percent). Only one reason was an outright rejection of marriage and only 56 percent of the singles choosing this option were almost equally divided between the never married (5 percent) and the divorce (7 percent).

Table 2.7 also confirms this idea that not being married is often viewed as a temporary position rather than outright rejection of marriage. Most respondents in both subcategories almost equally said they would marry when they found someone to love (26 percent). Almost an equal number would marry to escape the believed bugaboo of being single: being lonely and would seek companionship via marriage (24 percent). The next two reasons appear to contradict stereotypical beliefs held about singles, since the third most common reasons for marrying was sexual satisfaction (15 percent) and raising one's income (15 percent). Despite the seeming acceptance of having children sans marriage, 11 percent would marry in order to have children. Again, there is only one reason that indicates a seeming rejection of marriage, and it was a very limited selection: a stupid choice (5 percent).

Table 2.7. Why Would You Marry? (Three Choices)

	Current Study Never Married	Divorced	Combined
Companionship	25%	24%	24%
Desire Children	11	12	11
Raise Income	16	13	15
Love	25	27	26
Sexual Satisfaction	15	14	15
Stupidity	4	6	5
Other (Combined Replies)	3	4	3

The Acceptance of Singles?

Putting together the realities about both marriage and singles leads to a surprising conclusion: Being single is more acceptable today and people spend much more time unmarried over the course of their lives. The result of this is that the negative stereotypes of singles as lonely losers and social deviants are giving way to the belief that singlehood may be more than a passing stage of adult life. *Newsweek* has claimed that "single-hood has emerged as an intensely ritualized—and newly respectable—style of life" (1973). This, however, may be an optimistic conclusion, since many of the negative stereotypes applied to singles remain, as does the discrimination based on these stereotypes.

Chapter Three

Singles in the World of the Married

INTRODUCTION: NORMS AND VALUES

All social systems must have norms and values. Norms are agreed-upon rules of behavior that allow the group, organization, or community to attain its goals—those values that are considered important to achieve. In America, individualism—being responsible for our own actions and ideas—is an important value. An example of this is seen in this country's great emphasis on competition, which usually means that government-proposed or -run programs are generally considered inferior to those run by private enterprise. Another prized value is that of individuality—we are encouraged to think for ourselves. In pursuing these values, however, it is necessary to follow norms—otherwise there would be chaos. For example, there are numerous norms that must be followed in order to drive safely and prevent accidents. Similarly, there are other norms to protect the public from those who do not follow the norms in seeking valued possessions. As important as norms and values are, however, they do change over time: The value of a kingdom was exchanged for the value of a republic in the Revolutionary War; the value of slavery was exchanged for freedom for all in the Civil War; and the value of equal political rights was given to women when given the right to vote.

As America has grown larger and more urbanized in the twentieth century, it has also become more of an organizational society. These changes have transformed all aspects of social life and required the country to put a greater emphasis on norms—on conforming to the rules, whether written or simply understood as the way things are done. In regard to the prized value of individuality, this means that it cannot be carried beyond certain limits—for instance, one's pursuit of individuality cannot infringe on the rights of others—without

being restrained by the norms of conformity. Exceeding these limits brings
about penalties, either directly, by perhaps going to jail, or indirectly through the
application of negative stereotypes regarding that behavior and a resulting
shame. The simultaneous emphasis on individuality and conformity can lead to
contradictions and even problems, since values and norms change and may
change rapidly due to rapidly changing technology.

It appears that the penalties of violation of the norms are more likely to be
experienced by minority groups, since by definition they are different from
the majority. Thus, ethnic and racial groups may be discriminated against
because their language, dress, food, and values differ from society's norms. In
a system of rapidly changing values and norms, other groups often become
recognized as minorities and subsequently discriminated against. For example, it is only recently that such groups as the handicapped, the poor, and
women were recognized as minorities that were being discriminated against,
albeit in different ways. Although the discrimination was obvious, it apparently was accepted, since the majority believed the minority was inferior and
the minority believed that little could be done about it. Thus, it is only relatively recently that efforts have been undertaken to lessen and perhaps eliminate discrimination against these groups.

Considering how long it took to recognize these discriminated groups and
deal with the issues involved, it is obvious that changes in norms related to
discrimination are slow in coming. The result is that despite their growth in
numbers, the unmarried are still considered a minority of the population. Discrimination against singles is seen in the deliberate perpetuation by society of
what is believed be the dominant system of couples. Thus, singlehood is
described as a negative alternative to being married, and as a means of encouraging conformity to the marriage norm, singles are discriminated against by
specific acts and by the application of stereotypes.

Of course, sometimes the stereotypes are positive:

> If we're young and attractive and urban, the magazines call us "singles." Singles
> are said to live in a joyful flurry of other singles, racing each other through the
> surf, rising on the corporate ladder, and waking up in the penthouses of singles
> of the other sex. The darlings of a consumer society, we spend our incomes not
> on mortgages and disposable diapers but on electronic entertainment, clothes,
> and exciting cars. (Holland 1992)

The social changes that have made singles more numerous have also made
it somewhat more acceptable to be single—but only up to a certain age. Society recognizes that it is now important to attain higher education in order to
achieve economic security and that it is smart to build a nest egg for future
expenses before one gets married, and it has become acceptable to delay mar-

riage in order to attain these enviable aims—but ultimately one should marry. The age of thirty now seems to be the turning point. Beyond that age, singleness may become uncomfortable for both men and women. The truth is that we still live in a world of couples and families. Singles are still defined only in their relationship to marriage: Singlehood is the absence of marriage. The state of being single is still seen as a transitional in one's path toward marriage. Marriage is the norm for the community: the sanctioned means of having an intimate relationship, having children, and becoming a part of the family-oriented community. The result, as noted earlier, is that most people want to marry and do marry, and even remarry after a divorce.

This view of marriage as the most desirable condition for adults has also been held by those who were aware of the growing numbers of the unmarried. In the 1980s, sociologists did not write about them except in articles on dating, which is, of course, a means to meet a possible future mate. Lack of contradicting evidence from the scientific society means that explanations, in the form of stereotypical beliefs, are offered with regard to this failure to follow the norm.

The listing of why people do not marry is, then, a reflection of the belief that everyone should marry and that everyone can do so if they really want to. Even if none of these reasons for not marrying still apply, an excuse for not marrying is usually offered: The failure to marry must have been an oversight. For the married, it appears beyond belief that remaining single might have been a rational choice.

These beliefs have also led to descriptions designed to degrade the single and their lifestyle:

> The single person is a "poseur, a squander, a narcissist, a wastrel." His lifestyle consists of dancing "the hustle in the apartment's house party room" and "loafing on his plastic horse in the . . . swimming pool." He "lives for lotions, balms, and sprays." He is also a "non-stop lover, drinker, laugher, and more (or less)." (Rosenblatt 1977)

Table 3.1. Beliefs Regarding "Failure" to Marry

Belief	Result
Socially Inadequate	Failed in the dating game or are alcoholic or with other issues
Immature	Unwilling to assume responsibility
Homosexual	Hostile to the opposite sex
Focused on Economics	Believed to be too poor to marry
	Marriage is a threat to career
Limitations	Geographic, occupational, or religious
Unfit or Deviant	Moving against the approved value that defines marriage as the most desirable status adults can attain (Bell 1972)

Even when so-called positive images of singles are presented, they must be degraded. Thus, football star Joe Namath was presented as a positive image of the happy, swinging single, yet at the same time his singlehood had overtones of immaturity, selfishness, lechery, and social irresponsibility (Libby 1978; Stein 1976). At the other end of the spectrum are the "lonely losers"—those who live by themselves and drink a lot. Some of these descriptive terms applied to singles have been replaced with other descriptions of their behavior, but the main idea—that singles are different from the married in more than civil status—holds forth. Not surprisingly, it appears that the singles themselves often accept these descriptions of their behavior. The stereotypical terms singles themselves free-associate with the word "single" are "sex," "happiness," "loneliness," "fun," and "alone" (Stein 1976); these beliefs are seemingly confirmed in this study.

Stereotypes about singles are also applied to females. According to these beliefs, it is single women who are "saved" by marriage, since this is the only way she can find love and sexual fulfillment. Thus, it is important for women to marry, lest they face emotional and physical deterioration. In the past, it was widely accepted that single women were so because they were unattractive, handicapped, or incompetent (Deegan 1969), so they were people to be pitied, ridiculed, disliked, and ascribed a low status—except when needed, such as in times of war. These ideas are rapidly becoming passé as more and more women achieve advanced education and get better jobs, as well as due to the efforts of the women's liberation movement to break outdated beliefs. Still, it seems hard for married people to believe that these women are single simply because they do not want to be wives.

As a means of better understanding these stereotypical beliefs, it is necessary to sort them out into more specific groupings, since their large number results in stereotypes that are entangled, overlapping, and contradictory. In order to be fair, a reply to these stereotypes will be attempted by those being alienated and ridiculed—the singles from the adjunct sample of the singles organization.

DEVIANT

Perhaps the single most common approbation leveled at singles is that they are deviant. Since marriage is seen as the norm, adults past a certain age should be married. Therefore, in a strict sense, this charge is true—they are deviating from the cultural norm of marriage.

At the same time, singles are and always have been a substantial proportion of the population, and it seems strange to label such a large minority as deviant. Population trends indicate that this minority is growing rapidly as a result of an increasing age for first marriage and a slowly increasing divorce rate; it is possible that before long the minority will be the majority. Still, it is doubtful that the beliefs associated with being a minority will shift to the married. It would seem, though, that the large and growing numbers of singles belies the stereotype of deviancy.

FREE, WORKAHOLIC, AFFLUENT

These three stereotypes are so interrelated that it is easier to deal with them as a whole rather than separately. Since singles are not burdened with spouses and children, they are perceived as being freer, with more time and money to do as they wish. But this also implies that singles are less responsible: They can, if they wish, concern themselves only with having fun and looking after their own interests. Their lack of responsibilities and community ties also means that they are perceived as irresponsible and immature.

Freedom is actually a feature shared alike by both singles and married people—the freedom to divide their time between fun pursuits, office work, housework, and social responsibilities. But without the obligations of spouse and family, it is believed that singles have the freedom to spend more time at having fun or at work, which leads to the stereotypes that they are workaholics and affluent. This ignores the fact that the single is also solely responsible for household tasks and has only one income. Sadly, the stereotypes concerning singles provide a hindrance to his work ambition: It is the married who usually get promoted, since they are seen as more mature and responsible, as they are the ones restrained by the obligations of the family. The married are also more likely to be workaholics since they have greater obligations.

HAPPY OR LONELY

This is a mixed set of stereotypes. On the one hand, singles are pictured as happier because they have more freedom to make choices, to get out more, and to have more fun. This implies that they have fewer worries, which indicates that singles should be happier than married people. On the other hand, singles often live alone and have no permanent companion with whom to share. Therefore, singles are lonely and unhappy.

In reply to these opposite stereotypes regarding single life, singles note that life is not usually either happy or lonely for anyone, single or married. Just like married people, there are times when singles enjoy themselves and are happy, and there are times when they wish they had company, but they also glad to have solitude. Loneliness may be a problem at times, but it is a problem accepted in exchange for the perceived advantages of solitude and being single.

IMMATURE

Since marriage is seen as a normal stage of adult life, the "failure" to marry must reflect some kind of immaturity. A man who does not marry is seen as being tied to his mother's apron strings, whereas the woman, being a spinster, has failed to experience life's adventures. The sign of immaturity may be a reflection of their lack of altruism: Singles are selfish and unable to share. To refute such beliefs, one merely needs to point to the many singles—past and present—like Isaac Newton and Ralph Nader, who were experienced, selfless, and obviously mature.

SEXUAL DEVIANT

One of the most prevalent stereotypes is the approbation singles are "swingers"—lecherously hopping from bed to bed. Conversely, their sexual needs may be satisfied by acts of selfishness, such as masturbation, or acts of sexual inversion, considered unnatural, as in abstinence. What is ignored in these allegations is that such behaviors have also been found to be quite extensive in the married population (Kinsey, Pomeroy, and Martin 1948, 1953).

These beliefs are reflected in the impressions of singles as compared to the married held by the sample in the current study (see table 3.2). Singles are believed to have more fun (24 percent), have more sex partners (16 percent), be happier (17 percent), and be more sexually satisfied (12 percent). But they are also believed to be lonelier (10 percent), less sexually satisfied (7 percent), more irresponsible (9 percent), and more immoral (5 percent). The statistics indicate that more singles believe that there are positives to being single. Whether these beliefs are correct will be seen in chapter 12, when the stereotypes are reexamined in more detail.

These stereotypes also reflect the different values believed to be true by the married and the single. For the married, important values involve legitimate sexual activity, long-term stable companionship, parenthood, sharing a home, and sexual fidelity. For the single, in contrast, important values include freedom from parental responsibilities, personal independence, personal privacy, more discretionary income, and sexual variety (Reiss 1972).

Given these stereotypes and values, it is clear that Americans are socialized with the belief that to be truly happy and fulfilled, it is necessary to marry and

Table 3.2. Impressions of Singles Compared to Married People

Current Study *Impression*	*Never Married*	*Divorced*	*Combined*
They have more fun	23%	24%	24%
They have more sexual partners	17	13	16
They are happier	16	19	17
They are more sexually satisfied	11	13	12
They are lonelier	10	11	10
They are less sexually satisfied	7	7	7
They are irresponsible	9	6	9
They are more immoral	5	5	5
Other	1	4	2

take on the responsibilities of a family. That this is the norm is seen in the efforts by others to help singles meet the right person and the joy displayed by parents when an engagement is announced and a wedding takes place.

CHANGING FUNCTIONS

An important question to ask at this point is: Why? Why bother to discriminate against what seems to be a harmless group of people who, for the most part, will eventually join the majority? To answer this question, it is necessary to examine the functions of marriage believed to be valuable by society and, therefore, should be perpetuated. Despite the loss of many functions with regard to education, protection, recreation, and work, marriage is still seen as the means for aiding and maintaining life by providing for such personal needs as affection and security, socializing children, and providing the "matrix for the development of personality" (Ackerman 1972). In addition, the values sought in marriage are among the deepest human needs, for which there are no reliable substitutes: love, loyalty, and stability (O'Brien 1973). It is for these reasons that marriage is considered a valued part of the natural order of life's progression and that those who do not conform to this order are believed to threaten it. This being the belief, it becomes necessary to encourage conformity via stereotypes that discriminate against those not conforming to the desired norm of marriage. Marriage is presented as the norm: the only healthy solution to life's dilemmas. This is despite the facts that show that marriage as an institution has experienced a number of problems. The result of such beliefs has been the relegating of singles to the margins of society. They are seen as people who have failed to make the positive move into marriage. All of these factors contribute to the single viewing life through this lens and feeling deviant.

THE RAPID GROWTH IN THE NUMBER OF SINGLES

Despite these stereotypes and pressures, the singles population is rapidly growing. A better picture of this growth can be realized by looking at the totals. An adult singles population that was a mere 4 percent at the end of the 1950s had ballooned to a majority 50.1 percent in only sixty years. This large growth means that it is important to learn whether the stereotypes applied to singles are true. In short, it is important to know more about this large population grouping—the singles.

As noted, changing social values are responsible for these growing numbers:

- *Age*: The increase in the number of singles who have never been married is mainly due to an increasing age at first marriage—25.0 for women and 26.7 for men, an all-time high.
- *Education*: People are investing more time in educational endeavors necessary for "good" work in the changing technological society.
- *Freedom*: An emphasis on personal freedom means that obligations are undertaken voluntarily rather than being dictated by tradition.
- *Personal Growth*: Related to the emphasis on freedom and the need for more education for better jobs has been a change in life's goals to personal growth and self-fulfillment rather than long-term commitment to marriage.
- *Acceptance*: Casual relations outside of marriage are now more generally accepted.
- *Being Set*: Older people tend to become more set in their ways, making marriage a difficult adjustment.

Similar changes have added to the divorce rate. The divorce rate had tripled in the past fifty years and divorce is no longer a rare and stigmatizing event. Currently, there are 1.2 million divorces a year, comprising 24 percent of all existing marriages. Surprisingly, this is actually a lower percentage than that in the 1920s, but much higher than during the golden age of marriage in the 1950s. Some think the divorce rate is not as bad as it seems, since 75 percent of those who divorce will remarry. This may be wishful thinking, however, since half of those who remarry will divorce again. The reasons believed responsible for this increasing but now stable rate are:

- *Religion*: The influence of religion has declined.
- *Changing Norms*: "No-fault" has become the norm for obtaining a divorce.
- *Labor Market*: More women have entered the outside labor market—a factor believed to have made women less dependent on men. Thus, in 2006,

60.7 percent of divorces filed were by wives versus about half that amount (32.5 percent) by husbands.

A COMPARATIVE STUDY OF
MARRIED PEOPLE AND SINGLES

Historically, the current period is seen as radically different with regard to marriage as the norm for society. In reality, this period is merely an extension of earlier changes surrounding male and female gender roles, the propriety of sexual behavior, women's rights, and the relation between the individual, the family, and society (Skolnick and Skolnick 1977). The Great Depression and World War II interrupted these trends. The postwar demographic, economic, and historical circumstances led to what was perceived as the golden age of marriage and family of the 1950s, with its emphasis on family togetherness, a baby boom, and the increased domesticity of women. Actually, the norms emphasized during this period were radically different from what had preceded them, and the reality is that the so-called norms perpetuated in this period were not the norm at all. The 1950s was an anomalous period in the century with regard to the norms of marriage. Nevertheless, the norms of that period are what we currently perceive as being the "traditional" way that the domestic system should operate.

Scientific studies follow a natural lag from gradual development of awareness of an issue, to the formation of hypotheses about the issue, to the testing of those hypotheses. This meant that the social scientists did not really become aware of the problems created by the so-called norms of the 1950s, and especially their effect on adult singles, until the 1970s. As noted, the strong emphasis on marriage in the 1950s meant that singles were virtually ignored except in studies on dating. So strong were the norms of that period that even in the 1970s, family sociologists "seem[ed] to deny that change was possible in family structure, the relations between the sexes, and parenthood" (Skolnick and Skolnick 1977). The result is that it is only recently that the singles population has been perceived as a distinct social entity with its own "characteristics, dynamics, and unique features" (Adams 1976). The result is that studies designed to uncover the facts about singles were not begun until the end of the 1970s. Even then, since singles were still not perceived as a viable entity, the studies tended to not be very scientific, drawing samples from single students with no control categories of married people with which to compare.

At the time of the original study discussed here (1980), serious study of singles was only beginning. Thus, the negative stereotypes remained dominant, with the resulting consequences of serious and often unperceived discrimination:

- *Deviant*: Because they are deviant, singles choose a nonviable lifestyle in fulfilling personal goals.
- *Immature*: Because they are immature, they have difficulty in obtaining loans of any sort.
- *Lonely*: Because they live alone, they are morose and lonely.
- *Selfish*: Because they are selfish and uninterested in others, they have difficulty making friends.
- *Unstable/Odd*: Because they are unstable or odd, they lose out to the married in seeking organizational promotions.

It is necessary to study both the married and the single because the stereotypes indicate that there are differences between the two groups beyond their civil status, to determine whether the stereotypes regarding singles are myths or realities, and to see if there are really any differences between the two in the categories noted. It is important to discover whether singles are actually more likely than the married to be different with regard to:

- *Family Background*: Does their family background lead some individuals to remain single or remain single longer?
- *Loneliness*: Is loneliness a reflection of the single lifestyle?
- *Health*: Does being single have a negative impact on health?
- *Leisure*: Do the leisure activities of singles reflect loneliness, or fun and happiness?
- *Sexual Behavior*: Does the sexual lifestyle of singles reflect a propensity to "swinging"?
- *Fun Behavior*: Do singles' choice of fun things to do reflect their overall happiness?

The answers to these questions will help determine whether the claim by *Newsweek* (1973) that being single is a "respectable lifestyle" is true or just wishful thinking.

CONCLUSION: ANSWERING THE QUESTION

In attempting to make this determination, numerous studies were examined and a major difficulty was uncovered: There were studies of the married, and there were studies of the unmarried, but there were no studies comparing the two categories in order to note their commonalities and differences. It is only through such a comparison that it can be shown what stereotypes exist, whether they are myths or realities, and whether the beliefs in such stereotypes are still widely accepted. If they are not, then the claim by *Newsweek* can be accepted.

Being located in the Dayton, Ohio, metropolitan area turned out to be a lucky break, since that area in the 1970s was considered by pollster George Gallup to be one of the ten typical areas in the nation. He referred to this area as "a barometer for the nation" (1976). Thus, a comparative picture of these two categories could be easily obtained without conducting a nationwide survey.

In order to obtain a proper sample from the designated area, a probability proportionate to size (PPS) sample of four hundred households was drawn from the Dayton metropolitan area, which consists of the eastern two-thirds of Montgomery County and the urbanized western area of Greene County. After the total number of households in this area was determined, it was divided by 80 in order to obtain an interval number. Selecting a random number between 1 and the interval number allowed for a random starting point. The next step was the selection of a block area in a census track, utilizing the previously mentioned random starting number and adding the interval number until all 80 blocks were selected. Starting with another random number, five households in each block were interviewed. To ensure the probable inclusion of all segments of the population, interviews were conducted in the evening or on weekends. Based on a previously determined order, an adult female or male was interviewed. Households in which an adult was not home or declined to participate were replaced by similar randomly drawn households in the same block area. In this manner, the desired four hundred interviews were obtained. As a means of preventing interviewer bias, the questionnaire was designed to be self-administered. Questionnaire administrators were present during this process in order to answer questions and pick up the questionnaires. Questionnaires were collected in person to avoid the selective response that often results when questionnaires are mailed.

Since this was a comparison study of married and singles, the questionnaires were subdivided into these two categories and then further subdivided into the groups that made up each category—married and remarried for the married, and never married, divorced, and widowed for the singles. However, it was soon discovered that there were too few responses from the widowed to make for a viable category and so were replaced in both studies. In the first study 29 percent of the sample were never married (114), 9 percent were divorced (37), 51 percent were in their first marriage (205), and 11 percent were remarried (44).

It was the intention of this comparison study to test the stereotypes and, in so doing, develop an accurate description of singles as compared to the married.

Table 3.3. Civil Status

Early/Current Studies	
Never Married	29/26%
Divorced	9/14
Married Once	52/47
Remarried	11/13
Singles Total	38/40
Married Total	62/60

This would allow for a determination of the reality of the stereotypes. It would also reveal the extent of discrimination against singles and the needs of singles as compared to the married, and determine whether the claim that being single today as a viable lifestyle is realistic. Wanting to be on the safe side, a null hypothesis of no difference between the categories was selected.

After the data were codified using several independent variables and tested for significance via chi-square, they revealed further questions that should have been asked of the singles. With an anonymous sample, it was not possible to return to this group for the missing data. To deal with this problem, a set of questionnaires was mailed to a large singles organization, Group Interaction. An unbelievably large response was received—almost 40 percent, for a total of 603 questionnaires. In conversations with this group, we learned the reason for this large response: It was the first time that anybody had paid attention to them as singles, an attention for which there was much thanks. As we wanted to get a personal feel for their responses, we asked a group of about twenty to explain the reasons behind their responses.

The study was replicated in 2005 when two reporters called to find out whether any changes had occurred between the two groupings in the past twenty-five years. It appears that despite their growth in numbers, little attention is given to singles as a group. This may be a positive sign of acceptance,

Table 3.4. Civil Status and Gender

Early/Current Studies	Female	Male
Never Married	46/57%	54/43%
Divorced	32/64	68/36
Married Once	55/65	45/35
Remarried	52/52	48/49
Singles Total	52/53	48/47
Married Total	55/62	45/38

Table 3.5. Civil Status and Education

Early/Current Studies

	<HS	HS	College	More
Never Married	8/5%	28/61%	38/29%	26/5%
Divorced	19/0	17/56	39/40	25/4
Married Once	12/5	32/55	25/29	31/11
Remarried	18/6	36/24	32/57	14/14
Singles Total	11/1	25/59	38/33	26/5
Married Total	13/5	33/48	26/35	28/12

but it also maybe a sign that in the concentration on the divorced, the growth of the major group of singles—the never-married—had gone unrecognized. Therefore, their differences, if any, and their needs were not being dealt with. Finding the answers to these questions required a new study to update the material from the previous study, and to note any changes that may have occurred and the implications of such. The new study was conducted similarly, and for comparison purposes was also conducted in the Dayton metropolitan area, even though it was no longer considered a typical American city. The composition of the new study found that 26 percent of the sample were never married (100), 14 percent were divorced (56), 47 percent were in their first marriage (181), and 13 percent were remarried (51). Except for the responses from the never-married, this breakdown followed the demographic changes that had occurred in the previous twenty-four years, with increases in the number of divorced and remarried responses and a decrease in the married responses.

Chapter Four

A Changing Awareness

INTRODUCTION: BECOMING KNOWN

Given their rapidly growing numbers since the 1960s, it might be expected that there would be a growing awareness of singles as an entity. It could also be expected that this would lead to a growing awareness of the needs of this population group and in the development of a market to fulfill these needs. Awareness of the growth and needs of singles in general should be even more emphasized for the divorced, since there are constant reminders in the media of their increasing numbers, resulting in increased—perhaps disproportionate—attention paid to this group. Observation confirms these expectations for both the never-married and the divorced. The result is a large and growing number of organizations aimed at dealing with the needs of singles. A glance at advertising reveals that there are now outlets for companionship in clubs, dances, travel arrangements, websites, and numerous other programs to deal with the needs of the singles. At the same time, the ads also reveal a number of discriminatory conditions that affect singles; for example, the single buyer, who purchases in smaller quantities, subsidizes the cost of family-size discounts at the grocery store and family discount tickets at entertainment centers.

CHANGING PERCEPTIONS AND NEEDS

Simple observation, however, does not answer the question of whether the needs of this growing population have changed and whether the public has become aware of their changing needs. In order to note these factors, an examination of the titles in the *Readers' Guide to Periodical Literature* was

67

made from 1900 to the current period. Since the *Readers' Guide* provides the titles of all articles appearing in the popular magazines each year under numerous headings, it was believed that it would reflect what issues were considered important in the past century and the changing nature of what was considered important in the different stages of that period. In the first study, made in 1980, the main focus was on singles, so only titles under that heading were examined. In the twenty-four years after that study, the large decline in the married population meant that it was now also important to add this segment of the population in order to find out whether the print media was aware of this changing population figure for the married and what they considered this group's attributes. It was also believed that what was happening according to the titles discussing the married population would, in a sense, reflect the titles discussing what was happening with the singles population and that it would help explain the married population's beliefs about singles and how those beliefs may have changed with the passage of time. In short, this examination of titles gives both a quantitative picture of these changing population numbers and suggests a qualitative picture of the changes affecting both the married and singles populations.

There are, however, three problems in using the *Readers' Guide* for this evaluation:

- It does not provide quantitative statistics.
- There is confusion about whether interests changed or only the headings changed, since the title headings have changed and are often combined into new titles as some areas of interest faded and new subjects entered the realm of awareness.
- It cannot take into consideration the change in awareness created by the march away from popular magazines to television.

For example, the heading "single women" replaced "spinsters" as a description for unmarried women in 1960, but it took another five years for the heading of "single men" to replace the heading "bachelors" for unmarried men. In this time period also came the recognition that some titles applied to both genders, so the heading "single people" was added to encompass unmarried men and women. The result was that there were now three categories of singles: single men, single women, and single people, instead of the two outdated categories.

Actually, there was always an interest in singles, even while their numbers were declining in the first half of the 1960s. However, the interest during that period was almost exclusively devoted to the divorced rather than to the much larger population of the never-married. Most of the titles on divorce were related to how to obtain one. Remember that at this time "fault" had to be found in order to obtain a divorce, and only a few faults were recognized. The titles that were devoted to the never-married did not recognize this category as singles but rather the fact that they were candidates for marriage.

The growing number of singles and a growing awareness of their differences brought additional headings dealing with them. For example, the 1970s brought the realization that more and more couples were beginning their relationships in cohabitation. Many believe that this heading really belonged under a marriage category, since their behavior and problems are more similar to those of married couples than those of singles. Adding to this belief is the fact that cohabitation is merely a different term for what was formerly known as "common-law marriage"—a category that never found its way into the *Readers' Guide*. One wonders why this was so, since this type of relationship existed in relatively large numbers for several groups of people.

Another addition at this time was the title of single-parent family. Although single-parent families were not new—they have always existed, as a result of the death of a spouse, divorce, and out-of-wedlock birth—it was not until the 1970s that the heading appeared. The initial recognition of single-parent families also led to the realization that such families were mostly single mothers, so the heading "single mothers" appeared—but not single fathers, since it was believed that there were few single-father families at the time, and mothers were the much larger market. However, this was a temporary oversight, and the category "single fathers" was added shortly thereafter. And the large numbers of women entering the outside labor force meant a large enough increase that this group deserved a separate heading of its own. These additions of new headings tell us that common topics that arise in today's discussions of the married and singles were recognized as such thirty-five years ago.

Also interesting in the examination of *Readers' Guide* headings are the topics involved under these headings. Most of the topics under the various headings deal with the positives and negatives of this condition (210). Perhaps unsurprisingly, there are more negatives than positives regarding being single (135 versus 75). Apparently living single is not economically easy, since a large number of articles dealt with the economics involved with this civil status (145). Since singles encounter other problems, there are a large number of articles giving advice on how to deal with these (111). Interestingly, traveling alone is considered to be so much of a problem that it is given a separate heading (49), but apparently traveling is not a problem for the married since there are no articles with this heading under the married category. A final category appears to be a catchall of lists of things singles should or should not do (95).

The gender differences found throughout the examination of family history are also found in this examination of the history of singles. Although not reflected in large numbers, being a single male is considered more a negative experience than a positive one (20 versus 5). A greater number of articles under both the positive and negative headings appeared for single females, but there were also more negative items (37) than positive ones (27). It appears that it is not difficult economically to be a single male since there are only ten articles for them on this topic compared with twenty-eight for single females. Similarly, under lists of things do, there were only seven items for the males but nineteen for the females. There were also more advice articles aimed at women than there were for men (25 versus 10), and there were no articles about traveling alone for men, compared with twenty-two for women. These breakdowns indicate that it was believed during this time period that being a single woman was more difficult than being a single man.

The topics listed under single parenthood indicate a similar assumption that this lifestyle was more of a problem for women than men. As noted, there were only 14 articles devoted to single fathers versus a whopping 156 devoted to single mothers. The breakdown of titles into subheadings indicates a similar discrepancy. With so few articles aimed at men, it is not surprising that there were no titles on this topic about single fatherhood, but for single mothers there were 19 positive reasons versus 28 negative reasons for undertaking this lifestyle. Similarly, there were 83 articles about the economics of single motherhood but none about the single fatherhood. Advice on single parenting appeared for both groups, but slightly more for the women (22 versus 14). In general, there are more negatives associated with being a single parent than positives (18 versus 9), information on the economics of this lifestyle but despite its difficulties not much (14). There is, of course, a need for advice on how to live this lifestyle (20).

The increase in the number of articles devoted to singles overall indicates a growing interest in the singles' population, but although improved, the general perception of being single remains negative.

Generally, the image of unmarried men and women has changed from the belief that they were swinging bachelors and old maids to more general comments on their lifestyle. Thus, the number of articles on the problems of living as a single—articles on housing, money, and work—increased from five in the first half of the century to thirty-five fifty years later.

The stereotyped titles describing singles may have been dropped by the 1970s, but the stereotypes associated with them continued as articles focused on the supposed negatives of living single—it was not a happy lot (13 versus 13), and a very large increase in the number of titles on how to find a mate—from nine to thirty-four in the post-1950s period, a 277 percent increase. An interesting change occurred when the topic of sexual behavior became less taboo status after the 1950s—there were no topics prior to 1950 and eight after, for an 800 percent increase. Although it was still widely believed that the swinging stereotype applied only to singles, articles dealing with this topic

Table 4.1. *Readers' Guide* **Singles Headings and Their Main Subheadings: 1980–2000**

	People	Men	Women	Parents	Fathers	Mothers	Totals
Positives	13	5	29	9	0	19	75
Negatives	35	20	37	18	0	28	138
Advice	20	10	25	20	14	22	111
Economics	22	7	19	14	0	83	145
Travel	24	0	22	3	0	0	49
Lists	12	54	25	0	0	4	95
Totals	126	96	157	64	14	156	613

rated a separate subheading within headings dealing with marriage, but not within the singles headings.

Although the number of articles on singles grew rapidly in the period covered by the current study, it was no match for the number of articles dealing with the much larger market of the married. There are so many articles dealing with the married population that they had to be subdivided into several headings: The main heading, "marriage," contains 938 alone, 50 percent more than carried in all six of the main headings of the singles category (610). The other subheadings under the marriage category include "married couples" (1,241); "marriage counseling" (903), which indicates that it is not easy being married; and "marriage laws" (784).

Surprisingly, while there is a "married women" subheading containing 163 articles, there is no "married men" subheading. Almost all of the articles under the subheading "married women" dealt with employment issues—a major issue, since large numbers of what were formerly called housewives have entered the outside labor market. And since marriage implies a couple, there is another heading recognizing this factor: married couples. Their subheadings are the same as those noted below.

Like the articles on singles, the articles on marriage can be divided into several topic areas. Some of the topics are similar to those found under the singles category, but not in the same order of preference. Interestingly, articles about both singles and married people were mainly about major issues—but they were different issues. Perhaps recognizing the issues associated with living on a single income, the major issue for singles was economics (145) whereas for the married it was the topic of marriage itself (205). Since being married usually means having a family, it is perhaps no surprise that the next major topic for the married is that of religion (157).

There is some similarity between the listings for singles and married people: Both have headings dealing with the positives and negatives of the respective status, and for both, the number of articles dealing with the positives is far less

Table 4.2. Changes in Singles Articles

Topic	Pre-1950	Post-1950
Living	5	35
Not a Happy Lot	13	13
Find a Mate	9	34
Sexual Behavior	0	8

than those dealing with the negatives. For the positives, the singles category had 74 articles whereas the married category had 89; for the negatives, the singles category had 138 articles and the married category had 159 articles. And there were actually far more negative than positive articles for both categories, since the negative numbers should also include the first major topic of each group.

CONCLUSION: A CHANGING FOCUS

Despite the growing number of singles after the 1950s, emphasis in magazine articles remained on the value of being married. As noted, in the first half of the century, when marriage was seen as the only option, it appears that it was unnecessary to publish articles on mate finding; only nine such articles appeared during this time. After the 1950s, the growing number of singles was recognized, and perhaps even seen as a threat to the dominant belief in marriage, resulting in a 58 percent increase in the number of articles on mate finding. A typical title from the earlier period was "Why They Won't Marry the Modern Girl," implying that if a woman altered her behavior, she stood a better chance of getting married. The emphasis in the latter period was an assumption that women really wanted to marry but had trouble finding mates, and the titles reflected this shift: for example, "Eligible Bachelors for 1965" and "*Bazaar*'s A to Z List on Where to Find a Man."

The increase in the number of articles dealing with the different aspects of single life means that the publishers of these popular magazines were becoming aware of the growing numbers of singles and their market strength. Yet they seemingly also continued to support the emphasis on marriage by a lack of articles on the growing number of singles. There were only two demographic articles on the growing numbers in the singles population. A related omission was the absence of articles on why people stayed single. Both these omissions seemed to be related to the continuing belief that marriage was the proper role for adults. By failing to discuss the reasons people choose to remain single and their growth in numbers of the singles population, the publishers were not encouraging singlehood as a viable lifestyle.

Chapter Five

Behind the Titles

INTRODUCTION: A THEMATIC REVIEW

As noted, the *Readers' Guide* lists the articles under several headings dealing with the various aspects of married and single life. As a means of understanding these headings more fully, it was necessary to first code the responses in the *Guide* to see if they could be grouped under various themes and then to count the number of responses under each to indicate how important the theme was considered. As expected, the themes changed with changing conditions over time and with the growth in numbers of the singles population—growth came in both the number of articles and in the themes being covered.

THE EARLY THEMES: THE 1980 STUDY

Only six themes dealing with singles were uncovered from the early part of the twentieth century through the boom marriage period of the 1950s:

- Why Am I Single?
- Home Relations
- How to Fill Time
- Sexual Problems
- How Are Women Related to Men?
- Mortality

It is not surprising that there were so few themes, since there were few articles. Additionally, these articles were quite limited in scope because they were written by singles, for singles. The result was that these articles usually gave excuses for their authors' being single. This being the case, a single sample article will be sufficient to represent each theme. Beginning in 1930 and continuing to 1980, there were more articles and so three articles were chosen from each decade. The singles boom in the 1980s brought a large increase in the number of articles dealing with singles and an expanding list of topics. This expansion meant that it was no longer sufficient to limit the search to a limited number of articles. Thus, the new study examines all the articles in order to ascertain whether this large increase in numbers resulted in any additions to or changes in the themes. The selection of articles to be analyzed from the much larger number of articles in the current study was based on the generality of the title and whether it was representational of a theme.

In the earliest articles, a substantial majority of the articles were about the single woman, or "spinster," as she was then labeled. The representative article, from 1930, deals primarily with the theme of reasons the author has remained single; it is, in fact, titled "Why I am an Old Maid." It was written by a forty-five-year-old using a pseudonym. She answers this question by referring to a vow made not to marry except for love. Since the one person she loved did not ask, the vow seems retrospective. This claim also seems inauthentic, since she could not tell the man she loved this fact. The second theme, home relations, is discussed in poignant description: her disappointed mother, her sympathetic father needing care, her happy siblings and their children. The next theme, filling time, seems a strange issue to be included among the themes—until one realizes that what is really being said is that it is necessary to find things to do since there is no preoccupation with the usual tasks of marriage and parenthood. Not being married, the author fills time by doing what she claims to be interesting and useful work. Considering the time period in question, it is not surprising that no mention is made of sexual inhibitions or sexual problems of any kind. Despite this omission, the author claims in the next theme that she has no problems having male friends and relating constructively with them. Perhaps the idea of one's mortality seems like a strange theme in discussing singles, but it is quite real since the single person usually has no children to carry on after she is gone. For the single person, immortality is summed up by one's career—if it is useful and she is not a drag on society. This focus on a never-married woman for this time period does not mean that the other types of singles in this era—unmarried men, the divorced, and the widowed—did not have similar concerns, only that these did not usually reach print.

The condition of unmarried women changed little in the 1940s. The author of the representative article was still called a "spinster"—a fact that she did not recognize since she lived at home with her parents until their deaths, when she was in her thirties. Interestingly, this belief may have been enhanced by the fact that her parents only trained her to marry. This fact crops up in her explanation as to why she did not marry: She did not fall in love and her mother was disappointed that she did not marry. This is probably the most common explanation given for not marrying, and the parental reaction was typical. Living at home, she apparently did not recognize the things she did to fill time and so does not mention this theme. Her means of dealing with sexual problems is to assert that they do not exist. She believes that "the world has gone mad on sex" and claims that there are doctors "who, if called in by a spinster, would diagnose a broken leg as sex starvation." Perhaps this refusal to recognize sexual problems is not so strange, since during this time period women usually associated with and talked to other women. The opportunities to talk to men were limited and not usually initiated by women. Similarly, the author does not recognize her mortality as a problem, despite her desire for a career with a prestigious position. This may be due to the fact that she was less limited in her outlook because of her business and committee relationships.

The 1950s saw an increase in the number of articles about singles despite the declining singles population. It is perhaps for this reason that the increase in the number of articles did not mean a change in authors or themes—they were still written mostly by single women about single women, and only two of them were written by males. However, these two give us a different viewpoint of the life of singles. For example, the bachelor does not give the simple explanation of not having found someone to love as a reason for not being married. For him, there are a number of reasons: bad luck, dedication to his parents, illness, lack of maturity, military service, being in prison, or religious differences. The bachelor retains home relations not by living at home but by bringing his laundry to his parents' house. Filling time is not an issue male authors seem to be aware of; only the female writers mention this theme. Sexual problems are again dismissed by indicating the belief that it is no different from the married who want no more children. Gender relations seemingly were improving, since the female author no longer saw a need to comment on the one theme specific to her: how women relate to men. Only the woman is concerned with her mortality. She notes that with no descendents, she must do things herself that will have a lasting impact. The men saw no need to comment on either of the last two themes.

The 1960s and 1970s saw the beginnings of a growth in the number of singles as young adults began to delay marriage in order to further their education, and toward the end of this period the earliest of the baby boomers became adults. This growth in numbers led to more articles and the addition of eight additional themes:

- *The Normality of Marriage*: The larger number of singles led to the questioning of the idea of the normality of marriage. Singles challenged this idea by indicating that parents should teach their children that marriage is one of two options, and that both are normal and have advantages and disadvantages.
- *The Variety of Singles*: A larger number of singles also meant the recognition that there was more than one type of single: There were never-married men and women, cohabitating couples, divorced men and women, single parents with children, and widows and widowers.
- *Changes in Attitudes toward Singles*: Attitudes toward this growing population also changed as singles began to be recognized as a commercial market. The result was a growth in products marketed especially toward singles: apartments, cruises, dances, parties, and programs.
- *Changes in the Image of Singles*: The above added attractions led, in turn, to a change in the image of singles from being lonely and unfortunate to an upbeat image of the swinging single.
- *Freedom and Responsibility*: Singles had the freedom to travel, to join organizations, and even change jobs. The availability of all these options and activities aided their sense of freedom and at the same time their sense of responsibility, since they had only a single income with which to pay for these things.
- *Money*: Like any other group, singles could be free and happy if they have money.
- *Loneliness*: Perhaps the biggest bugaboo about being single can be summed up with the word "loneliness." It is a constant topic of conversation and concern.
- *Security*: A different kind of problem, perhaps on par with loneliness, is that of security. The threats to security lie in their awareness that they are single wage earners and that there is discrimination against singles by corporations in hiring and promotions, by landlords for rentals, and in other important areas of life.

ADDITIONAL THEMES: THE 2005 STUDY

Over the past twenty-five years a number of changes have occurred concerning the singles population. In the late 1970s and early 1980s, the singles population increased sharply as the baby boomers became adults. As descendents of the golden age of marriage, it could be reasonably expected that they would soon join the married ranks since there had been no change in the ideology favoring marriage. However, the belief that it was necessary to prepare oneself for a future of responsibilities by first going to college, finishing college, and even perhaps getting a steady job before marriage was becoming more widespread. This led to an increasing age at first marriage, and the delay in getting married led to a large increase in the number of young singles.

With different attitudes fostering the growth in number of singles, it seems proper to repeat the 1980 study in order to see whether other changes were also occurring with singles as compared with the married. Like the original study, this began with an examination of the publics' perception of them by again examining all the article titles that appeared in *The Readers' Guide to Periodical Literature* under the major headings related to being married or being single. The main interest was to see if the same themes would be repeated, to note whether particular themes had been dropped, and to see what new themes were now considered to be important.

The first noticeable feature is the expansion of general headings dealing with singles. There are now nine headings: single men (138), single parents (97), single people (162), single women (190), single fathers (49; started in 1984), single mothers (298; started in 1984), singles market (4; started in 1984), single parties (3; started in 1991), and single adoptions (16; started in 1993). Under these headings are nine subtopics. These include:

- Lists
- Clubs/Markets
- Economics
- Health
- Parenthood
- The Negatives of Being Single
- Advice on How to Deal with the Negatives
- The Positives of Being Single
- A Catchall List of Other Issues

These new themes, of course, do not mean that all the older themes are no longer relevant, only that they have been subsumed under more comprehensive listings. As the current list of themes is examined in more detail with specific titles, this will become more obvious. For example, excuses are no longer necessary to explain why one is single; home relations seem to be a nonissue, as most singles now live in their own homes; and immortality is tied more to one's career than family name. Similarly, greater equality for women apparently makes relations with the opposite sex, or, for that matter, sexual behavior, less important. And the growth in numbers of the different categories of singles means that it is no longer necessary to note this factor. With singles now seen as a market, filling time is less of an issue as clubs and other activities are available. The normality of marriage and the belief that singles suffer from loneliness are dealt with in numerous lists about where and how to find a mate. Similarly, many other problems noted in the earlier study—such as attitudes toward singles, freedom, images, responsibilities, and security—now come under the headings of the positives and negatives of being single. After examining the themes from the current study, the two sets of themes will be compared to note any differences.

Examining the New Themes

Lists

As indicated, the main idea behind these many lists is that singles are lonely and would like to be married, so lists are provided of where other singles can be found and even who they are. First are the lists of statistics that explain to singles why it is so difficult to find members of the opposite sex. However, the statistics are often contradictory, for example, "Why Fewer Men Are Available to Wed" and the "Sex-Ratio Squeeze" versus "Statistics Are Not That Bad for Single Women" and "The Great American Men Shortage Is a Lie." These statistics may be interesting—as well as confusing—but they are not really the lists that singles are interested in. Considering their numbers, the main lists of interest are the ones that indicate where available singles can be found and who they are. This leads to numerous articles on the whereabouts of singles, and even names of the cream of the crop: "The 14 Best Cities for Single Women" and "The 10 Best Cities: Where the Men Are." As indicated, it is also important to be able to locate the best ones in various categories, and the magic number is ten: the "10 Most Wanted Bachelors in America," the "10 Most Creative Bachelors," and the "10 Hottest Bachelors." There seems to be a gender bias in these lists of bests, since none list the best single females and where they can be found.

A belated newcomer to these lists appeared in the 1990s with lists on how to attract and meet other singles. Considering the above bias, it is not surprising that these new articles are also directed at women: "For Women Only: 10 Ways to Attract and Hold Affection" and "12 Rules for Single Women." Finally, with an increasing average age at first marriage, it is not surprising to now find articles directed specifically to the older singles: "Good Ways for Over 40s Singles to Meet Others."

Clubs/Markets

Another result of the growing number of singles is the perception of singles as a market to be exploited. In the 1980s, the large influx of single baby boomers created a need for apartments for singles, as well as such amenities as dances, cruises, and weekend conferences. Recognizing the fact that the singles business is a rapidly growing phenomenon, there are articles that tell marketers and businesspeople how to cash in on it: "The Singles' Industry," "Digging for Dollars in the Singles' Market," "How to Start a Singles' Club." One new way to cash in on this market is through computer matchmaking, including sites such as Hurrydate.com, Match.com, Truedater.com, and Atlasphere.com.

Economics

Singles are often stereotyped as affluent workaholics because they have time to work longer hours and have fewer expenses because they do not have families to support. This stereotype is challenged by such headings as "Financial Challenges of Singlehood" and "The Money Side of Being Single." Perhaps not unexpected is that economic issues seem to be more of a problem for women, since a number of articles deal with welfare and women—"Welfare Feminism," "War on Welfare Mothers," and "Welfare Moms Organize"—but none on welfare and men.

Health

The health of singles is not to be overlooked, even though most are part of a younger generation. For example, articles deal with the ideas that "Living Alone Can Be Hazardous to Your Health" and "Living Alone Could Shorten Your Life."

Parenthood

It is perhaps surprising that a list of themes for singles contains the topic parenthood. But remember, the word "single" includes a variety of different types of singles, including divorced people with families. Additionally, an increasing number of single persons are adopting and having children sans mate. Thus it is not unusual for a single person to be a parent. With young people beginning sexual behavior at an earlier age and the seeming disappearance of "shotgun weddings," there are articles discussing "Children Having Children" and "The Tragic Cost of Teenage Pregnancy." Dating issues specific to the single parent include "Single Parent: Double Trouble," "Sex and the Single Parent," and the "Dating Someone with Kids Challenge." Despite these problems, the articles assure us that "Single Parenthood Is Okay." In fact, it it has become "The New Choice: Single Motherhood after 30." It is surprising that the same gender bias found in the other themes are also found in single parenting. Considering that it is women who bear and usually get custody of the children, there are—surprisingly—more articles on the problems of single fathers than single mothers. Perhaps this means that men have more problems than women with single parenthood: for example, there is "The Reality of Teenage Fatherhood" and "What about Teenage Fathers?" Of course, single mothers are more common than single fathers, but rather than publishing articles specific to their concerns, magazines publish articles dealing with problems all single parents—male and female—face.

The Negatives of Being Single

On the negative side, we are told that single living is "Single Jeopardy" and that such living is also "The Punishing Life . . ." These factors also tell us "Why We Are Afraid to Be Single." The answer to this question seems to be that old bugaboo loneliness: "All Alone or Just Single" or "Home Alone, Still Single."

Advice on How to Deal with the Negatives

It is not surprising that the largest group of titles comes under the heading of advice on how to cope with the problems of living single. The articles on advice contained four main subjects: living and making it alone, how to deal with being alone by dating and other measures, dealing with the expenses of single life, and single parenthood. The articles on living alone imply that it is a problem, but more so for women: there is advice on making it "Without a Man," but none describing how to make it without a woman. Although there is "Help for the Single Man," readers are also told "How to be Happy Alone." If one does not like being alone, there are means of dealing with this problem. In fact, there are "Five Ways to Win" and that one can do so by going "Beyond the Bar Scene." Meeting others seems to be more of a problem for women than men, since there is advice about "How to Meet a Man," but not how to meet a woman. Help for the dating lifestyle is available in "Six Ways to Enjoy the Adventure," and "Financing the Single Way of Life" gives advice on economics. With a trend toward solo parenting, there is a need for advice for "Mothers on Their Own" and even "Help for the Supermom"—but no such help for the single father. Interestingly, these articles are not necessarily written based on marriage as the ultimate goal. A number of articles discuss meeting others, but it is not until the new century that information appears on how to find a mate: "Want a Spouse? Read This Book."

The Positives of Being Single

Despite the problems associated with single life and the need for advice on how to deal with this lifestyle, more and more people are staying single for longer and longer periods. This raises the question: Why? What are the positives of being single? For one, it allows for "Being Myself" and it is also means that I am "Betting on Myself" and that living alone is not necessarily a bad experience since there are those who have found "Living Alone and Liking It" and even "Liking it Too Much." As a single female, it is "A Declaration of Female Independence" and it also means that I am "Making It without a Man" and "That We Are Not 'Old Maids.'"

A Catchall List of Other Issues

The final category to be examined in the list of topics consists of topics that do not easily fit into the other themes. Some of these concern men but are probably of interest to women: "Your Basic Bachelor," "Who Has a Bachelor Pad," and "The Bachelor Speaks Out," including "Confessions of a Persistent Playboy" and "The Secrets of a Single Man." Since women are believed to be "saved" by marriage, it is not surprising that articles appear justifying the single lifestyle: "New Look in Old Maids" and "Play Homage to the Spinster," and even the "Other Women." Any new path requires learning the ropes, and so articles discuss "Pleasures and Perils of Being Single Today" and "What's Best, Scary about Living Alone." Because not everyone will remain single forever, some articles focus on marriage: "Psyched to Get Married" and "Why are you Still Single?" Even couples sound off on the issue of being single: "Couples Views Singles: Who Is Better Off?" Apparently, the decision on staying single is being made in the affirmative since "More are Single Longer" and the experts say that the "U.S. May Become a Society of Singles." You finally decide that it is okay to stay single but that you still would like to be a parent. This decision will get you involved in the big debate of the 1990s: Dan Quayle versus Murphy Brown.

A COMPARISON OF THE THEMES

It is interesting to note the differences and similarities between the two lists of themes dealing with singles—one developed from the articles before the 1980s in the first study and one from the 1980s until today in the current study. Many themes have been considered important more or less continuously, while others have dropped out of sight and others have become important as the issues dealt with by singles have changed.

The themes that have been continuously important include:

• *Marriage as the Norm*: The norm of marriage as the role for adults can be expected since marriage is still the cultural norm in society, and the much larger market.

- *Variety of Singles*: The recognition that there are a variety of singles—the never-married, the divorced, single parents, and the widowed.
- *Image*: Changes in the image of single—such terms as "spinster," "old maid," and even "bachelor" have disappeared, and singles are no longer seen as lonely or defective.
- *Economic Issues*: In one respect singles are no different from the married: They have money worries.
- *The Negatives*: Loneliness is still a major issue, but this is not the only problem for singles. Because of this, loneliness and other problems have been lumped into one category labeled the "negatives" of single life.
- *The Positives*: The good points of living single—like "freedom" and "responsibility"—have also been combined into a single theme dealing with the positives of this lifestyle.
- *New Topics*: The carryover themes did include some new topics within these theme areas such as safety and security.

An Important Addition

Since the actual studies were a comparison of singles with the married in several areas of life, it was important to also see what the writers of the current period considered important issues for the married and to note the differences in themes. This was not done in the earlier study due to the lopsided majority of articles aimed at the married. Thus, it was easier and more accurate to do a comparison of married and single titles with the increased number of titles appearing under the singles headings during the current study period.

Because the married population is much larger, there are more headings needed to cover the topic, but it is also important to note that many of these headings are quite limited in scope and in the number of articles:

- Age Starting in the Late 1990s
- Counseling
- Couples
- Customs/Rites
- Laws
- Marriage
- Priests
- Proposals
- Women

Also new in this period and even more limited were some titles that did not last very long:

- Mixed Marriages (only in the early 1980s)
- Common-Law Marriage (only in the early 1980s)

In common, the topics in both the singles and married articles contained lists, the problems of economics, family, sex, negatives, advice, positives, and catchall.

Lists

Both categories contain lists, but that is where the similarity ends. Whereas the lists for the singles are the names of available singles and the cities in which they can be found, the lists for the married have a negative slant, dealing with ways to improve marriage. Once again, ten seems to be the magic number: "10 Ways to Improve Your Marriage" and "10 Ways to Keep Your Marriage Strong." Since the 1990s, articles indicate that it now takes twenty-five ways to accomplish this task: "25 Ways to Superglue Your Marriage," "25 Ways to Strengthen Your Marriage," and "25 Ways to Make Your Marriage Sexier." Although not as prominent as in the lists found in the single articles, there is still a bias toward men. There are "28 Little Ways to Make Your Husband Feel Special," but no such advice for husbands. Continuing this negative slant, numerous quizzes and tests appear to let readers know if their marriage is on track: "Test Your Marriage" and "The Love and Understanding Quiz." From the number of lists and quizzes on the subject, it appears that marital sex is a major issue with couples: "The Husband and Wife Sex Test" and "Test Your Sex." Many of the problems indicated in these quizzes are apparently the result of misunderstandings: "8 Wrong Ideas about Sex: His and Yours."

Economics

It is not surprising that problems with economics appear in the themes of both categories. For singles, it is mostly about the financial difficulties of a single-income household, whereas for the married it appears to be the opposite problem of dealing with two careers and two incomes: "The Truth about Two Job Marriages," "Two-Career Couples: How They Do It," "Career and Family: Making Both Work." The main problem with this type of household appears to be the sharing of roles: "Shared Roles Take Their Toll" and "The Myth of Male Housework." There are, however, other issues that can crop up in this type of household: "When the Wife Makes More," "Are Working Wives Hazardous to Their Husbands' Mental Health?" and even "Does a Working Woman Really Need to Be Married?"

Family

Family is a common theme in both categories, but finding the topic of under the singles heading was somewhat of a surprise. However, the number of articles under the topic "single-parent families" illustrates that family has become a major element in the life of singles, although perhaps not recognized as part of an emerging lifestyle for singles. A 1990s article under the marriage category reminds us that there has been a "Demise of the Shotgun Wedding" and a rise in the number of unmarried mothers. In fact, there were almost as many articles on single parenthood under the marriage category as there were under the singles category. But the issue was treated differently in the two different categories. For singles the main question is "Raising a Child Alone." The answer seems positive since a 1990s article affirms that there is a "Single-Mommy Track" On the other hand, the question for the married seems to be: "What Will a Baby do to Your Marriage?" and the main concern seems to revolve around sex: "Is There Love after Baby?"

Sexual Behavior

Although sexual behavior is a subject of interest for both categories, it is seemingly more so for the married—there were many more articles on this subject within the marriage heading, requiring a separate thematic heading. Despite all the stereotypes regarding singles and sex, it was not a theme found to be necessary under the singles category. As expected the articles focus on couplehood: "Couples" and "The American Way of Loving"; but it is a troubled way of loving: "Don't Let Those Sex Myths Ruin Your Marriage" and "Keep Your Marriage Sexy: 10 Mistakes to Avoid." Some articles offer lists to help readers become more assertive and positive about sex in their marriages by taking: "6 Steps to Better Sex," or, better yet, "10 Steps to More Satisfying Sex." In fact, readers have their choice of 1, 4, 5, 9, 10, 12, 15, 16, 21, or 23 days or secrets to better marital sex, and one article even promises "The Sexy Marriage from A to Z." In examining other topics it has been noted that there was a bias toward men, and it was no surprise to find a similar bias when examining sexual behavior. Thus, there are articles revealing "Six Mistakes Most Wives Make" and "What Married Men Want from Sex," but there are no articles on the mistakes husbands make or what married women want from sex. Maybe that is the reason for another article: "Husbands Are Lousy Lovers."

Negatives

The earlier examination of stereotypes concerning singles led us to believe that most negative factors would be concentrated under the singles' heading.

But there seemed to be as many negative topics concerning marriage. In fact, as early as 1948 the *Ladies' Home Journal* felt it necessary to publish a regular marriage advice column called "Making Marriage Work." Most were quizzes that helped readers deal with a specific marital problem, for example, "What Factors Favor Good Sexual Adjustment and a Happy Marriage?" and "Are You Enhancing Your Appeal?" Both the married and single headings had similar negative themes, but there were also some differences: for example, there are "Troubles That Pull Couples Apart," the "Six Thoughts That Sabotage a Marriage," "The Five New Problems That Threaten Every Marriage," "The Four Biggest Stress Points in Marriage," and "Love Blunders: Mistakes That Can Wreck Romance." In the face of such problems it is no surprise to read that some authors regard marriage as "The Impossible Commitment," yet, there is also "Breakups—Is the Fever Dropping?"

Advice

With numerous negatives in both categories, it would be expected that both categories have a thematic site giving advice on how to deal with these problems, and they do—lots of it. With singles, this advice concerns mostly ways of locating and keeping dates. For the married, the concern is how to maintain the marriage: "Keys to a Loving Relationship," "Ingredients of a Happy Marriage," "60 Seconds That Can Save Your Marriage," "The Two-Minute Marriage Saver," "Words That Can Warm Up Your Marriage," and even "Six Questions That Can Warm Up a Cool Marriage." Articles also tell "What Every Marriage Needs," or, put another way, "What No Marriage Can Do Without." Perhaps a way to resolve these issues before they even begin is given in the article "How to Pick a Wife"—revealing the same bias as the other topics, since there is no information on how to pick a husband. This bias similarly shows itself in the article "How I Got Him to Marry Me"—but not how I got her to marry me.

Positives

The negative attributes do not preclude also having positive ones, of course, and this must be so because people keep getting married and staying married. Titles extol "The Benefits of Marriage" and "The Best Things about Being Married." There is also the assertion that "Marriage Is Better" since it brings "Endless Love." To ensure a happy outcome, readers can learn "What Happy Couples Do Right" and the "4," "6," or "8 Secrets of a Successful Marriage." All of this explains the "1," "8" or "13 Reasons Why Marriage Is Cool"—or, perhaps, "Why Marriage Is Hot Again."

Catchall

Like the singles heading, there are topics found under the marriage category that do not fit into the previous themes. These catchall items can, however, can be generally separated into the subtopics of marriage, gender differences, and potpourri.

Marriage.   Under this grouping is found, to no one's surprise, that there are "Great Expectations in Marriage" and that "Marriage: It's Back in Style." Despite these optimistic claims, there are questions as to "What is This State Called Marriage?" and "Is Marriage Better?" However, it is not until the 1990s that it is necessary to learn "The Truth about Love and Marriage." It is this discovery that will allow for "The Reinvention of Marriage" in order to have "A Thoroughly Modern Marriage" and it is not until the new century that it is learned that there is "Life after Marriage."

Gender.   Many subjects under the marriage heading illustrate gender differences, and, as with the singles heading, it is a gender bias toward men. For males, for example, there is "What Men Want from Marriage" whereas for women, it is a question "Does Marriage Give Today's Women What They Really Want?" On the other hand are articles extolling the benefits of singlehood: "Single Women in 30s Happy, Not Old Maids." Perhaps the negative response to the marriage question—for women, at any rate—lies in the fact that "Studies Show Men Do Better in Marriage Than Women." This difference may be what leads to "The War between Men and Women."

Potpourri.   Remaining under the miscellaneous category are a number of potpourri titles. The 1980s told us "How to Marry a Millionaire," that the "The Computer [Is a] Rival," and that there is "Politics [in] Housework." Surprisingly, some topics that first show up in the 1990s deal with important topics: "Does Dating Work?" "Living Together: Does It Help or Hurt a Marriage?" The answer appears to be: "Living Together Was So Much Easier Than Being Married," and "Cohabitation Blues." Considering all the problems associated with marriage, it should be no surprise that articles deal with "What Happens in Marriage Therapy"; the surprise is that it took until the 1990s for this subject to come up—and that there is no similar topic for singles. Only two headings dealing with the married category were different from any found in the singles category.

Contracts

This topic is the result of a rather recent idea that has seemingly become de rigueur for making marriage stronger, or at least safer: the prenuptial agreement. Titles include "Put It in Writing," "I Still Love You, Sign Here," and "For Better, For Worse—But on the Dotted Line." Since this is a relatively new idea, it needs to be explained, and is still being debated: "The Pros and

Cons of Prenuptial Agreements"; arguing that it will "Cut the Divorce Rate" or that it is best to "Take a Pass on the Pre-nup."

Customs

Another different but limited theme began to appear in the 1990s—the customs surrounding marriage. In America, there are "Love, American Style" and "Choosing Mates—the American Way." In China, there are "New Family Values." Other titles about international customs include "Bombay Bliss" and "Brides of the Sahara." Most customs, however, are listed under a religious heading: "An Ecumenical Strategy Statement" and "Cohabitation: A Perplexing Pastoral Problem."

Table 5.1. Singles Subheading Titles: 1980–2000*

Lists
Pleasures . . . Perils of Being Single
The 14 Best Cities for Single Women
What's Best, Scary, Fun about Living Alone
Where the Men Are: The 10 Best Cities

Economics
The Singles Industry
Money, Sex and the Single Life
Digging for Dollars in the Singles' Market
Financing the Single Way of Life
Financial Challenges of Single-hood

Parenthood
The Missing Father Myth
Mothers on Their Own
Single . . . with Children
The Out of Wedlock Question
Don't Stereotype Single Moms
Single Moms and Dads on the Dating Scene

Sex
Sex and the Single Man
What Makes Single Girls Tingle
Never to Old for Love
Love for Sale

Negatives
Sex Ratio Squeeze
Living Alone
The Punishing Pace of the Single Life
Why We Are Afraid to be Single
A Lonely Bachelor
Life in the Alone Zone
Stress and the Single Girl
Single Jeopardy
Living Alone Can Be Hazardous to your Health

Advice
Help for the Single Male
Beyond the Bar Scene
How to Start a Singles' Club
Making It without a Man
How to Be Happy Single
The Single Man's Guide to Dating
The Art of Flying Solo

Positives
Single and Loving It
A Declaration of Female Independence
Single and Sensational
Living Alone and Liking It Too Much
Goodbye Miss Lonely-hearts
The Coming of the Singles' Society
Being Single, Being Myself

Catchall
Sex-Ratio Squeeze
Catch 39
Who's Winding the Marital Clock?
U.S. May Become a Society of Singles, Experts Say
Dating at 40
Traveling Solo
They Didn't Go 2by2

*Listed in chronological order

Table 5.2.   Married Subheading Titles: 1980–2000*

Lists	Negatives
Premarital Test Can Reduce Problems	Marriage: The Impossible Commitment
10 Tips for a Happier Marriage	This Is Marriage?
Who Are the Happiest Couples?	How to Avoid Love and Marriage
The Love and Understanding Quiz	The Power Structure in Every Marriage
New Ways to Tell if Your Love Will Last	Being Married Is Not Always Bliss
20 Truths Super-Happy Couples Know	Married Myths: What We Know Hurts
	Myths That Can Ruin Your Marriage

Economics	Advice
Love You for Your Money?	After the Wedding
How to Marry a Millionaire	How Marriages Can Last
The Marital Money Wars	Your Marriage Survival Kit
Does He Love You for Your Money	Do Marriage Contracts Help?
	Loves That Last: How Do They Do It?

Parenting
How Motherhood Can Threaten Marriage
How to Baby-proof Your Relationship Before You Get Married
How a Baby Tested Our Marriage
Changing Attitude toward Marriage and Parenthood
Do Your Parents Haunt Your Marriage?
Working Mothers' Anti-Guilt Guide

What Makes Marriage Work
The Love and Understanding Quiz

Positives
Marriage Is Better
Married Bliss
Creative Moments in Marriage
For Longer Life, Take a Wife
What Happy Couples Do Right
Why Married Couples Live Longer and Do Better Than Singles
The Benefits of Marriage

Sex
Is Marriage Becoming a Sexual Turnoff?
Sexual Delight: How to Keep It Alive in Your Marriage
Sex, Money, and Housework
Sex and the Married Woman
Dr. Ruth Says, "Have More Fun in Bed"
Babies and Sex

Catchall
Wildest Fantasies in Every Marriage
Marriage versus Just Living Together
Choosing Mates—The American Way
Does Dating Work?
Motherhood Can Threaten Marriage

*Listed in chronological order

As a means of better understanding the subheadings, two tables were prepared in an orderly representative list. Table 5.1 covers the topics under the singles category, and table 5.2 covers the topics under the marriage category.

CONCLUSION: THE DEVELOPMENT OF STEREOTYPES

Having examined the themes and specific topics for both singles and the married, it is now possible to compare the two categories and make a preliminary judgment as to the truth of the stereotypes concerning singles. These stereotypes are: deviant, immature, free/workaholic/affluent, sexual deviant, and happy or lonely.

Deviant

Since marriage is considered to be a normal stage of adulthood, singles are by definition a deviant group. This stereotype would appear to be confirmed by the mere fact that there are stereotypical beliefs about singles but seemingly none about the married. This stereotype is also seemingly confirmed by two of the major listing of topics—lists and clubs. Under the list topic, it is noted that there are numerous places where singles can be found as well as the quality of singles that are available. In addition, there are numerous articles about how to meet and attract other singles. Adding the topic of clubs tells us that there are numerous organizations both available and growing in number to aid singles in their quest to meet other singles in order to develop relationships, perhaps to cohabitate or even get married. This indicates that being single is considered a temporary condition, now being extended for various reasons, but still temporary. The belief is seemingly confirmed by the fact that the overwhelming majority of singles—more than 90 percent—will get married at some point in their lives, and 75 percent will remarry following a divorce. Yet because their lifestyle is not the norm of the majority, they are nonetheless a deviant group.

Immature

A second stereotype—immaturity—is one that is believed to cause singles to deviate from the norm. This stereotype implies that the reason singles do not marry is that they are tied to their mothers' apron strings. As noted, however, most singles will marry, but later in life, which actually may be a sign of maturity since it allows the individual to be better prepared for the future, married or not. Since this is the case, if the apron string exists, it is short. The large number of where-to-meet articles among the lists implies that it is not immaturity that keeps people single, but rather simply not having yet met the right person.

Free/Workaholic/Affluent

Also believed to be related to their deviancy is seemingly the strange stereotype that singles are workaholics; that is, they are so preoccupied with their work that they do not have time to seek and court a mate. Related to this stereotype is the belief that singles must be affluent, since they can work more and do not have the expenses of a family. However, the thematic review revealed no articles dealing with either of these stereotypes except for one—"How to Marry a Millionaire"—that does not tell readers how to become one on their own. So it would seem that these related stereotypes have no basis. Also countering the belief that singles must be affluent is the fact that a large number of them are heading single-parent families, and a large number of articles discuss the economic difficulties of this type of family, especially those headed by single mothers. The word "welfare" is found only in articles discussing the single mother. In fact, the married tend to be more affluent than singles since they usually benefit from two incomes, but this is also not a sure sign of affluence, since there are numerous articles on economics for the married. A related stereotype is that singles have the freedom to do as they wish, and this would seem to be true. Seemingly confirming this belief is the large list of clubs and organizations available to singles. For the married family in which both parents work, the major problem is not income as much as it is time to schedule and tend to all of the tasks in the family home. Thus, articles aimed at married people have advice on how to deal with this problem.

Sexual Deviant

The deviancy involved in remaining single also leads to another stereotype regarding the sexual behavior of singles. If the definition of sexual deviancy is any and all sexual behavior outside of marriage, then singles are by definition sexual deviants since their sexual behavior is necessarily outside of marriage. However, studies of sexual behavior reveal that the vast majority of the public start their sexual experiences long before marriage. Thus, it would appear that the problem with the stereotype is with the definition of sexual deviancy and its extreme restrictions. By definition the stereotype of sexual deviancy by singles is true, but the fact that so many people, married and single, also fit the definition makes it a useless description of deviant sexual behavior. It would be more appropriate to apply the stereotype to specific activities by small groups, both married and single, since then it would be truly descriptive of deviancy from the majority. Seemingly confirming this proposal is the fact that sexual deviancy is not listed as a topic under either of the major headings. In fact, the subject of sexual behavior is not found under the singles heading at all, whereas it is a much-discussed subject under the married heading. The major interest for the married in this regard is in learning ways to improve their married sex life. Whether this exclusion under the singles heading means that their sex lives are more satisfactory than those of the married will be discussed in chapter 7, which deals with that topic, as will related subjects such as number of sexual partners and intercourse frequency. It can be said, however, according to the titles appearing under the singles heading, it appears that for singles sexual behavior is not a topic necessary to discuss. With more people spending longer periods of time in singlehood, this may change.

Happy or Lonely

Perhaps the stereotype concerning singles most often bandied about is that they are lonely. As has been noted, a major topic under the singles heading is dealing with being alone. The assumption is that those who live alone must be lonely; since married people have a partner to share activities with, they are presumed to be not lonely. This belief is confirmed by the fact that there were no titles with this topic listed under the married category. Of course, a large percentage of singles are now living in single-parent families, so they have the company of children, but this is not what is meant by loneliness. Since this is a major stereotype about singles, it was made a part of both studies and is discussed in chapter 10.

Another, related stereotype claims that singles, having fewer responsibilities than the married, are happier. The stereotype is a difficult one to apply to either category, since both married people and singles have periods when they are happy and when they are sad. Also, there are few titles on this subject under either of the two major headings. Therefore, the answer to this stereotypical belief will have to wait for the discussion of the findings on this topic in chapter 9.

Other Stereotypes

A clue as to whether other stereotypes can be added to this list comes with the topics not found in common under the two major headings. As noted, titles under both the married and single headings discussed economics, the negative aspects of being married or single, how to deal with those negatives of their civil status, and the positives of each lifestyle. Both headings also discern gender differences and the titles in both categories imply that there are more difficulties for females than for males in this regard. As noted, both categories surprisingly have subheadings dealing with marriage. For singles, it is a consideration of whether the pleasures of living single outweigh its difficulties and, therefore, a consideration of marriage. This may be taken as a confirmation of the stereotype about happiness, and it also implies that singles wish they were like the majority—married. This belief is seemingly confirmed by the large list of titles about how to meet eligible others. For the married category, the subtopic of marriage deals with the question of what marriage is, and therefore a stereotype of its own—marriage is an unknown. This answer also applies to the future since both groupings see themselves as the wave of the future.

Part III

LIFESTYLES

ARE SINGLES DEVIANT?

Major themes found in sociological studies are that of deviance and discrimination. Various groups throughout history have been labeled as deviant since in some manner they were acting differently or were physically different from the perceived norms of the time period. In most situations, those labeled "deviant" will suffer from discrimination. Those labeled as such may, over time and with great effort, change the label and lessen or eliminate the discrimination. Sometimes, the label and the discrimination that follows are unperceived. For example, there have always been handicapped people, but they were simply people with physical problems who were ignored by all except their caretakers until the label "handicapped" was applied. The label led to improvements for these people through increased access to buildings, jobs, and wages—but it also indicated that they had been discriminated against in these areas, and they are still discriminated against in other areas. Another unperceived area of labels and discrimination was seen in the chapter 1, when noting the difference in treatment experienced by females versus males. Since they were different from men, women have been denied many rights throughout history. Some think that the label "female" no longer carries this negative implication—but the women know better. Think of the terms applied to the sexual behavior conducted by men and the same behavior by women. Which carry a negative connotation?

Singles, the main subject of this book, have also been labeled as deviant and have been discriminated against, and like many such labels and acts, this has gone unperceived, for example, the question, "What is your marital status?" Through the use of the term "marital status," singles are denied an entity of their own—they are labeled as deviant from the majority, the married. So unperceived is this discrimination that no one protests that the question should really be "What is your civil status?" The census data continue this unperceived discrimination by using the category "singles" as applicable only to the never-married. The divorced and the widowed have their own category headings, but their common civil status with the never-married goes unrecognized. By identifying themselves as a particular civil status along with their growing numbers, singles are providing awareness and organizational structures that have aided a reduction in the perception that they are deviant and thereby help to reduce discrimination. However, at the same time, they are also making us more aware of an identifiable category that can be consciously or unconsciously discriminated against. What is being seen is that in calling attention to discrimination, the fighters against this discrimination call attention to the category being discriminated against, and this may make them a more visible target for discrimination against even as it provides a means for recognition and change.

As the earlier chapters noted, singles are labeled "deviant" since they are not following norms that have defined marriage as the most desirable status for adults. However, this label is not applied equally to the three main segments of this category, and so the problems faced by these groups are different as is their treatment. For example, the never-married must first recognize that their civil status is the problem and that, according to the married credo, it is necessary for them to make an effort to marry. On the other hand, the divorced followed the prescribed path and tried marriage. Their problem involves the failure to reconcile their marital differences, and failure always brings irreparable damage and stigma. To rise above the label, the divorcée must do what the never-married must do: join the majority in being married, even if it is preceded by a "re." The widowed are not normally discriminated against since they are only part of that category through what would be called a normal stage of development—they followed the prescribed route of being married and remained married until the death of a spouse.

Singles are now beginning to challenge the label "deviant" and, in so doing, are bringing more attention to themselves. The material in chapters 4 and 5 confirms this increased and changed attention as illustrated by an increased number and variety of articles listed in the *Readers' Guide to Periodical Literature* over recent years. Some singles may challenge the label by pointing to their rapidly increasing numbers as proof that they are now part of the majority and thus are not deviant. That is, they can eliminate the label of being deviant by redefining it. Other singles may accept the label with pride—they are different from the married and accept both the negative and positive aspects of this label.

The advocates of singlehood note that there are many positive attributes to living single. They claim that without the responsibilities of marriage, they have more freedom to pursue leisure activities. One of these activities is the participation in a greater variety of sexual encounters. The result of having more time to do that which they desire and being able to enjoy sexual variety is greater fun and happiness. These three supposed positive features of single life—freedom, sexual endeavors, and fun—will be examined in chapters 7, 8, and 9.

The negative aspects of single life include not having a steady companion and resulting feelings of loneliness. Loneliness is believed to be so pervasive for singles that it has been called the great bugaboo of this lifestyle. Another major reason it is considered the great bugaboo is that loneliness can lead to both physical and mental health problems. Therefore, it is important to check on the health claims of the different categories as related to their claims of loneliness, since the literature of the period may have led singles to overestimate the impact of loneliness—and led the married to underestimate its impact—since the married have supposedly made a pact against its intrusion. Finally, it is important to check on health claims in order to note whether the divorced, having committed a deviant act, report greater health problems than the other categories. These two supposed negative features of single life—loneliness and health problems—will be examined in chapters 10 and 11.

Since both the married and singles categories are made up of different subgroups, it will be important to see whether these negative and positive features of their lifestyle also vary according to their status. However, before examining these supposed negative and positive features of the singles lifestyle, it is necessary to ask whether the lifestyle was freely chosen or was an outcome of a particular family lifestyle. This will then be discussed in chapter 6.

Chapter Six

Family Background

INTRODUCTION: IMAGES

> Our family comes first. For us without families, our job comes first, but often they don't. Our friends, lovers, and even our apartments come first. (Holland 1992)

There are two contrasting images of singles that are quite common. On the one hand, there is the belief that people who are unmarried after a certain age remain so because they are immature. Although statistics indicate that the never-married are, on average, a much younger component of the singles sample, this is not what is meant by immaturity. In this context it is a behavior reflected not by age, but by behavior—by the very act of not getting married. In short, it is a label defined by itself—one is immature because one is not married, and one is not married because one is immature.

People may also remain single because they are reluctant to leave home. Thus the "silver cord" remains intact because singles are so comfortable at home that they are unwilling to leave this nest—to leave home and take on the responsibilities of a single or married household. This reluctance to leave home and take on responsibility is then taken as proof of immaturity. The idea of the "silver cord" can be applied to either gender: The female is tied to her mother's apron strings or her parents selfishly foster her singlehood in order to have someone to look after them in their old age; the male's mother is interested in her future care and so works diligently at preventing any woman from usurping her position in her son's life. The author Phillip Wiley referred to this situation as "momism."

This belief regarding a reluctance by singles to take on the responsibilities of marriage brought a mixed reaction from the large sample in the adjunct singles

97

organization study. The divorced were particularly forceful in their belief that singles were as responsible as the married. One divorced woman noted: "Most of the singles I know have enormous responsibilities. There are a lot of single men and women who are like me; I have a child that I am raising. I have a house that I have to keep. And I am holding down a job." Asked about those who have never taken on the responsibilities of marriage in the first place, these individuals reiterated that taking on the responsibilities of a household is not a sign of maturity.

On the other hand were those that agreed with the stereotype of immaturity, but felt that it also applied to the married. As one divorced gentleman remarked, "There are divorces that occur because of immaturity. There are an awful lot of immature divorced people and that is a cause of the divorce. I don't think we can not stereotype divorces by saying all divorces are okay. This is the same as saying all marriages are okay. Because they are still married doesn't mean they've got their act together."

Another divorced man suggested that the belief about immaturity is true "mainly for the married because they depend on the one or the other of two people that are in the relationship and they are not responsible to themselves, whereas most singles are very responsible to themselves."

Unfortunately, none of these observations from the adjunct sample deals with the "silver cord" immaturity belief, since this belief applies to those unmarried people who have not left their parents' home and there were too few of those in this sample to make a conclusion in this regard.

Contrasting with the image of singles remaining single out of immaturity is that of the swinging single. This image is of a single who remains unmarried because of the endless sexual endeavors involved in being a swinger—the lascivious bachelor who enjoys the sexual benefits of marriage sans marriage. In the past, this image was usually applied to men, since single women were perceived as "prim spinsters," but with the development of more varieties of effective birth control, the swinger image is no longer limited to men. The prim spinster has now become the liberated woman—one who leaves her parents' home and sets up her own abode complete with endless possibilities for leisure activities. This image—for men and women—has been enhanced by images of the singles condominium, porno movies, and celebrities who engage in this type of behavior.

Although the stay-at-home, immature single and the swinging single are contradictory, both images are possibilities for the lifestyle of the single, since, as with the married, there are a large and growing number of different types of singles listed under this rubric: the never-married, cohabiters, the divorced, and the widowed. With large numbers and several types of possibilities, it is thus possible to have both "stringers" and "swingers" in the singles community. This is true also for the married, since there are also several types of marriages: first marriage, remarriage, commune marriage, commuter marriage, same-sex marriage, and sexually open marriage, to name a few. As a means of examining these two images, this chapter will be devoted to examining the "stringer" image by looking into the relationship between our respondents and their parents. Chapter 7 will be devoted to examining the "swinger" image. Are singles likely to have numerous partners, or is this merely an image fostered by the media? So in addition to questions about their own number of sexual partners, the respondents were asked about what they believed regarding the number of sexual partners others in their own civil status had. An adjunct to the "swinger" image is the question of whether there are benefits to this lifestyle, so respondents were asked whether it was more satisfactory. A related belief is that singles have more freedom to pursue leisure activities such as swinging; this will be taken up in chapter 8.

HOUSEHOLD RELATIONS

The basic belief with regard to civil status and parental relations is that a lack of warmth in such relations can lead to hostility toward the opposite sex and a resulting preference to remain single for those raised in such households. It is also true that even with a lack of warmth, the family may still provide safety and security for its members—advantages members may not wish to lose by leaving the family home.

The sample from the adjunct study of a singles organization thought that these issues were not a factor in their current status. One divorced male called it "baloney." He thought that this belief was way out of proportion: "Both parties, females and males, need each other." Another recently divorced male added, "It's all according to the kind of experiences you've had from a kid on with the opposite sex. If you've had trouble with 'em from the time you were a child, you'll have a hostility toward them." An early study by Rawlings (1966) seems to support these comments. Rawlings found that there was no significant relationship between having parents perceived as being affectionate or cooperative and one's civil status. As a means of checking on this belief, several questions on this issue were asked of the respondents: what their relationship to their parents were like, whether their parents were open in their relationship toward them, and what their current relationship with their parents was like.

Past Relations

Prior to examining past relations, it is perhaps best to discover what sort of abode is their current residence. Another study done at about the same time as our early study indicates a number of types of residences, illustrated in table 6.1.

Table 6.1.   Residence Type

	Men	Women
Alone	47	35
Cohabits	14	11
Cohabits—Same-sex	11	7
Family	23	45
Group	5	2

(Simenauer and Carroll 1982)

The replies to the questions about parental relationship seemed to confirm that such relationships do not affect civil status, since all groups except the divorced had similar majorities claiming loving and warm relationships with their parents in the early study. However, there was one seeming contradiction. The divorced had almost as many parental relations that were conflicting and cold (42 percent) as had loving and warm relations (47 percent). On the other hand, the remarried had the highest proportion of any group claiming loving and warm parental relations (72 percent) and the lowest number claiming conflicting and cold relationships (18 percent). This positive picture of parental relationships by the remarried made a complete reversal in the current study. Now only 48 percent claim such positive relationships—a whopping 24 percent decline. This turnabout for the remarried is reflected in an increase in those who describe their parental relationships as conflicting and cold (26 percent). This shift also occurred with the never-married: Their positive perception of past parental relationships in the early study declined from a majority of 64 percent to 49 percent in the current study—another large decline of 15 percent. Again, the divorced seem to be bucking the trend: In the current study slightly more perceive a positive parental relationship (58 percent). Those divorced respondents perceiving a negative parental relationship remain relatively high (37 percent), but it is now more in line with the other categories.

The pressure to marry was greater in the post-1950s period because of a carryover glow from the golden age of marriage, and it is likely that this pressure increased as this population delayed marriage. The findings from the current study indicate that what was a friendly pressure from parents toward marriage became not so friendly as their children ignored the cultural emphasis on marriage and perhaps scared their parents into a belief that their singlehood would be permanent. Yet in both studies, both the married (M) and single (S) respondents reported generally positive relationships with their parents (M: 64 percent and 59 percent; S: 60 percent and 52 percent) Since both categories had positive images of family relations from their own experiences,

Table 6.2. Parental Relations*

| | Early Study/Current Study | |
	Warm-Stable	Cold-Conflict
Never Married	64/49%	28/30%
Divorced	47/58	42/35
Married Once	63/62	29/26
Remarried	72/48	18/42
Singles Total	60/42	31/42
Married Total	64/59	27/30

* For ease of clarification, figures from those who had only one parent
  were omitted.

it can be said that the "stringer" stereotype does appear to be true, but to a very limited degree since almost as many singles reported negative relationships with their parents.

Openness in Family Relations

A large majority of both the married and single respondents reported similarly open relationships with both parents in the 1980 study (M: 46 percent; S: 45 percent). Again, the divorced noted a different type of relationship with their parents, since an equal number claimed that they had an open relationship with neither parent (39 percent). As can be seen, these figures are not as positive as they were for the earlier question on relationships. This may be due to the fact that here the respondents could note the relationship with both parents or with just one parent. If the open relationships with one of the parents were added to those having open relationships with both parents, than the positive open-type relationships would be even higher than the recollection of past relationships. Not surprisingly, more of the sample reported open relationships with their mothers than their fathers (25 percent versus 7 percent). Again, the divorced revealed a different picture, since only 14 percent claimed open relationships with their mothers, a much lower figure than the claims of the other respondent categories.

Although the figures regarding open relationships were similar in the current study (M: 36 percent; S: 41 percent), they again reveal a slight decline from those reporting positive relations with both parents in the original study. The decline in openness with both parents is the result of a switch to a particular parent—not surprisingly, the mother. Both the married and the singles had an average increase of 10 percent in those claiming open relationships with their mothers. Unfortunately, the findings do not indicate why there was a decline in those reporting open relationships with the fathers. These results

Table 6.3. Household Emotions: Open

	Both	Early/Current Studies Mother	Father	Neither
Never Married	47/38%	27/39%	7/4%	19/19%
Divorced	39/46	14/24	8/0	39/30
Married Once	49/41	24/32	6/4	22/23
Remarried	35/18	35/49	12/4	19/29
Singles Total	45/41	24/33	7/3	24/23
Married Total	46/36	25/36	7/4	21/24

were confirmed by similar findings from the adjunct study of the singles organization, a group comprised of mostly divorced singles. Tentatively, it appears that the lack of openness between parent and child may be reflected in the child's socialization and thereby affect her ability to communicate with others as an adult. The difficulty with this assumption is the findings of the remarried—a mostly formerly divorced group that reported opposite findings from the divorced. Apparently, being remarried improves memories in both warm relationships and openness. Of course, the poorer relations and emotions recalled by divorce could be a reflection of the divorce itself and the parents' reaction to it; this reaction could be improved by remarriage, improving the relationship.

If open relationships can be defined as meaning good and warm relations, the stringer image appears to be a factor for all except the divorced, since all had similar numbers reporting openness either with both parents or with one or the other. It would appear that open relationships with one's family may have something to do with marriage preference.

Current Relations

It is only when the study turns to respondents' current relationships with their parents that a large difference is seen between the married and the singles. In the early study, an overwhelming 70 percent of the married reported warm and stable relations with their parents, but only 45 percent of the singles claimed such a relationship. However, this large gap in parental relations between the two categories closed in the current study as relations improved for the singles and declined for the married. This changed relationship is reflected when it comes to fights with the parents: The singles show a decline in this behavior (31 percent to 18 percent) whereas the married show an increase in this behavior (13 percent to 18 percent). Considering the other findings in this chapter, it is not surprising to find that in the early study a larger percentage of the

Table 6.4. Current Parental Relations

| | Early/Current Studies | | |
	Warm/Warm	Cool/Cool	Fights/Fights
Never Married	46/58%	26/21%	28/21%
Divorced	44/52	18/35	38/13
Married	71/64	16/22	13/14
Remarried	65/47	22/26	14/27
Singles Total	45/56	24/26	31/18
Married Total	70/59	17/23	13/18

divorced reported fighting a lot with their parents (38 percent) than any other group. A surprise comes in the current study, where this claim is lowest for the divorced of all the categories (13 percent). Another surprise comes with the remarried, which showed a large jump in the number fighting with their parents, from 14 percent in the early study to 33 percent in the current study.

It is only with the question of current relations with their parents that the stringer stereotype is shown clearly to not apply, since more of the singles than the married in the sample reported not getting along with their parents— but this does not explain why there is a decline in the number of married people noting warm relations with their parents.

CONCLUSION: NO STRINGS

The findings on family background, the openness of family relations, and current family relations reinforces previous research on the "apron strings" stereotype: There is apparently little relationship between an individual's parental relations and whether or not he or she chooses to marry. No one would ask an older married man why he did not stay single, since he is a "mama's boy," or muse that an older married woman might have remained happily single but for an obligation to her family to marry. What these questions would imply is an assumption that close relationships affected their choice to marry. On the other hand, such questions seem common to attempts to understand why one stayed single. As noted, these wonderings usually involve ideas of immaturity and parental attachment. The exception to these stereotyped beliefs is mostly found with the divorced, who tended to report poorer relations with their parents than the other categories. Whether this means that those who have divorced married in order to escape their families, and in so doing made poor choices, can only be based on conjecture. If this remains as an explanation for the findings regarding the divorced, then how do we explain the findings on the remarried—a group both previously married and divorced? They, like the other married group and the other single group, reported high positive relations with their family. Thus, remarriage might be explained by these warm relations with their parents, both when they were married and when they were single—but this explanation also does not appear to be satisfactory.

On the other hand, there does appear to be a relationship between family socialization and divorce. Socialization theory indicates that children who felt that communication with their parents—especially with their mothers—was blocked may continue to have communication problems in their own marriages. This impression is reinforced by the cool or conflicted relationships the divorced report in current relationships with their parents. The hypothesis that a parental communication block can be a factor in a future divorce remains, then, a need for further study. Another, seemingly more important factor than parental relations with their children were parental relations to each other—the perception that a parents' marriage was a happy one should lead to a more favorable attitude toward marriage.

Chapter Seven

Sex in the World of Singles

INTRODUCTION: CHANGING MORES

Adult sexuality begins at puberty. For females, this usually starts around the age of twelve and for males it is at age fourteen. However, most societies attempt to restrict biological sexual impulses until marriage. Currently, this happens at an average age of twenty-five for females and twenty-seven for males. The result is approximately thirteen years of sexual stress—a longer period now than in the past due to the increasing age at first marriage. Perhaps, then, it is no surprise that sexual mores have undergone changes leading to a more permissive attitude regarding sex outside of marriage.

A HISTORY OF SEXUAL BEHAVIOR

The early patriarchal societies of the Hebrews, Greeks, and Romans recognized sex as necessary in itself, but only for the men. Men's desires were considered innate and strong. Restrictions on sexual expression for women began to crumble in the Greek and Roman societies as a result of their many wars and the absence of men. With the dominance of Catholicism came a period of sexual restrictiveness for both sexes. In Christianity there is a general taboo against sex going back to St. Paul, which has been carried through to St. Augustine and Catholic theology. The only type of sexual relations accepted—and rather reluctantly—during this historical period were those conducted in lawful marriage, and only for the purpose of procreation rather than passion. This belief gave a strong boost to marriage, since it was the only legitimate expression of sexual behavior. The early Protestants maintained

105

this restrictive view regarding sex, seeing sexual permissiveness as a threat to one's dedication to his or her "calling." The Victorians added to this restrictive view of sexual behavior, viewing sexual behavior as dangerous to one's health as well as to one's marriage: "In fact, graham crackers and Kellogg's Corn Flakes were created during this period to replace foods that were believed to inflame lust" (Clanton 1984). These features of early history led to a mostly antisexual morality.

Since men held all the power at this time in history, they were able to refashion sexual beliefs to fit their supposedly greater sexual needs. Thus, in addition to the patriarchal double standard, sexual relations were dictated by husbands without any regard to the feelings of their wives. The result was a sexual code that allowed men to enjoy sexuality under all situations—premarital, marital, and extramarital—but also denied these sexual freedoms to women. Thus, the price a "decent" girl paid for sex was the same one she paid for a home, children, and social position—marriage. If, however, women did not engage in premarital or extramarital sexual behavior, a majority of possible partners for the men were eliminated. This meant that the double standard of freedom for men and sexual restriction for women would be covertly modified, but it also meant that sexual behavior was secretive and guilt ridden.

Modification of the double standard came with the development of the ideal of romantic love. The sinful behavior of nonmarital sex could be excused if it was done for the sake of love. Love became the justifier and purifier of sexuality, primarily for women, since men needed no such excuses. Historically, then, sexual behavior has been ruled by this double standard rather than by abstinence.

The Christian ideal, although powerful, has consistently been violated throughout the centuries. Sex is still not considered a topic suitable for everyday conversation, but the sinful prohibition of sex had become a limited factor by the beginning of the twentieth century. A number of factors were involved in this departure from the ideological tenets of the traditional romantic view:

- *Birth Control*: The pill and other methods of contraception were readily dispersed by physicians and college medical personnel.
- *Improved Contraception*: Improvements in contraception separated sex from reproduction and made sex for pleasure possible.
- *Court Rulings*: Early in the twentieth century, court decisions regarding freedom of the press made discussions of sex in books and magazines more acceptable. Thus, more information about sexual desires and techniques were disseminated, as well as information on the development of improved methods of birth control.

- *Freud*: Early in the century, Sigmund Freud's radical ideas regarding sex pervaded society's thinking, giving an air of respectability to people's behaviors and feelings regarding sex. This meant that a more naturalistic interpretation of sexual behavior became more widely accepted. The major tenets of this new view of sexuality included the idea that sexual desire is normal, since its ultimate goal is physical pleasure and psychological intimacy, and so it is not a threat to moral character for either men or women. This being the case, a wide range of sexual behavior can and should be accepted if it does not involve force or fraud.
- *Industrialization*: In the twentieth century industrialization became a major factor of change. The development of the automobile, for example, and its ability to become a "bedroom on wheels," as well as a means of transportation to other locations where privacy was assured, gave couples more freedom to explore their sexuality.
- *Women's Lib*: Aiding the movement into freer sexual behavior has been the women's movement, with its strivings for social equality. It was during the last half of the twentieth century that sex for the single woman was first declared to be a basic human right—and shortly thereafter a necessity.
- *War*: The two world wars in the twentieth century, with the uncertainties about life they produced, led to a loosening of sexual morality.

In a society where men and women were becoming more equal, sexual behavior was demanding greater attention and interest from the women. Sexual liberation meant that an increasing number of women began following male initiatives in a more elaborate multipartner sexual script. The historical requirements that women postpone sexual gratification, be exclusively heterosexual, and be possessive and faithful are indicators of the traditional double standard and signs of oppression. Thus, challenges to the sexual double standard led to more privacy for young, never-married people, both at home and away at college—the influx of married women with children to employment outside the home meant that their children would be at home and unsupervised, and the in loco parentis role of colleges was also eroded.

In order to eliminate any feelings of guilt about supposedly banned behavior, the negative term "promiscuous" was replaced with the more neutral term "socially active." It was claimed that "chastity was a health risk; the unbedded withered emotionally and physically. . . . It was a sign of hostility, too; women who slept alone in this unnatural way hated the world and should seek professional help." It was also believed that sex was good for us. It put "roses in the cheeks and spring in the step and toned up the system and protected us from various illnesses, possibly psychosomatic, and the milder forms of madness" (Holland 1992).

The result of these changes is that recreational sex has gained ascendancy over procreational sex. There is now a more permissive attitude regarding sexual behavior, which has resulted in changes in both premarital and extra-marital sexual activity. Studies have shown that there has been an increase in premarital sexual behavior overall, particularly coitus; a decrease in the aver-age age at the onset of coitus; and an increase in the number of sexual partners among those who are experienced. These changes in sexual behavior were "uncovered" in the findings of the two Kinsey books, *Sexual Behavior in the Human Male* (1948) and *Sexual Behavior in the Human Female* (1953). Among Kinsey's findings were that about 90 percent of men and some 50 per-cent of women had engaged in sexual intercourse without benefit of matri-mony; adding masturbation and "petting," the figure rises to 64 percent of women achieving orgasm without benefit of marriage; and a considerable portion of the population had engaged in alternatives such as homosexuality. Emphasizing this movement into freer sexual behavior was the fact that few reported guilt over these behaviors.

More recent statistics also underscore this movement of freer sexual activ-ity: At the beginning of the twenty-first century, two-thirds of all males and half of all females reported engaging in sexual intercourse by the age of 18. And since the average age for the timing of first intercourse is 16.6 years for males and 17.2 years for females, a large number of these groups actually started their sexual relations at a much younger age (Cox 2002). These figures indicate that the vast majority of Americans now have coital experience prior to marriage. This change in behavior was accompanied by an attitude change—seen in both the under- and over-thirty groups—that saw premarital sexual relations as immoral.

This acceptance of impersonal sex with unknown partners that began in the late 1960s came to a crash in the 1980s with herpes and AIDS. The emergence of AIDS, in particular, led to a reevaluation of America's sexual behavior by many. Naturally, the increase in earlier sexual behavior was blamed on a decline in individual morality and an abandonment of traditional values, rather than earlier physical development and the social changes noted previously.

As indicated, the sexual revolution appears to have begun in the post-1950s period. Although authorities continued its support of the "traditional family," maintaining that sexuality had the potential to ruin families, the Kinsey's stud-ies of sexual behavior among men and women and other surveys were pro-viding vivid evidence of the sexual changes noted earlier. Kinsey not only demonstrated the pervasiveness of sexual behavior but also that in practice it violated accepted moral standards. Kinsey believed that these findings proved that the categories applied to sexual behavior were meaningless. What is con-sidered socially acceptable or unacceptable, normal or abnormal, heterosexual or homosexual, depends on those doing the assessing. In reality, sexual behavior operates on gradations of extremes. What worried the defenders of the "traditional family" was the fact that the Kinsey data reflected the behavior of average, respectable men and women rather than that of deviant minorities. In a survey conducted in 1972, premarital sex was approved of by 65 percent of adults and by 50 percent of females—a vast change from the 22 percent who approved of premarital sex in 1959 (Hunt 1974). Considering the Kinsey reports and other surveys, it is clear that changes in sexual behavior had been undergoing a slow, gradual shift since the turn of the century and did not constitute a revolutionary change in attitudes.

These changes in sexual behavior were not limited to the unmarried. Extramarital sex has historically been condemned by almost all Western societies because it was believed to have a negative effect on marriage. This belief is consistent with research showing that in at least one-third of divorce cases, one or both spouses had been involved with another person (South and Lloyd 1995). Apparently, however, the attitude change toward greater sexual permissiveness has also impacted the views on marital sex. For example, Kinsey (1948) found that half of all married men had engaged in extramarital affairs by the age of forty-five. This seemingly surprising finding was confirmed when Nass, Libby, and Fisher (1981) found that 60 to 65 percent of all married men and 45 to 55 percent of all married women had at least one extramarital experience. Other studies done at this time revealed similar figures. However, these figures are subject to challenge due to the technology utilized for drawing their interview samples. For example, Kinsey used nonrandom, selected volunteers who were young, college educated, and middle-class. Similarly selected samples were taken from the readership list for the studies conducted by Hite for *Ms* and *Penthouse*. These questionable samplings cast doubt on the findings of the studies, but they do, however, indicate that the greater sexual freedom found among the singles population is also a factor among the married.

In addition, the earlier one begins to date, the earlier one becomes involved in a relationship that leads to sexual intimacy. Since about 90 percent of all young people begin to date before their seventeenth birthday and about three-quarters of these become involved in a steady relationship by the age of eighteen, the resulting intimacy figures are not surprising. Thus, the rush into a monogamous relationship may be explained by the anxieties customarily related to dating—the fear of rejection and the fear of such sexually transmitted diseases as AIDS. Rather than going to bed with strangers, one is now expected to set up a relationship, have a specific discussion about sexual history and go together to have an HIV test, and to promise to sleep with no others during the duration of the relationship. Of course, this is not being promised for emotional reasons but rather for reasons of health.

For those who are older and perhaps divorced, the so-called rule of not starting a sexual relationship until the third date has fallen by the wayside. The belief now seems to be that if you are comfortable with your partner, why wait? The sequence prior to the mid-twentieth century was dating, going steady, exchanging class rings, becoming engaged, and getting married. This led to earlier marriage; by 1950, the average age at first marriage was twenty years for women and twenty-two for men—the youngest average of the twentieth century. This early start into a monogamous relationship also seems to lead to the likelihood of a cohabiting relationship—a likelihood increasing rapidly. Thus, by the year 2000, there were 3.8 million cohabiting couples, up by 900,000 from 1990. These figures imply that cohabitation has now entered the sequence as a stage prior to marriage. Since most such relationships are relatively short—half last longer than two years—it is likely that many of the individuals involved in such relationships will have been involved in more than one cohabiting relationship. Thus, by the age of thirty, 54 percent of adults had shared a home, including 45 percent of those currently married and 65 percent of those currently divorced.

In chapters 4 and 5, the *Readers' Guide to Periodical Literature* was examined in order to note the changing image of singles over time. A similar examination, with sex as the topic, revealed a similar changing picture and in a sense confirmed the previously mentioned findings. Prior to World War II, most of the articles on sex in the *Readers' Guide* were medical in nature. The heading for this topic was "Sex (Biology)," and the subtopics covered dealt with venereal diseases and sexual selection in the animal world. After the war, the word "biology" was replaced with two main subheadings—"Sexual Behavior" and "Sex Relations"—with a jump in coverage. These new subcategories were added in order to accommodate the increasing number of articles that treated sex as a cultural factor instead of a biological condition. In fact, so many articles were being written on this topic that many experts concluded that Americans were obsessed with sex.

Since singles do not have steady sexual partners, their sexual liberties can be understood—but what excuse can be made for the married, who supposedly have steady sexual partners? According to a study by Ruben (1986), both personal reasons and societal conditions are involved in the increase in extramarital sexual relations. Personal reasons include curiosity about something that appears to be exciting, a desire for sexual reassurance, imitation of a role model, and revenge against a real or imagined infidelity. It appears most people do not engage in extramarital relations because of serious problems in their marriage. Nor are such people "immature," "narcissistic," "neurotic," or "sick." As was seen when examining the stereotypes applied to singles, society tends to apply labels to people who participate in "deviant" acts. Abetting these personal reasons for extramarital relations are:

- *Anonymity*: Urban living provides a greater degree of anonymity and a lower chance of "getting caught."
- *Birth Control*: The development of improved birth control techniques made such activity less risky.
- *Boredom*: Longer life spans, resulting in a longer period with the same mate, increase the potential for sexual boredom.
- *A More Mobile Society*: Greater mobility provides more opportunities for such behavior.
- *Permissive Attitudes*: More permissive attitudes toward premarital sexual may be having a carryover effect.
- *Women in the Workforce*: Greater participation in the labor force by women provides them with the opportunity and freedom to engage in such activities.

Interestingly, extramarital affairs do not seem to have a negative effect on a marriage since there is no scientific proof that sexually monogamous couples are happier or healthier than those participating in extramarital sexual relationships, nor is there any scientific proof that such behavior is destructive of marriage (Myers 1977). In fact, it is claimed that such behavior may actually enhance marital relations by motivating the other spouse to become more attractive, by making more of an effort in the marriage, by removing the need to participate in sexual relations when there is no desire, by providing diversion, and by making a sexually mediocre marriage more bearable (Myers and Leggett 1972).

Sexual behavior can be encompassed within four classes of sexual expression:

1. *Comfortable Monogamy*: no other sexual partners
2. *Venturesome Cohabiters*: serial monogamy with numerous partners
3. *Moderate Polygamists*: both partners have multiple partners
4. *Enthusiastic Polygamists*: both partners have a large number of multiple partners (Laumann and Youm 2000)

Based on this classification, a 2000 study gives us a clue as to the differences in sexual behavior according to civil status (Laumann and Youm 2000).

The greater range of sexual behavior now part of the moral structure is reiterated by two factors: a large percentage of married men (37 percent) and an even larger percent of married women (44 percent) do not practice

Table 7.1.　Civil Status and Sexual Expression

| | *Men/Women* | | | |
| | Class | | | |
Civil Status	1	2	3	4
Never married/not cohabiting	28/39%	40/32%	5/17%	28/12%
Never married/cohabiting	23/43	68/13	0/5	9/39
Divorced/separated/widowed/not cohabiting	35/39	33/27	6/15	26/19
Divorced/separated/widowed/cohabiting	52/38	45/23	0/8	3/31
Married	63/56	36/22	0/1	1/21
Overall	50/50	38/24	2/5	10/20

monogamy, and more women than men tend to serially cohabitate with a larger number of multiple partners. It appears that both men and women are now part of the sexually liberated. This claim is reinforced by a nationwide study that indicated that 72 percent of men and 70 percent of women have engaged in extramarital affairs (Hite 1976). In reality, the formant over sexual scripts and behavior is an attempt to bring social practices into cohesion with existing biological and technical realities.

There remains a cultural lag between current behavior and the scripts seen as appropriate. Despite these changes in sexual behavior, our parental admonitions still reflect traditional values and so these behaviors may result in feelings of guilt. Despite these changes, our sexual language is still defined by marriage. Thus, sexual behavior is labeled as "premarital" or "extramarital" and there is no label for sex that occurs when a marriage ends in divorce or widowhood. Premarital and after-marriage sexual relations are still considered something bad: something that will bring about an unwanted marriage, the likelihood of unwanted children, and sexually transmitted diseases. What, then, should the unmarried do with their sexual energies? Should they repress their desires? That is unhealthy, and sexual desires are bound to be expressed in some manner. Should they take cold baths? What an old-fashion idea. Should they masturbate? Ugh! It's a dirty habit. Should they practice voyeurism by buying adult books and/or going to X-rated movies? Sad, ludicrous! Should they violate the norm by bedding every person of the opposite sex that is available? Then they are considered lecherous. Or are they queer?—in which case they are considered to be contemptible and pitied. It appears that no matter what the unmarried do with their sexual energies, it is unacceptable.

An interesting aside must be added at this point, since the topic of the following material was not found in the 1980 study on this topic. Discussion concerning singles at that time dealt mostly with the young baby boomers of that period. With the passage of time many of those singles are now older, necessitating a new topic: sexual relations and the older single. Twenty-nine percent of adults between the ages of forty-five and fifty-nine are now single, as compared to only 19 percent during the eighties. Sexual relationships are still of interest for these now-older singles, and so they date regularly. Sexual relations outside of marriage may be officially frowned upon, but with more single middle-aged people than ever before, they are being recognized as a market. A new industry has arisen to help them in sexual endeavors, from sex toys to drugs for erectile dysfunction.

Another new industry has developed around the need of singles to meet others. Older singles may still meet in the older ways—through friends, neighbors, or relatives—but they are also increasingly turning to online searches. There are now websites designed especially for these older singles, such as PerfectMatch.com, PrimeSingles.net, and the Match.com site for people over fifty. Since older singles may have more specialized requirements, there are also religious sites such as BigChurch.com for Christians and Jdate.com for Jews, SciConnect.com for science nerds, and even OurPersonals.com for gays.

Since these people are older, what they seek from potential dates are not necessarily potential mates. Most are better educated and more affluent than previous generations, so their aims do not necessarily include marriage. A survey by the American Association of University Professors (AAUP) indicates that only 22 percent of men and 14 percent of women are looking for someone to marry or cohabit with. It appears that the network of friends developed in college, the workplace, and community service has negated the fear of being lonely in old age.

One of the main problems with the current dating scene is the result of an issue that arose after the baby boomers came of age—the HIV epidemic. Most never learned about the use of condoms or how to ask a partner about HIV testing, or know that older women are at greater risk due to body changes. The result, according to the AAUP survey, is that most (61 percent) of those baby boomers engaging in sexual endeavors are having unprotected sex.

This change to greater sexual permissiveness raises several questions. Although less is written about the sexual behavior of singles than the married, but is there really a difference in the number of "swinging" singles and their married counterparts? The answer to this question would seem to be obvious—it is not surprising to find that singles have had more different sexual partners than the married, since they do not have sexual partners exclusively reserved for them. However, raises the question: What is the difference in the number of partners? Seeking partners also relates to the question of frequency—does the one actually lead to an increase in the other? Since the end result of all this seeking in numbers and frequency is sexual satisfaction, another question becomes relevant: Is the sexual lifestyle for either category more sexually satisfying? This question is, in reality, more important than the ones about numbers or frequency.

THE SWINGER IMAGE

Before turning to the indelicate question of number of partners, we believed that a clue to this answer could be provided by checking on the respondent's stated liberalism toward sexual behavior. According to the swinger image, the important point is numbers, and not love. This being the belief, it follows that the swinger would commit to having sex for any reason. It was felt that a more telling answer to this question would be afforded by dealing with two supposedly problem areas for singles: finding love and dating, rather than asking about having sex for the fun of it. Since these were issues supposedly affecting only singles, only they were asked these sexually related questions.

Almost half of the sample in both studies (48 percent) did not feel that it was necessary to be in love in order to have sex. There was also very little difference between the never-married and the divorced with regard to this issue: 49 percent of the never-married versus 46 percent of the divorced held this opinion. The respondents from the adjunct singles organization reinforced the replies from the true sample. As one divorced male put it, "I have had sex with women whom I didn't necessarily like. It's an activity, sometimes, that's separate from all other dimensions." Another divorced male did not believe that sex was any different than other types of activities: "It's like any other activity. Sex is sex. This business about casualness is a bunch of baloney. I mean, the fondling is good when it's going on, right?" A divorced woman of about the same age bracket disagreed: "I think it's easier for men to live that way than women. I think we have to have more compassion for the results of our situation. What if we have a baby? Is the kid going to be illegitimate? If we've got six boyfriends, who do we know is the father?" Not all the women agreed, however; another woman noted: "Oh, but not with the contraception and information that's available to women today! It's an individual thing."

These responses raised a question as to the propriety of the question itself. Would there have been a more positive response to the acceptance of sex on a casual basis if a less emotional term like "affection" had been used? It was too late to test this question in the study, but it was not too late to toss it at the adjunct singles organization. It appears that with this group, it was first necessary to define the terms being utilized. To the question "How do you define love?" a younger divorced person replied that it was "an emotional attachment. That you really care for people." An older man said that it means "you have to have a deep desire to please the person." On the other hand, affection was likened to the word "like." A young woman suggested that "you like a person; you enjoy being with him. You don't have to be in love with him."

From these responses, it appears that there is a willingness among singles to engage in sexual relations without marriage, but that some positive feelings have to be involved. The implication is that they will not have sexual relations alone as the price of the relationship. These replies do not gel with most people's interpretation of "swinging": that in order to have sex on a casual basis there should be strong, affectionate feelings but not necessarily the exclusive or possessiveness of romantic love. In sum, it appears that premarital intercourse is acceptable for both men and women under such conditions as a stable relationship marked by an engagement or love and when strong affection is present (Moneymaker and Montanino 1978). An author quoted in the earlier study goes so far as to claim that the "one-to-one young adult, heterosexual, consensual, affectionate relationship" has been completely accepted by America. Whether this is so will be clarified by a look at the numbers related to sexual encounters.

Another aspect of this same question is whether the situation dictates the feeling. What this question asks is whether a desired situation will make one believe that affection is involved and so allow for a sexual engagement. To answer this question, the sample was asked whether they would have sex in order to keep a date. Dating was chosen for this sexual situation since it is a very important element in the lives of singles. Thus, it came as a surprise that only 24 percent of the singles in the 1980 study would engage in a sexual encounter in order to keep a date. But it appears that this study was ahead of the curve of permissible sexual behavior, because twenty years later this figure had doubled to 48 percent.

Another study done at around the same time as the early study carried the dating question a step further by asking whether their sample would have sex on a first date. A somewhat surprising answer is that almost 75 percent of the men were indifferent or actually opposed to sleeping with a woman on a first

Table 7.2. Sexual Affairs (Yes)

| | Early/Current Studies | |
	To Keep a Date	Without Love
Never Married	24/48%	49/49%
Divorced	24/47	46/46
Totals	24/48	48/48

date. However, by the third date almost two-thirds of men and 50 percent of women have had sex with their partner (Simenauer and Carroll 1982).

SWING YOUR PARTNER

Technically, "swinging" is defined as a married couple having sexual relations with at least one other individual. Thus, swinging is not the same as adultery, since both partners are accorded equal privileges whereas adultery usually involves only one partner. The philosophy underlying swinging is that love and sex can be separated. The result is sexual involvement with others with little emotional involvement. This philosophical claim for swinging maybe true, but for other swingers there are other conditions underlying the effort. Modern society usually means that we live in more urbanized environments in relative isolation. Since sex is not an impersonal act, some swingers may use it as a means of gaining intimacy. Other benefits of swinging include:

- It is less time consuming and emotionally demanding than an affair.
- It offers sexual variety.
- It is sexually educative.
- It is honest and democratic, since both partners are involved.
- It is less dangerous with regard to losing a spouse than infidelity.

Swinging, however, is not without its drawbacks:

- Lack of emotional closeness may inhibit enjoyment and/or performance.
- Denial of ego satisfaction, since the partner was obtained by being available rather than charm.
- A worried air since the spouse's partner may be sexier and better looking and this may inhibit ability and enjoyment of the sex act.
- Philosophy involves having an affair only once with each new partner, there is an ongoing search for new partners that can be fatiguing.
- Subliminal fear that swinging can lead to venereal diseases (Murstein 1974)

Besides, swinging is hard work.

It would appear that swinging is neither a sexual paradise nor a practice that is practical. For these reasons, swinging appears to be a transitory stage in some marriages.

The discovery that love is not needed to engage in a sexual relationship and that singles would engage in a sexual relationship in order to keep a major aspect of their social life—dating—led to the belief that singles would, indeed, be the swingers compared to their married counterparts. And so it was, but with some interesting sidelights. However, two questions arose prior to administering the questionnaire to the sample. First, would the sample answer such delicate questions as to how many sexual partners they have had, how frequent were their sexual interludes, and how satisfied were they with their sexual lives? To those of an older generation, sexual behavior was a private matter, little discussed and believed to be of little involvement. Thus, it was believed to be rather uncouth to ask strangers, even anonymously, about their sex lives. With this belief, it seemed to be best to leave such questions until the end of the questionnaire, with the hope that after answering sixty-six questions, respondents would be encouraged to continue through these more sensitive questions. Whether this was the reason for the high rate of response (88 percent) to these questions is unknown, but answer they did—with seemingly no more hesitation than they did the questions on outing preferences: I would prefer to go to the theater over the movies but I selected the movies since it is more affordable; I remember eight partners but two of those were disasters and perhaps should not be counted. Another important question was at what point is the actor considered a swinger—having had more than one sexual partner, having had more than five sexual partners, or having had more than ten sexual partners? Obviously, quantitative interpretation depends on perception, and that perception depends on one's own experience. This being the situation, any figure chosen to represent swingers would encourage a debate.

No matter what figure is chosen, however, singles have had more sexual partners. In the 1980 study, 35 percent of the singles noted having no or only one partner, but by the time of the current study, this figure dropped to 16 percent. On the other hand, the numbers on the high end—of eleven or more partners increased—from 16 percent in the early study to 28 percent in the current study. A similar change is seen with the married. In the early study, half of the married (50 percent) had one or no sexual partners, whereas only 20 percent reported having few partners in the current study. Like the singles, there was a jump in the numbers of those claiming eleven or more partners: 11 percent in the early study versus 19 percent in the current study. These results confirm the belief that sexual behavior is becoming more acceptable for both married and singles.

It seems that in the early study, the label "swinger" might be applied to anyone who had more than one sexual partner, whereas a higher number would be more realistic by the time of the current study. However, the label is still not widely applicable, since the majority of both married and singles were limited to two or three sexual partners (M: 41 percent; S: 33 percent) or four to ten partners (M: 23 percent; S: 20 percent). It is only those singles with eleven or more partners who could claim that they were the true swingers, since they had had more sexual partners (26 percent to 19 percent). In both studies, it is the divorced who actually take the honors as swingers, since they were far more likely than those in the other categories to claim more than ten sexual partners. In the early study, they were twice as likely as the other singles category—the never-married—to make this claim (31 percent versus 16 percent) and five times more likely than the married categories (31 percent versus 5 percent). These figures, as they relate to the never-married, may come as a surprise, since the divorced were supposedly restricted to one partner during the time when they were married.

The biggest surprise regarding number of partners comes, however, with the current study in two categories: All groups show an increase in those claiming eleven or more sexual partners, and this was particularly true for the married (early study: 6 percent; current study:19 percent). In fact, the increase was so large for the married that they were more likely to claim the label "swinger" than the never-married (19 percent versus 17 percent). A recent federal study confirmed that the double standard that permitted sexual experiences for males but not females is also going by the wayside. Almost 18 percent of unmarried women and slightly more than 13 percent of married women have had at least ten sexual partners (Statistical Abstract of the United States 1999). It appears that the claim made earlier regarding the acceptance of heterosexual, consensual, affectionate relationships by Americans is true and becoming more so by the married, and that this claim also holds true for women.

As an added check on this assertion of the acceptance of heterosexual sex, the adjunct singles organization was asked to describe their ideas in this regard. It was believed that they would add some extra depth to the discussion, since most of them were divorced and the divorced are the most likely to be swingers. A divorced man and woman began the following duet regarding what they believed to be the unique situation of the divorced. The man started: "I see the divorced people, as a whole, in a situation in which they want no strings attached, they treat sex on a very casual basis."

"Right! And not on a personal basis."

"Right!"

"And, therefore, they can hold that on a level where they don't put any . . ."

"Human . . ."

"Human holds on the opposite person's . . ."

"Feelings. They don't put anything."

The idea of no strings attached may be an aftereffect of the divorce itself. A younger woman indicated that she thought a lot of it was due to cheating: "Men find other women and women find other men." However, another young woman disagreed: "I think when one person in a marriage seeks somebody outside, the marriage is already in trouble."

Others noted that there is a searching process going on: "A lot of times if you were satisfied with your sex life when you were married, you look for the same thing." Another person chimed in, "And that's hard to do because it took years to build up."

Other ideas tossed out by the group regarding the increased sexual activity among the divorced included such aspects of human behavior as our strong sex drives and that sex is a natural activity. There is also the need to reaffirm one's sexual attractiveness and to dull the pain of the divorce, loneliness, and boredom. An older woman believed that such sexual activity tapers off after a time: "When you are going through a divorce, one of the stages is affirming your manhood or your womanhood, and that does involve sexual activity. But then it tapers off as you realize how unsatisfactory one-night stands, or whatever you want to call them, are. Then moderation and selectivity sets in. So it's skewed to the first several months of a divorce and then it changes as you grow as a human being." This idea was seemingly confirmed by another woman's belief that those sexual relationships are not as casual as they sound: "To me, after six or seven times over a span of six months or more with the same partner, that's not casual sex."

Since this study compares the behavior of singles to that of the married, it was necessary to expand the married/single comparison by analyzing the other two categories of the sample—the divorced and the remarried—because of their distinct contribution. If swinging is defined as those people who have had more than ten sexual partners, then the early study, taken at the beginnings of a boom in the number of singles, reveals that it was a limited behavior: only 6 percent of the married and 19 percent of the singles claimed this many partners. In each category, the figure is high due to the activity of one of the two subgroups involved: The remarried were twice as likely as those married once to have this many partners (10 percent versus 5 percent) and the situation is similar when comparing the divorced to the never-married (31 percent versus 16 percent). By the time of the current study, following a period of rapid growth in the number of singles due to the increasing average age at first marriage and the increasing rate of divorce, it could still be said that swinging behavior is limited, even though the number of those participating in this behavior had doubled since the early study: 23 percent versus 11 percent. A trend toward increased numbers engaged in swinging behavior is indicated, since the numbers who were swinging had increased for each category involved: the never-married from 16 percent to 17 percent, the divorced from 31 percent to 44 percent, the married once from 5 percent to 17 percent, and the remarried from 10 percent to 22 percent. It should be added, however, that the increase in the numbers of those having more than ten sexual partners for the married does not automatically translate into a belief that more married are

Table 7.3. Number of Sexual Partners: Self

| | Early/Current Studies | | | |
	0–1	*2–3*	*4–10*	*11+*
Never Married	42/21%	21/40%	22/22%	15/17%
Divorced	14/4	31/37	25/14	31/45
Married Once	66/24	15/41	14/18	5/17
Remarried	23/4	38/38	28/36	10/22
Singles Total	35/16	24/35	23/21	19/28
Married Total	50/20	21/40	19/22	11/19

engaging in extramarital affairs, since their multiple partners may have come with their later age of marriage, and thus an increased period of singleness.

SEXUAL PARTNERS: OTHERS

Is this increase in the number of sexual partners a trend occurring in society in general, or a fluke of this particular sample? This seemed like an important question to ask since it would give a clue as to the truthfulness of the earlier statement that affectionate heterosexual behavior is now an accepted fact of American life. To answer this question, each segment of the sample was asked how many sexual partners they thought that others in their same category had had. In the 1980 study, none of the categories could believe that others in their category had had none or only one sexual partner. This was especially true for those in a first marriage: 66 percent claimed having this few sexual partners, but only 39 percent believed this was true of others in this category. This trend was reflected when looking at the other end of the sexual partner spectrum, those having more than ten sexual partners: Only the divorced did not believe that others were as likely to have this many partners. Although the divorced stood out from the other categories, with 31 percent claiming eleven or more sexual partners, only 14 percent could believe that others in their category had as many sexual partners. The other component of the singles segment, the never-married, seemingly believed that the stereotype of swinging was true but that they individually were just unlucky: 16 percent claimed eleven or more partners, but 39 percent believed that others had this many partners. Both of the married segments also believed that others in their category had more sexual partners: 6 percent versus 11 percent.

By the time of the current study, the swinging image had apparently become an accepted fact for all segments in the sample. Despite large increases in their own numbers claiming eleven or more sexual partners, the belief across the categories was that even more people were engaging with as many at least as many partners. This was especially true for the group with the

Table 7.4. Sexual Partners: Beliefs about Others in Their Category

	0–1	*2–3*	*4–10*	*11+*
		Early/Current Studies		
Never Married	12/5%	35/40%	31/26%	23/28%
Divorced	6/6	34/34	43/28	17/33
Married Once	27/6	45/42	18/32	10/20
Remarried	13/2	40/31	28/47	20/20
Singles Total	11/5	35/38	34/27	20/30
Married Total	19/5	41/40	26/35	15/20

largest number claming this many sexual partners: the divorced. It was noted that 44 percent of the divorced had claimed having had at least eleven sexual partners but a far larger number, 77 percent, believed that other divorcées had been involved with this many sexual partners. There was also a large increase in the number in other categories who believed that others in their category had eleven or more partners: among the never-married it increased 28 percent, and among the married once and the remarried it increased 20 percent. It would appear that the swinger image may be partially true and that it is becoming more so, but in the minds of all the categories as represented in the sample, it is not a stereotype but a true fact.

FREQUENCY OF SEXUAL RELATIONS

The findings on numbers brought about the question of why this seeming non-relationship. A number of ideas were examined and, while probably true, did not provide the hoped for one-to-one relationship being sought. This led to the idea that greater frequency of sexual encounters would lead to greater satisfaction with one's sex life. In short, was there a relationship between frequency of sexual intercourse and one's feeling of sexual satisfaction? The author had already taken a deep gulp over asking what appeared to be the indelicate questions of numbers of sexual partners, and so now turning to what seemed to be an even more delicate question was not a drawback, despite the need to phrase the question for the computer thusly:

During the past six months, how often have you had sexual intercourse?

1. Almost never
2. Once or twice a month
3. Once or twice a week
4. Three or more times a week

Table 7.5.   Sexual Frequency: Past 6 Months

| | Early/Current Studies | | |
	1/Week or Less	2	3+
Never Married	67/48%	21/37%	12/18%
Divorced	42/69	22/16	36/15
Married Once	35/45	37/35	28/20
Remarried	43/33	33/50	25/17
Singles Total	61/56	21/29	18/15
Married Total	36/43	36/38	28/20

Apparently, this question did not faze the respondents, since almost 88 percent answered it. Perhaps it is no surprise that the married report that they have sexual intercourse more often than the single, since they have an available sexual partner nearby. In the first study, 28 percent of the married claimed a sexual frequency of three or more times a week, compared to only 18 percent of the singles. Interesting is the fact that for both groups, there was a decline in the number claiming such frequency by the time of the second study—a time of seeming even more heightened sexual promotion: In 1980 28 percent of the married claimed this high number versus only 20 percent in the current study and 18 percent of the singles claimed this number in the earlier study but only 15 percent in the current claimed this frequency. This change in frequency is also seen at the other end of the scale. In the first study, a whopping 61 percent of singles indicated a sexual intercourse frequency of only once per week or less, compared with 56 percent in the current study. Interestingly, fewer married respondents noted a frequency of once per week or less (36 percent), but with more partners in the current study, the number claiming this frequency increased (43 percent). These results tie in with national sex surveys on frequency: Forty-three percent of married men report having sex at least twice per week, whereas only 26 percent of noncohabitating single men claim this frequency. The results are similar for married women (39 percent) versus single women (20 percent).

These figures for both the married and the single—especially the divorced—confirm the suspicion that it is not the number of partners that count in producing sexual satisfaction, but rather its ongoing frequency.

SEXUAL SATISFACTION

The acceptance of affection rather than the deeper feelings of love as a reason to engage in a sexual relationship seems to have translated into an acceptance of individuals having more sexual partners. It does not, however, translate in all cases to more sexual encounters per week. This seeming contradiction leaves open the question of sexual satisfaction. If singles have more adventurous sex lives with regard to having numerous partners but less frequency, does this type of activity provide greater sexual satisfaction than the less varied but steady sex life of the married?

Prior studies indicate that variety is not the spice of sexual life. *Redbook*, in a "startling new report" reassured us that the number of sexual partners is not a valid index of satisfying sexual relationships (Tavris 1978). The results of the National Sex Survey seem to agree: Married men and women were more satisfied with sex than were sexually active singles. As the examination of this question will show, whatever the advantage in numbers, divorce does not seem to improve one's satisfaction with regard to sex.

In the two studies, all of the groups seemed to agree that quantity was not directly related with satisfaction. In the 1980 study fewer married respondents claimed to have had more than ten sexual partners, yet a whopping 80 percent of them claimed to be sexually satisfied; only about half (53 percent) of the singles made this claim. The current study notes a vast increase in the number of both married and singles claiming more than ten sexual partners, but the numbers claiming sexual satisfaction declined slightly (M: 65 percent; S: 46 percent). This lack of correlation is probably best illustrated by the divorced. When it came to having multiple partners, this category that stood out in the early study, yet they were far less likely than the married to claim sexual satisfaction (61 percent versus 80 percent). The current study showed that the number of divorced claiming more than ten sexual partners had increased substantially, yet the number claiming sexual satisfaction had dropped to 47 percent.

Confirmation that there is no correlation between number of partners and sexual satisfaction is also seen with the married. Although there is a large increase in those claiming to have had more than ten sexual partners in the current study, there is also a decline in the number claiming sexual satisfaction (80 percent versus 65 percent). Although the number claiming sexual dissatisfaction was small in both studies for all groups (M: 6 percent, early study and 13 percent, current study; S: 18 percent, both studies), these numbers did not decline as the numbers of those not sure of their sexual satisfaction did. Thus, those ranking their sexual satisfaction as satisfactory or unsatisfactory increased from 15 percent to 23 percent for the married and from 30 percent to 36 percent for the single. Supporting this seemingly limited sexual satisfaction with, another study on singles done about the same time as the 1980 study noted that only 39 percent of the men and 25 percent of the women rated their sex lives as "good" (Simenauer and Carroll 1982).

These findings on sexual satisfaction raise the question: Why participate with such large numbers of partners if there is no increase in satisfaction? This is the question that was posed to the adjunct singles organization. According to them, having multiple partners was not a situation of gamesmanship. Respondents spoke rather of the positives gained from sexual participation: feelings of being attractive, acceptable, and worthwhile, and the resulting feeling of personal power. All these positive feelings add to their self-esteem and thereby provided them with a sense of self. These feelings are especially important to the divorced, who are often suffering from a sense of rejection. Other thoughts were that the game of catch-as-catch-can is less emotionally demanding, eliminates sexual boredom, and can be less time consuming. The singles also mentioned a need that is satisfied: sex was a habit that they had gotten used to and so "like an itch, wants to be scratched."

Despite these benefits, they noted that swinging may not be satisfactory since it involves a constant search for a new partner, there is the increased possibility of sexually transmitted diseases, and the lack of emotional closeness may prevent the ability to perform the act or to perform it adequately. Thus, it appears that swinging has its benefits but also its drawbacks. Whether the resulting behavior is satisfactory or not depends on the individual's basic reasons for having numerous partners. As noted, the divorced are most likely to have numerous partners, but they are also more likely to be dissatisfied with their sexual excursions. The reasons given for this indulgence may all be true, but it may not be what the divorced person is actually seeking in the affair. Considering the usually rather quick turnaround from divorce to remarriage, what really may be sought is an enduring intimate relationship. Perhaps, then, it is no surprise that in the first study the remarried had the highest satisfaction rate of all the groups, even those in first marriages. The satisfaction rate for the remarried dropped in the current study, but is still far higher than the singles category: 65 percent versus 46 percent.

Table 7.6. Sexual Satisfaction

| | Early/Current Studies | | |
	Satisfied	Neutral	Dissatisfied
Never Married	49/45%	32/37%	18/18%
Divorced	61/47	22/35	17/10
Married Once	78/65	16/22	6/13
Remarried	83/62	12/26	5/13
Singles Total	53/46	30/36	18/18
Married Total	80/65	14/23	6/13

CONCLUSION: THE SEXUAL PICTURE

Beliefs regarding sexual behavior in this country are divided between traditional late-Victorian values and contemporary values. About 20 percent of American adults disapprove of premarital sex, believe that masturbation and homosexuality are shameful and that sexual pleasure is sinful, and condemn extramarital sex. When it comes to adultery, the double standard is the norm, since women are expected to be more forgiving of cheating husbands than men of cheating wives. In short, for participation in sexual behavior, marriage is required—without any extras. Since marriage and having children are the norm, divorce is considered a tragedy. Perhaps, not surprising, these people tend to be religious conservatives.

The remaining 80 percent of the population have a more liberal set of sexual values that are almost the opposite of the traditional values noted earlier. Sexual pleasure is viewed positively, masturbation is considered a source of pleasure, and premarital sexual intimacy is believed to be appropriate for most adults and especially for those couples who are "in love" or planning to get married. Since people are waiting longer to get married, it is recognized that many people will engage in several sexual relationships prior to marriage. Thus, unattached sex with multiple sexual partners has become more acceptable; marriage and family are still the norm, but having few children or remaining child-free are not condemned. In line with this more positive view of sexual behavior comes a toleration of homosexuality. But it is important to realize that these newer patterns have not replaced the traditional ones; they have joined them to create a more pluralistic view of sex, marriage, and family.

This pluralistic view of sexual behavior does not, however, completely describe the beliefs regarding the sexual behavior of singles. The typical sexual stereotype of the single person is that he—and in today's sexual climate, probably she—is a swinger. In other words, singles are thought to be likely to have a continuous number of sexual partners. The change in the sexual climate also means that this is something to brag about rather than a source of shame. In an age of supposedly easy sex, not having someone to have sex with means that there really is something wrong with you. This view of "easy sex," however, seems contradictory to reality. The studies reveal that the bragging rights belong to few singles and fewer married people, despite an increase in those claiming multiple partners in this seemingly more sexual liberal period. Even here the figures are misleading, since it is mostly one group—the divorced—that skews the overall numbers this high, and even in that group a majority do not report having more than ten sexual partners. Thus, the stereotype of singles as being swingers may be partly true, but only for the divorced. The never-married report similar figures as the married, but this may change since the average age at first marriage is increasing. The number of married people who report having had multiple partners is increasing rapidly, but this fact has not been recognized by a shift in the stereotype. Thus, it appears that when the public, especially the married, thinks of the swinger—the lecherous movement from one sexual partner to another—the image remains fixed on the never-married and not, as it should, on the "gay divorcée."

The increasing number of sexual partners reported by all four categories of the sample raises the question: Why? What has encouraged this movement toward what appears to be greater sexual permissiveness? A number of factors have contributed to this libertine movement of easier availability of sexual partners. Perhaps the most important of these are the ease of use and widespread availability of birth control. Another major factor in encouraging more liberal sex was the development of the women's movement, which, probably more than any other factor, eased the restrictions of the double standard regarding women. A final major factor affecting this shift is the seemingly earlier sexual maturity of teens. Teens today start dating earlier, and earlier dating leads to earlier experimentation with sexual intercourse. The old progression of dating, going steady, becoming engaged, and then getting married appears to be passé. All of these changes led to a change in the terms for engaging in sexual encounters—one no longer needs love for such an engagement; simply liking someone is enough for this affectionate response. Thus, this seeming revolution in our sexual heritage was not created by the media but by advances of technology and society: more reliable methods of birth control, easier conditions for obtaining a divorce, and the disintegration of the idea of community that accompanied increased mobility. However, the media did encourage the sexual revolution ideals of sex without love or marriage by publicizing and popularizing it—the *Playboy* philosophy of "swinging liberation" became more acceptable and desirable.

The movement toward more swinging behavior raises a second question: What are the benefits of such behavior that encourage its interaction? For singles, it may be their only way of getting steady sex, which it is assumed is a given for married couples. Overall, this appears to be true since more married respondents than singles reported greater frequency of sexual intercourse per week despite a fewer number of partners. However, doubt is cast on this finding when the sample is broken down into its various segments. This breakdown reveals that larger numbers of the divorced group reported having more frequent sexual relations than the married, and, as was noted, the divorced were far more likely to have multiple sexual partners. Seeming to confirm this relationship were the responses of the never-married, who as a group, were the least likely to report multiple sex partners and high sexual frequency. By the time of the current study, doubt is cast that there is any relationship between number of partners and frequency of intercourse: All the categories in the sample reveal that more of their members are engaging in sexual intercourse with more different partners, yet all groups reveal a decline in frequency of sexual intercourse. Thus, it appears that the hoped-for goal of having more sexual partners may be increased frequency of sexual intercourse, but that this is rarely the outcome.

The conclusions reached in examining numbers and frequency leads to another possible reason for swinging—greater sexual satisfaction despite the lack of frequency. The findings on the two previous questions seem to confirm this possibility: Although increasing in numbers, the married were still less likely than the divorced to have multiple sexual partners, were as likely to have multiple frequencies of sexual intercourse per week, and were far more likely than either single category to report that they were satisfied with their sex lives.

If sexual satisfaction is not based on number of partners or frequency of sexual intercourse, why, then, is there this movement toward greater number of sexual partners? Strange as it may seem, it may be based on the belief that this is what other people in their category are doing. This conclusion seems to be true in the 1980 study, since all groups reported believing that others in their category were likely to have had more sexual partners. However, with the increase in sexual encounters with more partners by all groups noted in the current study, this belief has seemingly faded. Now, only the never-married are likely to hold such beliefs.

As noted, the major stereotype held by the public regarding the sex life of singles is that they are "swingers"—lechers who hop from bed to bed. If you want to meet a swinger, however, your best bet is to talk to a divorced person. As a divorced man from the adjunct singles group explained, "A lot of times you were satisfied with your sex life when you were married and so now you look for the same thing." Another divorced man added, "And that's hard to do because it took years to build up." This may explain why marital sex has a number of advantages over nonmarital sex: It is confined to an available and steady partner, it is conducted in a favorable environment, and it meets with social approval and so is free of guilt. As noted, more married persons rated their sexual satisfaction higher than did singles of all categories. This also seems to explain why swinging rarely leads to increased frequency of sexual encounters and sexual satisfaction. Despite the lack of relationship between numbers, encounters, and satisfaction, it is unlikely that the pursuit of numbers will decline, since most people do not understand the relationship and so they will continue to be encouraged to seek numbers by those who profit from this business.

Chapter Eight

The Use of Leisure Time

INTRODUCTION: DEFINING "LEISURE"

"Leisure" has been defined as "the various recreational activities that people engage in." This definition sees leisure as activities conducted in one's free time. Another definition of leisure might be considered a social class refinement, since it adds the idea of improvement of oneself through the "cultivation of self, meditation, and the development of true spiritual freedom" (Kando 1975). During the 1950s, a shortening of the workweek and a seemingly inexhaustible material affluence led to the emergence of almost endless free time in which to pursue leisure activities.

Does more free time mean a change in activities? A Roper poll found that a move to a four-day or three-day workweek would mean that:

- People would get soft and lazy with all that leisure time (20 percent).
- People would simply get bored having too little to do (20 percent).
- People would find things to do so that they would be just as busy as they are now (32 percent).
- People would enjoy the extra time, relax more, and be happier (24 percent). (deGrazia 1964)

As can be seen, having more leisure time is not necessarily a positive condition. Proof of this is seen as the century wore on. Economic pitfalls and new consumption practices meant that women began to work outside the home, and others used their free time from the shortened workweek to moonlight on second jobs. Even without the extra burden of extra work, the individual actually has little spare time during the day for leisure. It has been estimated that out of a twenty-four-hour day, one spends about eight hours on the job; another two hours and forty minutes commuting; an average of ten and a half hours on such subsistence activities as dressing, eating, and sleeping; and about twenty minutes per day on miscellaneous activities. The result is that one has an average of two and a half hours per day of free time for leisure activities (deGrazia 1964). It appears that the term "leisure" is little understood or thought about. Still, people have leisure time, whether recognized or not. Thus, the question to be answered in this chapter is whether the activities engaged in during this limited free time is different for married people and singles. In short, do singles actually have more fun, because they have more time to have fun?

THE GRASS IS GREENER

Some of us never go out and some of us never stay home. The crouchers and the wanderers. The inert and the restless. (Holland 1992)

In reflecting on their activities during the past week, married people will take a gulp and wonder how they managed to accomplish all the tasks with which they were confronted. In addition to work—now usually performed by both partners—there were such household tasks as meal preparation, grocery shopping, cleaning, doing the laundry, mowing and other yard work, and, perhaps, cleaning the garage. For those who are parents, there are the tasks related to the children—helping with their homework, taking them wherever they need to go, sport coaching involvement, dealing with their medical needs, going to parent-teacher nights, taking time to listen to them talk about their activities and complaints, and dealing with whatever other of their needs and wants that arise. Added to all this are the required visits to church and the in-laws. Families are time consuming, and married people often believe that the grass is greener on the other side. It seems that their single friends are always on a weeklong round of fun activities. To listen to them, their single friends are always getting together with other single friends in the condo for drinks, playing games, and enjoyable conversations about sports and the opposite sex. They always seem to be off on a walk in the park or on a leisurely bike ride or going away for a weekend trip. Of course, none of their conversations with their single friends would be complete without tales of their numerous affairs—after all, they are supposed to be swingers.

A discussion with these same singles, however, would reveal that this vision is overly romanticized. Singles must also work, and are often expected to take work home with them and even take classes as a means to obtain a promotion. They also have to do all the requisite household tasks—and without the help of a mate. Granted, because they don't have the obligations to children and spouse, they can go out anytime they desire, but it really is not as simple as all that since there is often no pleasure in doing these things alone and so it is necessary to make arrangements with others for such excursions. This may mean having to change plans to fit other people's schedules or facing the "downer" of rejection. In short, having fun for singles is a production, and working hard to have fun takes away from it. Of course, a large number of singles are the divorced, who have the added responsibility of raising children on their own or making time to spend with noncustodial children. As one divorced woman from the adjunct singles organization sample noted, "I'm supposed to be going to discos every night? I couldn't. I'm going to college full-time."

Each of the images portrayed earlier has a certain amount of plausibility. As a means of determining whether one image or the other has more feasibility, several questions were asked regarding the frequency of social outings and, as a check on the fun question, what sort of activities are involved. Of course, the main reason for these varied activities is to have fun. As a further check on the fun question, chapter 9 is devoted an attempt to answer this question by asking the sample to self-rate their various outlooks in such areas as happiness and getting fun out of life.

THE ROAMERS

It is not surprising to find out that those in the married category report going out socially less often than those in the single category. Singles, if they are to avoid the old bugaboo of loneliness, must go out socially. Thus, in the two studies, 29 percent of the singles reported going out socially three or more times per week, as compared with 8 percent of the married. Going out infrequently appears to be mostly in the realm of the married or formerly married. An average of 42 percent of those in a first marriage in both studies reported going out socially less than once per week, and another 45 percent reported managing a social outing once per week. Not quite as restricted in social outings are the remarried and the divorced, where an average of 88 percent of the remarried and 72 percent of the divorced in both studies claimed a social outing once per week or less. Probably what these three groupings have in common are children; the difficulties and expense of getting a sitter may not be worth the hassle. Still, if the divorced desire adult companionship, they must go out socially, and an average of 26 percent in both studies reported doing so to the tune of three or more times per week.

Table 8.1.   Going Out Socially

	Early/Current Studies		
	< 1/Week	1–2	3+
Never Married	21/11%	48/59%	31/30%
Divorced	30/36	48/36	22/29
Married Once	41/43	51/40	8/17
Remarried	30/37	61/55	9/8
Singles Totals	23/20	48/51	29/29
Married Totals	39/42	53/43	8/15

Another possible explanation for the infrequency of social outings noted by the married is seen when looking at where they prefer to go on these social outings: Respondents in both of the married categories chose visiting relatives. Perhaps, then, another possible explanation for this infrequency of going out socially is that visiting relatives is not considered by the married to be a social outing. Adding to this explanation is the fact that in the current study, those reporting visiting relatives declined by 14 percent (from 42 percent to 28 percent) for the married, while those reporting going out three or more times per week doubled (8 percent to 17 percent). Although their visitations to relatives also declined for the remarried in the current study (from 43 percent to 37 percent), they report going out less frequency, with a decline from 9 percent to 8 percent. Perhaps the explanation for this difference between those married once and those who are remarried lies in the term "combined family."

The belief, then, that singles have more freedom seems to be confirmed by the greater frequency of their social outings. However, this may be changing, since the number of those married once reporting social outings three or more times per week doubled between the two studies, from 8 percent to 17 percent, and the number of never-married reporting this frequency declined from 31 percent to 30 percent.

LEISURE-TIME ACTIVITIES

Knowing what singles do in their leisure time might reveal whether the social activities are for fun or a means of escaping loneliness. In short, the question is whether the findings here add to those found in the chapter on happiness (chapter 9) or the chapter on loneliness (chapter 10). Knowing what people do on their social outings might also allow for an understanding of the stereotype that singles have more fun. If the activities selected by singles are different from those selected by the married, are they also be considered to be more fun?

A long-ago survey of leisure activities indicated that the top ten actually engaged in on the previous day included:

- Watching television (57 percent)
- Visiting friends or relatives (38 percent)
- Working around the yard (33 percent)
- Reading the newspaper (27 percent)
- Reading books (18 percent)
- Driving for pleasure (17 percent)
- Listening to music (14 percent)
- Going to meetings (11 percent)
- Engaging in hobbies (10 percent)
- Going out to dinner (8 percent)

Since individual respondents may have engaged in more than one activity, the totals add up to more than 100 percent. Less popular activities included sports, playing cards, music activity, movies, dances, plays, and concerts (deGrazia 1964).

The list derived from the two studies here will be different from the previously shown list, since the questionnaire asked what respondents' favorite social activities were, not what they actually did the previous day. Also, the samples in the studies were given a list of activities for ranking and so may have inadvertently left out some favorite activities. Thus, watching television was not included since it was not considered a social activity. However, there were some similarities since people usually do most what they like the most.

The most popular choices for both the married and the singles in both studies were visiting friends, going to restaurants, and going to the movies. In this age of impersonality, personal relations have supposedly been eroded by urbanization and television. To a point this appears to be true, since the impersonal television watching led all other activities by far in the study noted above; however, activities that include personal relations such as visiting friends were next in popularity. Confirming the popularity of personal relations is the fact that in the first study, more than half (55 percent) of both the never-married and the divorced selected socializing with friends as their favorite social activity. However, for the married, visiting friends was a second choice to going to restaurants (58 percent versus 55 percent). Going to restaurants was a much less popular choice for singles than it was for the married (43 percent versus 58 percent) and was almost tied with going to the movies as a desired social outing (42 percent). Since going to a restaurant or a movie may also involve friends, the importance of friends in social outings becomes even more pronounced. However, the importance of friends in social outings appears to be declining for the married. By the time of the current study, visiting friends as a social outing had declined from 55 percent to 47 percent, while the preference for going to restaurants increased from 58 percent to 69 percent. In fact, for the married, visiting friends was actually tied with going to the movies—a choice that almost doubled in popularity, from 25 percent to 47 percent. Since there was no such change for the singles, it appears that friends are somewhat less important to the married than to singles for social outings. This might be explained by the fact that married people have partners to join them at restaurants or the movies, whereas the single must seek a partner and friends are always there.

Another surprise was the finding that going to a restaurant was more popular with the married than with singles. It was believed that singles would spend more time at restaurants than the married, since meal preparation is a hassle after a day at work and eating alone would seem to be lonelier than eating with a group of strangers. Perhaps singles do go to restaurants more often than the married but simply do not interpret everyday eating out as a social outing. On the other hand, with both partners in a marriage usually working, eating out is both more affordable and a break from the routine of meal making after work. Regardless of which of these ideas is correct, eating out at a restaurant has become, by the time of the current study, the overwhelming first choice for all the categories in the sample.

It is only in turning to the less popular choices that a difference in selection for social outings among the categories is noted. These differences involved preferences for visiting relatives versus going to a nightclub (bar). In the 1980 study, almost half of the married (42 percent) chose visiting relatives as a popular outing, whereas only 18 percent of the singles found this a desirable outing. When it came to visiting nightclubs (bars), however, the opposite was true: 36 percent of singles chose this option as compared to only 20 percent of the married. However, by the time of the current study, the differences between these selections were less pronounced. For visiting relatives there was only a difference of 7 percent (30 percent to 37 percent) as this option became far more popular with the divorced (24 percent versus 41 percent) and far less popular with those married once (36 percent to 17 percent). One wonders if the increase in visiting relatives by the divorced means that divorce has become more acceptable to those relatives. The decline in visiting relatives for those married once appears to be tied with a big jump in preference for going out to a restaurant, from 56 percent to 69 percent. On the other hand, going to a nightclub (bar) was always a lesser preference for both married groups (20 percent and 16 percent), whereas for the singles this preference increased by the time of the second study (from 36 percent to 49 percent). This change came about due to a large decline by the remarried (from 27 percent to 14 percent) and a large increase by the never-married (from 35 percent to 53 percent) in selecting this option. It appears that for the married, leading what appears to be a staid life, the restaurant is probably thought of as a nice social pleasure, allowing one to escape the drudgery of the kitchen. On the other hand, a nightclub (bar) is an exciting, exceptional place to visit on occasion. However, for the single the nightclub (bar) has a primary function not needed by the married: meeting possible partners. The owner of a singles bar explains: "For city dwellers, the bar scene fills an immense vacuum. Let's face it, people don't meet at church anymore" (*Newsweek* 1973). This being the case, many singles set aside a regular part of their budget for drinking and socializing (Brooks 1981). It is this role of meeting others that probably explains why going to a nightclub (bar) has overtaken going to a movie as a preferred social outing by singles (49 percent to 42 percent).

Before turning to a summary of the findings on social outings, it should be noted that a number of other possible outing choices were offered, but they received few selections by the sample in either study despite the fact that they included going to church. Perhaps, church going is not seen as a social outing by either segment of the sample.

Asked to give their top three choices for a social outing, the main choices for singles in the 1980 study were visiting friends, going to restaurants, going to the movies, going to nightclubs (bars), and visiting relatives. The only difference in these choices between the two singles categories was seen with the divorced preferring going to a nightclub (bar) over going to a restaurant or a movie. Twenty years later, two major changes in preference by the singles had occurred: going to a restaurant moved ahead of visiting friends as a first choice (60 percent versus 53 percent) and going to a nightclub (bar) was now in third place, ahead of going to the movies. This was primarily due to nightclub (bar) going vastly increasing in popularity for the never-married (from 35 percent to 53 percent).

Turning to the preferences for social outings of the married in the 1980 study, it is seen that their main choices were similar to the singles only in the preference of friends and restaurants for the first two choices. Whereas the singles selected going to the movies as a third choice, the married chose visiting relatives next in the order of preference. The popularity of going to nightclubs (bars) is similarly lower than visiting relatives or going to a movie. In the current study, the ranking of these choices for the married remained the same.

The noted differences in preferences for social outings raise the question of what shapes these choices. Since the major difference between the two major segments of the sample is that members of one group have a mate and the other do not, a major factor shaping choices appears to be the need for singles to find companionship. Thus, singles spend more time visiting friends and in such buffer activities as going to nightclubs (bars) while finding their way into new relationships.

This seems to be a greater problem for the divorced, who often find themselves deserted by their friends from their former marriage. The situation was summed up by a divorced respondent in the adjunct singles organization, who noted: "I had what I thought were close married friends right in my neighborhood. We were partying back and forth. I've been divorced for two and a half years. I've never been invited over; they never call up. I run into them once in a while and that hurts. When you feel they were friends of yours and when you are divorced, they don't want to hear from you." Despite the hurt, the divorced respondents believed they understand the reason for this rejection by their former married friends' insecurity: "The insecurity lies in the people that don't invite you to their homes. If people are secure in themselves, they'll invite you."

Another divorced woman explained that this insecurity is based on the belief by married women that "single women become creatures in negligees." Many of the other divorced women could not understand this insecurity, since there always seemed to be a separation of the sexes whenever they got together: "If you think back on the married parties you went to, the men are in one room discussing sports and the women are in the other room. So what is the threat if they invite a single woman?" A divorced male tossed out the idea that maybe that is what the married women are afraid of—"[that] you'll be in there with the sports."

But another woman reminded the group that it is not all one-sided. The singles must also take some responsibility, since they may be excluded because an escort is more appropriate at a particular affair. This rejoinder is a reminder of the biggest need and desire of singles—a companion to join them on social outings. This has been, and maybe still is, a greater problem for women. As one woman explained apologetically, "I'm not that aggressive. You know, I still cannot call a man. I'm back some years ago when men called women." But having a partner does not mean that married people have an open choice of social outings, either; the partner's preference often shapes couples' choices for social outings. As one divorced woman explained, "My former husband was antisocial. Therefore, I either had to do things alone or stay home."

As an added check on the question of preferred social outings, respondents were asked how much time they spent per week actually doing these activities. Since visiting friends was a main social outing choice, it was compared to the major independent activity: watching television. It was not expected

Table 8.2. Preferred Social Outings

			Early/Current Studies			
	Restaurant	Friends	Movie	Bar	Relatives	Theater
Never Married	44/62%	56/53%	45/48%	35/53%	17/19%	20/19%
Divorced	38/55	51/54	32/30	41/43	24/41	14/9
Married Once	1/11	56/69	52/47	23/46	36/17	42/9
Remarried	68/69	66/45	34/47	19/13	43/37	12/12
Singles Total	43/60	55/53	42/42	36/49	18/37	18/10
Married Total	58/69	55/47	25/47	20/16	42/30	12/8

that respondents would report spending more time visiting friends than watching television, but rather that the comparison would provide some idea of the importance of visiting friends. It is seen that visiting friends is indeed very important for both categories, since almost as much time was spent on this activity as watching television, and it seems to have become more important over time since there was a large increase between the studies in the number of respondents reporting spending three or more hours per week visiting friends: Singles reported 25 percent in the 1980 study and 77 percent in the current study, while married respondents reported 18 percent in the early study and 61 percent current study. This large increase in time spent visiting friends was true for all four of the categories examined. It is not surprising that singles spent more time visiting friends than the married since friends provide their major source of companionship.

But no one can go out every evening to visit friends or visit other places that take up energy and money. This leaves the very passive time user of watching television. A national study indicates that singles have the tube on an average of twenty-nine hours per week (de Grazia 1964). This is not the same as watching television, however, because many singles automatically turn on

Table 8.3. Leisure Activities (Hours per Week)

	Early/Current Studies					
	TV			Friends		
	0	1–2	3+	0	1–2	3+
Never Married	7/2%	51/17%	42/81%	6/2%	55/18%	39/78%
Divorced	6/2	58/18	36/80	10/4	69/20	21/76
Married Once	9/3	49/17	42/80	15/5	64/34	18/61
Remarried	7/2	48/16	45/82	16/6	63/31	21/63
Singles Total	7/2	53/18	41/80	7/5	58/19	25/77
Married Total	8/3	49/17	42/80	17/5	64/34	18/61

their televisions when they come home; with its constant yammering, it provides the impression that they are not alone. When it is watched, it is more for the purpose of having something in common to discuss at the water cooler, a shared experience that binds us.

DATING

Most singles prefer to spend their leisure time on outings with someone else to share in the enjoyment. This usually means finding a date. Of course, there are preferences in seeking a date. In a study conducted in 1977 among college students, both the men and women agreed on their most valued qualities in someone to date: looks and personality. Another area of agreement was on the asset of good conversation; both agreed that its importance was seventh out of eight choices. The other attributes were arranged in different order of preference. For the men, intelligence was a fourth choice after sex appeal, whereas the women placed intelligence in last place and omitted sex appeal all together. Both agreed that a sense of humor was important, but the men put it in sixth place after good companionship while the women placed it fourth, after thoughtfulness. A final choice was that of honesty. Again, the women valued this asset more higly than the men; in this case they made it a fifth choice, whereas the men had it last. In sum, there were two items ranked by the men but not mentioned by the women: sex appeal (3rd) and good companionship (5th). The women also listed had two assets that they believed to be important that were not mentioned by the men: thoughtfulness (3rd) and respect (6th; Saxton 1977).

The current study also asked the singles what attributes they preferred in a date. Since it can reasonably be assumed that the married are not looking for

Table 8.4. Qualities Most Valued in a Date, by Rank

	Men	Women
Looks	1	1
Personality	2	2
Sex Appeal	3	—
Intelligence	4	8
Good Companionship	5	—
Sense of Humor	6	4
Good Conversation	7	7
Honesty	8	5
Thoughtfulness	—	3
Respect	—	6

Table 8.5. Qualities Sought in a Date (Current Study)

	Never Married	Divorced	Total
Looks	16%	14%	15%
Humor	15	14	15
Finances	15	10	13
Sociability	14	14	14
Consideration	13	14	14
Being Healthy	12	12	12
Other (Combined)	16	21	18

dates, the findings were examined according to the subcategories of the singles heading only. The most interesting finding in the current study in this regard is the fact that there are small differences in the attributes preferred by the never-married and the divorced. Like the respondents in the other study, the sample also chose looks and sense of humor as important attributes. On the other hand, the sample included such considerations as finances and health as issues and ignored such selections as sex appeal, intelligence, good conversation, honesty, and such added female selections as respect. An important question at this point revolves around an explanation for this wide disparity between the two studies. Since the earlier study was among college students, the average age was younger than the people in the current study. This may explain why the earlier sample chose such esoteric ideals as intelligence and honesty, while the older, working sample in the current study chose realistic concerns such as finances and health.

Another question on dating is: Where do singles meet people with these valued attributes? Two surprises show up with regard to the selected locations. It was thought that with a large variety of matchmaking websites, the computer might be preferred by many of the singles, but it ranked at the bottom (6

Table 8.6. Where Meet Others (Top Three Choices)

	Never Married	Current Study Divorced	Singles' Total
Bars	27%	20%	51%
Blind Dates	11	18	13
Church	14	16	15
Computer	5	8	6
School	25	3	19
Singles Organization	6	10	7
Other (Combined)	11	25	18

Table 8.7.   How Meet Others (Most Frequent)

Most Frequent	Less Frequent
A friend	Blind dates
At parties	Singles bars
A hobby/interest	Bars
School/work	Social/community function
Talking to a stranger	Joining a health club
	Answering/placing an ad (Barkas 1980)

percent). It appears that the sample prefers to meet people face to face rather than through computer ads, despite the fact that the ads are basically positive in their descriptions. The first choice by both segments of the singles category was that old standby—the bar (51 percent). School, the second choice of the never-married segment (25 percent), is not much of a choice for the divorced (3 percent), probably reflecting the age differential between the two categories and the fact that the never-married are more likely to still be students. Two other old standbys for finding dates are still somewhat popular—church (15 percent) and blind dates (13 percent). With singles organizations being chosen by only 7 percent of the group, it would appear that the singles of today still prefer the tried-and-true means of meeting others to the newer, unproven methods.

Comparison with a study done in the 1980s reveals the changes in dating preferences over the past twenty-five years. This difference may be accounted for in part, however, by that study's considering singles as a whole rather than separating it into subcategories (see table 8.7; Barkas 1980).

An overlooked but important aspect of dating is it is, in itself, an enjoyable social outing. A study done at about the same time as the early study indicates that it is a positive experience for most (67 percent), and that men and women almost equally rated it positively (Simenauer and Carroll 1982).

CONCLUSION: A SATISFACTORY LIFESTYLE?

A final question in this regard seems appropriate: How satisfied are the respondents in each category with their leisure lifestyle? In both studies, both single and married respondents were overwhelmingly personally satisfied: In the early study, 87 percent of married and 72 percent of single respondents, and in the current study 89 percent of married and 71 percent of single respondents, reported being satisfied with their lifestyle. As can be seen, more married respondents than singles report being personally satisfied. Their advantage in

Table 8.8. Personal Satisfaction

| | Early/Current Study | | |
	Satisfied	Neither	Dissatisfied
Never Maried	73/70%	20/17%	7/13%
Divorced	70/73	19/22	11/6
Married Once	88/91	9/6	3/4
Remarried	80/81	7/11	14/8
Singles Total	72/71	20/19	8/10
Married Total	87/89	7/7	6/4

this regard seems to lie in the fact that they are following the preferred cultural route, and this may also indicate that they are more settled, whereas the never-married are younger and so may still be drifting and thus less likely to report personal satisfaction. The divorced have had a major disruption in their goals and lifestyle, so the surprise here is that so many claim to be personally satisfied.

That such a large number of respondents claimed personal satisfaction raised some doubts about their claims. Perhaps, the term "satisfaction" is not a true measure of how people feel about their lifestyle; perhaps it is something that is simply easy to agree to. To deal with these doubts, the respondents were asked to compare their personal satisfaction to their impression of the satisfaction of their single and married acquaintances. This theory was somewhat proven in both studies by the fact that a larger number of both groups indicated that their single acquaintances were more personally satisfied than those that claimed to be personally dissatisfied by almost a three-to-one margin. A similar result is seen when the sample was asked to compare their personal dissatisfaction with that of their married acquaintances, only this time it was only the singles who showed this discrepancy. By an almost three-to-one ratio, far more singles saw their married acquaintances as more satisfied than the relatively few who claimed to be personally dissatisfied. An interesting

Table 8.9. Impressions of Personal Satisfaction: Single Acquaintances

| | Early/Current Studies | | |
	More	Same	Less
Never Married	26/17%	57/57%	18/26%
Divorced	29/19	43/62	27/19
Married	13/10	58/43	29/47
Remarried	30/17	49/46	21/37
Singles Total	26/18	54/59	21/24
Married Total	16/11	55/43	25/46

Table 8.10. Impressions of Personal Satisfaction: Married Acquaintances

| | Early/Current Studies | | |
	More	Same	Less
Never Married	31/88%	41/6%	28/6%
Divorced	24/80	38/14	38/6
Married	8/88	76/8	16/4
Remarried	16/81	61/8	23/12
Singles Total	27/87	40/9	33/6
Married Total	9/87	74/8	17/5

finding is indicated in the current study, since there was a huge jump by both married and single respondents indicating that their friends were more satisfied than they were (M: 9 percent versus 87 percent; S: 27 percent versus 85 percent), whereas for their single acquaintances the shift went in the opposite direction (M: 16 percent versus 11 percent; S: 26 percent versus 18 percent). It would appear that life is getting less satisfactory for both groups as compared to married acquaintances, but not as compared to their single acquaintances—an indication that marriage may be returning to the image acquired in the 1950s. In both studies, it appears that both singles and the married were somewhat more likely to overrate their personal satisfaction.

Chapter Nine

Do Singles Have More Fun?

INTRODUCTION: THE PURSUIT OF HAPPINESS

National studies indicate that those who claim to be very happy are less likely to claim being depressed. However, a review of two studies done in 1972 and 1994 shows that only about a third of the population claim to be very happy, and that this number has declined during the twenty-two-year period between the studies (to 31 percent). Since this was a time period when the singles population was rapidly growing, the question is whether there was a relationship between the growth of this population and the seeming growth in unhappiness. Studies indicate that having a partner is a strong cause of happiness and, in turn, being happy makes having a partner more likely. In fact, when it comes to happiness, the married are very advantaged. National studies consistently show that married people are happier than the unmarried (Glenn and Weaver 1988): 40 percent of the married claimed to be very happy as compared to 22 percent of the never-married, cohabiters, or widowed; 18 percent of the divorced; and 15 percent of the separated (Waite and Gallagher 2000). This finding is a recognition that people primarily get happiness from other people—it is their affection and their opinion of us that most influence this mood. Yet one stereotype applied to singles is that they are happier than married people.

WHAT IS IMPORTANT TO HAPPINESS?

In order to answer the question of happiness, it was important to ask questions related to what we get from relationships: children, friends, love, marriage, personal growth, religion, and sexual satisfaction. In the 1980 study, the two most important factors for happiness were, for both subcategories of singles, friends (54 percent) and personal growth (52 percent). In the current study, the importance of friends grew to 65 percent and personal growth grew to 69 percent. Perhaps not surprisingly, in the early study the married reported that their marriage (69 percent), love (61 percent), and their children (61 percent) were more important to their happiness than either friends or personal growth, and this was also true in the current study (67 percent, 81 percent, and 73 percent, respectively).

It is not surprising that it was the subject of marriage that brought the widest disparity between the married and the singles in both studies (early study: 69 percent versus 23 percent; current study: 67 percent versus 25 percent). Also not surprising is that the role of children in happiness brought wide disagreement between the married (61 percent) and the singles (26 percent) in the early study. However, a surprise shows up in the current study. The gap between the two categories remains—73 percent versus 58 percent—but the importance of children to happiness increased considerably for the singles (26 percent to 58 percent). This also may explain the vast increase in single-parent births and adoptions. It appears that as the never-married got older, children became more important to their happiness (23 percent to 50 percent).

Actually, the role of children with regard to happiness shows some interesting discrepancies. Among the four subcategories there was at least a 10-point difference between the two singles subcategories in both studies—23 percent for the never-married versus 44 percent for the divorced in the early study, and 50 percent versus 73 percent in the current study. A similar difference was noted between the two married subcategories in the early study—64 percent for those married once versus 54 percent for the remarried in the early study, and 75 percent versus 65 percent in the current study.

Two other factors with regard to children and happiness are also of interest. Children seem to be of less importance to happiness to the divorced (44 percent) than the remarried (54 percent) in the early study, but this is not true in the current study (77 percent versus 65 percent). This raises an interesting question, since most of the remarried were formerly divorced. Perhaps in the early study the responses of the divorced reflected the difficulties of raising a family on one's own, and it is getting easier to do so. Another interesting change had occurred with regard to children and happiness by the time of the current study: The importance of children had risen to a position of greater importance for both subgroups of singles; in fact, it was now the most important factor for the divorced.

Another surprise is the very low ranking of marriage as a happiness factor by the singles (23 percent in the early study versus 25 percent in the current study) in light of the fact that 90 percent thought that they would marry in the future.

Table 9.1.   **Factors Important to Happiness**

	Never Married %	Divorced %	Early/Current Studies Married %	Remarried %	S. Tot. %	M. Tot. %
Children	23/50	44/73	64/75	54/65	26/58	61/73
Friends	54/66	60/64	36/53	32/57	54/65	34/54
Love	43/50	43/33	63/80	63/85	43/44	61/81
Marriage	2/30	23/16	69/70	78/57	23/25	69/67
Per. Gr.*	51/71	57/60	49/61	40/48	52/69	46/58
Religion	26/43	9/34	37/54	32/65	21/40	36/57
Sex	38/47	51/26	42/54	42/51	40/40	41/53

*Personal Growth

Turning to the other factors indicated as important to happiness, the only difference is seen with regard to religion. For the never-married, the divorced, and the married, religion has a low ranking in importance for happiness in both studies, and so it comes as a surprise to find that it has a very high ranking in both studies for the remarried. This high selection by the remarried may be a reflection of their return to the fold. As mostly a formerly divorced group, they may have either lacked religious orientation or felt outside of a structure set up mostly for families: Toughest of all is going to church alone with two teenage daughters. Like the neighborhood cookout or the Saturday-night dinner party, most churches still function on "traditional family" togetherness (Brooks 1981). Thus, it is not surprising that the divorced ranked religion as the lowest factor in their happiness of all the groups in both studies.

ARE YOU HAPPY?

The previous question tells us what the single and married respondents believe is important to their happiness, but it does not indicate whether they are happy. To determine this, the respondents were asked to self-rate their degree of happiness. In the early study, it seemingly made little difference if respondents were single or married, since at least 70 percent of each category rated themselves as either very or moderately happy with their lifestyle. This does not mean that the rest of the sample was unhappy; more people selected "neither" (13 percent) than the "unhappy" (6 percent). Since the stereotype sees singles as carefree and happy, it was a bit surprising to see that more of the married than the single respondents claimed that they were happy—86 percent versus 72 percent in the early study and 72 percent to 64 percent in the current study. The current study also produced a surprise with regard to personal happiness. It was assumed that with the large growth in their numbers

Table 9.2. Self-rating: Happiness

| | Early/Current Studies | | |
	Happy	Neither	Unhappy
Never Married	73/69%	20/27%	7/4%
Divorced	70/54	19/41	11/5
Married Once	88/76	9/20	3/4
Remarried	80/61	7/27	14/12
Singles Total	72/64	20/32	8/5
Married Total	86/72	8/22	6/6

since the early study and the added benefits of being perceived as a market, happiness with the single lifestyle would increase, but instead it decreased for both the never-married (from 73 percent to 69 percent) and the divorced (from 70 percent to 54 percent). But it also declined for both categories of the married (from 86 percent to 72 percent). It appears that the period between the two studies was one of high but nonetheless declining happiness for both married people and singles. However, this was not a question of being unhappy with their status—the number reporting this are still quite low (5 percent)—but more question of being happy or unhappy overall. Another seeming contradiction is noted in the fact that those married once were the happiest in both studies, even though divorce rates increased during the period between the studies. Unfortunately, because this was a random sample study it was not possible to go back and find out why there was such a drop in happiness with the lifestyle for all categories.

ARE YOU HAVING FUN?

Suspecting that the respondents might take the easy way out by selecting the happy response, since it required less thinking about their true feelings, it was decided that a supplemental question was necessary. It is assumed that if you get a lot of fun out of life, then you are happy, so respondents were asked "Do you get a lot of fun out of life?" This was a straight yes-or-no question, with no waffling allowed. The replies in the early study supported the answers to the prior question, since 75 percent of the singles and 80 percent of the married replied in the affirmative. There was, however, a contradiction in replies by the time of the current study. In a period when the overall claim of happiness declined slightly, the number of those claiming they were getting fun out of life increased for both the singles (from 75 percent to 80 percent) and the married (from 80 percent to 87 percent). It would appear that it is possible for

Table 9.3. Gets Fun Out of Life (Yes)

	Early/Current Studies
Never Married	76/81%
Divorced	70/79
Married Once	81/87
Remarried	74/89
Singles Total	75/80
Married Total	80/87

people to have fun in life without believing they are happy overall. What can be said at this time is that all categories claim to be happy and get fun out of life, but, in contradiction with the stereotype of the happy, carefree single, this is more so for the married than the singles.

THE HAPPINESS OF OTHERS

To find out how positive respondents felt about their affirmations of happiness, two more questions were asked on this subject. It was believed that by comparing their state of happiness with that of their married and single friends, the respondent would reveal this information. In the early study respondents overwhelmingly saw their single friends as being as happy as they were themselves (M: 56 percent; S: 54 percent). Except for the never-married, about a quarter of the sample across the categories saw their single friends as more happy than themselves: divorced, 27 percent; remarried, 21 percent; married once, 29 percent; never-married, 13 percent. The current study confirms this negative view of the sample regarding their happiness as compared to their single friends. The once-married stood out: fewer respondents in this group saw similarities in happiness with their single friends (43 percent) and more saw their single friends as being less happy (11 percent). By small margins, singles saw themselves as happier than their single friends in the early study, but unhappier in the current study (26 percent versus 21 percent unhappier; 18 percent happier versus 23 percent unhappier). These findings tie in with the earlier findings that showed fewer claims of happiness in the second time period. On the other hand, the married saw their single friends as more happy than themselves in both studies (16 percent versus 28 percent happier in the first study; 11 percent versus 46 percent happier in the second study). This appears to be a contradiction to the claims on happiness of the married in the current study. It appears from these figures that the singles and the married in the current study were less likely to see themselves as being

Table 9.4. Personal Happiness Compared to Single Friends

| | Early/Current Studies | | |
	Happier	Same	Unhappier
Never Married	26/17%	57/57%	17/26%
Divorced	30/19	43/62	27/20
Married Once	13/10	58/43	29/47
Remarried	30/17	49/46	21/38
Singles Total	26/18	54/59	21/23
Married Total	16/11	56/43	28/46

as happy as their single friends (S: 23 percent versus 18 percent; M: 46 percent versus 11 percent). These findings support those findings on declining happiness during the second time period.

A somewhat different picture is seen when the groups compared their happiness to that of their married friends. Singles were more likely, by a slight margin, to see their married friends as happier in the early study (33 percent unhappier versus 27 percent happier), but this was completely changed by the time of the second study (9 percent unhappier than married friends versus 75 percent happier than married friends). It appears that singles, as a group, are happier than their married friends. The married had similar findings to the singles when comparing themselves to other married friends in both studies: In the first study, 17 percent rated themselves unhappier than their married friends, compared to 10 percent happier; in the second study 87 percent considered themselves happier than their married friends and only 5 percent were unhappier. So it also appears that married people see themselves as happier overall than their married friends. The problem with these findings is that life appears to have been getting happier for both categories at a time when in general it was not getting so for a larger number of them. It would appear that the old cliché about the grass being greener on the other side is not believed by either the singles or the married as it relates to personal happiness.

Table 9.5. Personal Happiness Compared to Married Friends

| | Early/Current Studies | | |
	Happier	Same	Unhappier
Never Married	31/74%	41/6%	28/10%
Divorced	24/80	38/14	38/6
Married Once	8/88	76/8	16/4
Remarried	16/81	61/8	23/12
Singles Total	27/75	40/9	33/9
Married Total	10/87	73/8	17/5

CONCLUSION: THE FINDINGS LIE

As noted, the sample for both categories in both studies indicated that they considered themselves to be happy, with more of the married than the singles making this claim in both studies. Very few overall noted that they were unhappy. Respondents substantiated this claim by noting that they get a lot of fun out of life, and again it was the married that were more likely to make this claim. These figures mean that only 20 percent of the married and 25 percent of the singles reported getting no fun out of life in the early study, and 13 percent of the married and 20 percent the singles made the same claim in the current study. These claims of happiness and fun seem slightly contradictory to those shown when the sample was asked to rate their personal happiness as compared to their single friends and their married friends. Compared to their single friends, 28 percent of the singles and 21 percent of the married noted that these friends were happier than they were in the early study—a much higher figure than those claiming they were unhappy, 8 and 6 percent. Similar findings show up in the current study: Only 5 percent of the singles and 6 percent of the married claimed that they were unhappy, yet 23 percent of the singles and a whopping 46 percent of the married claimed they were unhappier than their single friends. Similar findings appeared when the sample was asked to compare their happiness to that of their married friends. In this regard, in the first study 33 percent of the singles noted that their married friends were happier than they were, yet, as noted, only 8 percent noted being unhappy. These contradictory findings on happiness are again confirmed with the questions on fun, since very few noted not getting fun out of life.

How can we explain these seeming contradictions in regard to claims of happiness? It would appear that when people are asked about their personal happiness, their first impulse is to think of happy and fun things that have been occurring recently in their lives and so believe that they are happy and having fun out of life. If the question had been changed to ask whether they were unhappy, a different type of response might have been received. Although most of both categories are happy, it is clear that the stereotype that singles are happier than married people is not true.

With so many of the married noting being happy, a question arose regarding any differences between those in a first marriage and those in a remarriage. Similarly, there was a question as to any differences in happiness between the never-married and the divorced among the singles. It was also decided to add gender to these categories in order to determine differences between females and males regarding happiness in these categories.

Among the married females, those who are in their first marriage are far more likely to note being happy in their marital position than were remarried

Table 9.6. Married Groups Happiness Differences (Current Study)

	Happy	Neither	Unhappy
Married-once Females	81%	17%	2%
Remarried Females	58	25	17
Married Females Total	78	18	4
Married-once Males	71	22	8
Remarried Males	63	29	8
Married Males Total	69	24	8

females (81 percent versus 58 percent). Although the difference is smaller, married-once males are more likely to note happiness with their current marital status than remarried males (71 percent versus 63 percent). In general, being married is a happier position for females than males (78 percent versus 69 percent).

Among the single females, the never-married are more likely to note being happy with their marital position than the divorced (66 percent versus 54 percent). An opposite claim is noted when examining the claims among single males. Among males, it is the divorced who are more likely than the never-married to note happiness with their position (68 percent versus 58 percent). Although the differences are minor, single males are slightly happier with their position than single females (62 percent versus 60 percent).

Married females are more likely to be happier with their marital status than married males (81 percent versus 71 percent). On the other hand, single males are slightly more likely to be happy with their status than single females (62 percent versus 60 percent). In general, females are somewhat more likely to claim happiness than males (70 percent versus 65 percent).

A final question in regard to happiness would be which group has the bragging rights as being the happiest with their status? In order, married-once

Table 9.7. Single Groups Happiness Differences (Current Study)

	Happy	Neither	Unhappy
Never-married Females	66%	31%	3%
Divorced Females	54	37	9
Single Females Total	60	34	7
Never-married Males	58	35	7
Divorced Males	68	27	6
Single Males Total	62	32	6

Table 9.8. Happiness Differences among the Married and the Singles

	Happy	Neither	Unhappy
Married Females	81%	17%	2%
Single Females	60	34	6
Females Total	70	26	3
Married Males	71	22	8
Single Males	62	32	6
Males Total	65	28	7

females claim this position with 81 percent making this assertion. Married-once males cement this claim on happiness with the next-highest number of 74 percent. Apparently, remarriage is not as happy as first marriages since next in line for claiming happiness are divorced males (68 percent) and never-married females (66 percent). Bringing up the bottom half on the happiness scale are remarried males (63 percent), remarried females (58 percent), never-married males (58 percent), and divorced females (54 percent).

An interesting aside to these findings would be a question regarding surprises. Where there any surprises in the findings? Why? An explanation for the findings will be left up to the reader, since one's own beliefs will affect the answer.

Although most respondents in all categories are happy, what has not changed is the fact that the stereotype that singles are happier with their status than the married is not true.

Table 9.9. Who Are the Happiest? (Current Study)

	Happy	Neither	Unhappy
Married-once Females	81%	17%	2%
Remarried Females	58	25	17
Never-married Females	66	31	3
Divorced Females	54	38	9
Females Total	69	25	6
Married-once Males	74	17	10
Remarried Males	63	29	8
Never-married Males	58	35	7
Divorced Males	68	26	6
Males Total	65	26	8

Chapter Ten

Loneliness: The Great Bugaboo

INTRODUCTION: LONELINESS—WHAT IS IT?

Loneliness has been interpreted as the result of a deficiency in two different social needs: a sense of attachment through an intimate relationship and a sense of community with a network of friends who share our interests and concerns (Rubin 1979). Thus, "you are lonely when you feel there is nobody upon whom you can rely on to augment you, especially in conditions of stress or threat" (Lear 1980). These ideas confirm that loneliness can be painful, but being alone can also be pleasant and valuable.

A supposed asset of being single is that singles have the freedom to do as they please: snacking when hungry, staying up late to read, doing things at their own pace, and the like. However, this freedom can also lead to chaos. There is no one around to tell them to check the refrigerator, that they are wearing mismatched socks, or when to spring ahead or fall back. As we found in examining the stereotype of singles as swingers, this examination of a supposed benefit of being single reminds us that there are always two sides to a coin, and supposed benefits can have drawbacks. Another example of this process is seen with the stereotype that singles are swingers. But the freedom to search for a partner for the evening at a singles bar is often seen as a sign of loneliness—the hope of meeting someone, anyone—even if it is only for the evening, even if it means a casual assignation. Yet those using sex to achieve intimacy and avoid being alone often end up feeling even lonelier. Casual sex actually has different effects for men and women. Very early women find that casual sex produces low self-esteem, and this may result in increased feelings of loneliness and unhappiness.

These different perceptions of the same activity raise the question as to which perception is correct. Is the interpretation that the single life is a lonely life correct, or is it part of a belief system that favors marriage? A divorced man in his forties from the adjunct singles organization believed the former to be the case: "I do something because I feel that way and I want to do it and not because I'm trying to offset loneliness. If I want to talk to Mary or not talk to Mary, or talk to Jane or not talk to Jane, I do it not because I am offsetting loneliness but because that person is interesting to me or I want to communicate with that individual and I resent being put into this slot that says, 'The only reason you're talking to Jane is you're suffering from loneliness,' and that's bullshit." These differing perceptions also raise two related questions: Why is being alone believed to be so painful that all activities are interpreted as a means of avoiding this predicament? And which perception is closer to the truth?

In truth, a lack of human contacts results in pain. The fact is that people need frequent confirmation of their identity, intimacy, a sense of worth, and warmth. Without fulfillment of these human needs, we feel emotionally empty and lonely. Without someone to confide in and with whom to share our feelings and thoughts, we experience loneliness. Loneliness is a subjective feeling, so only you know when you feel lonely. This feeling is like a hunger pain—a natural sign that we are lacking intimacy and companionship.

The conditions of modern society mean that these feelings are not unique—it has been reported that some 35 million Americans suffer from loneliness each month (Rubenstein and Shaver 1982). A more recent study revealed that one-quarter of all Americans report that they have nobody to talk to about "important matters" (Smith-Lovin 2006). In fact, the most common idea associated with being single by numerous respondents is that of loneliness.

As important as these figures are in indicating loneliness in America, it is not the most important fact being reported from these studies, and a comparison reveals that that in two decades the number of people who report having no one to share with remains unchanged. What is it about modern society that causes so many to be deprived of closeness and community? A number of explanations have been suggested:

- *Changes in Entertainment*: Technological change means that entertainment now consists mostly of watching television and movies at home rather than spending time face to face with others in the community.
- *Changes in Relational Time*: Technological changes have also changed the way we use our time—personal and business transactions that were once done face to face are now conducted over the phone or on the Internet.
- *Changing Values and Needs*: Changes in community values have made divorce more acceptable, so the divorce rate has increased.

- *Changes in the Job Market*: Some 5 million Americans move away from their friends, acquaintances, and communities each year. This often results in isolation in a new community where there is no one that we know or trust.
- *Changes in the Workforce*: In the 1950s, most married women stayed and worked at home, and friends came from a small pool of similar type neighbors and coworkers. All of this togetherness began to change in the 1960s with the great influx of women into the outside workforce.
- *Greater Educational Needs*: Industrial changes brought about a need for increased education, and the resulting delay in marriage brought about a delay in finding a mate to share the good and the bad.
- *Modern Living Conditions*: Modern life makes little provision for ordinary human contact on weekends—there are no butchers, milkmen, or other delivery people to break the solitude.

The result of these changes is that the problem of loneliness is becoming more and more pervasive, and a countless number of people are searching for a solution to put an end to this emptiness and the fear of loneliness that threatens to engulf them. Our cultural traditions and personal needs lead many to believe that marriage will resolve the problem. One of the major themes parents use to convince their children to get married is that of loneliness, pointing out that if they do not marry, they will end up in the world alone. Indeed, loneliness is both a major fear as well as an actuality for those people who are single. It is believed that marriage means that one will be cared for and loved. This, in turn, not only reduces the level of stress experienced but also buffers the impact of stress on health. However, when marriage is used merely as a defense against the oppressively empty feeling of being alone, it becomes a negative bond since the reason for the marriage is not the desire of two people for each other.

A CASE OF PERCEPTION

Her loneliness—My God, had this always been so?—had been largely caused by her sense that she was supposed to have a man, supposed to have someone, or else be the pathetic woman in the rain, staring into a lighted house. (French 1978)

A major difficulty in dealing with the topic of loneliness is that people are hesitant to admit that they are or ever have been lonely. This is a result of their desire to suppress ideas of loneliness and the pain associated with this emotion. Also, loneliness engenders feelings of worthlessness—one may feel like a failure and thus unworthy and weak. Yet the significance of any act depends on perception and interpretation. A study of loneliness revealed a number of distinct reasons for feelings of loneliness:

- *Being Alone*: Coming home to an empty house
- *Being Unattached*: Having no partner
- *Social Isolation*: Needing friends
- *Social Forces That Create Dislocation*: Moving often and being far from home
- *Forced Isolation*: Being housebound or hospitalized, or having no transportation

Being alone, then, is a common reason for loneliness. In this study, two questions were asked in order to determine whether the various components of our sample had different interpretations of being alone. Respondents were asked both whether they were depressed and whether they were unhappy when alone. In both studies, singles were more likely than the married to report that they were depressed when alone (early study: 23 percent versus 15 percent; current study: 21 percent versus 18 percent). Regarding unhappiness, there was a reversal of findings. This time it was the married in both studies who were more likely to report feelings of unhappiness when alone (early study: 19 percent versus 12 percent; current study: 11 percent versus 9 percent). Responses to the question about unhappiness were a surprise, since it was the never-married who were, by a wide margin, the least likely in the current study to note being unhappy when alone.

Granted, the differences are minor on both questions, but it was in the expected direction when it comes to depression. In fact, the difference between the two categories on these two questions provide a clear picture of what it is like to be divorced rather than being single or married. The divorced in both studies were, by a large margin over the other categories, more likely to claim being depressed (early study: 33 percent; current study: 31 percent) and being unhappy when alone (early study: 25 percent; current study: 18 percent).

These differences add another dimension to the question about feelings of loneliness—the why of these feelings. There are now a large number of activities available to singles, since they are now considered a large potential market. This availability of numerous activities may mean that they are not often alone, and when it occurs it may be a welcome respite. At the same time, they could feel depressed over their efforts to prevent being alone. Those who are married have companionship most of the time, so being alone may be perceived as a gap in this easy way of reaching out for someone to talk to or to touch. Thus, they may believe that they would be both depressed and unhappy

Table 10.1. Reflections on Loneliness

| | Early/Current Studies | |
	Depressed	Unhappy
Never Married	20/14%	8/3%
Divorced	33/31	25/18
Married Once	14/15	18/11
Remarried	18/16	21/13
Singles Total	23/21	12/9
Married Total	15/18	19/11

when alone. This may explain why the divorced report such high levels of unhappiness when alone: They had enjoyed constant companionship in their prior married life and so are acutely aware of the difference. One wonders whether these conditions surrounding being alone are getting better, however, since both conditions were less likely to be acknowledged by all components of the sample in the second study.

LONELINESS ACTIVITIES

The sample was also asked some direct questions about their activities as a means of resolving the question of whether certain activities are accurately interpreted as being signs of loneliness. Of course, these questions tell us only whether singles are more likely to engage in these activities and not whether they are doing so to avoid feelings of loneliness. Another part of this chapter, then, is an effort to deal with the term "activities" and determine whether it is true that no matter what singles do, it is an effort to counteract the loneliness they endure.

Two questions were asked about everyday activities that might influence those feelings of depression and unhappiness: dining alone and entering an empty room. One would think that the task of eating, being a natural require-ment for life, would bring only thoughts regarding what and perhaps where to eat, not thoughts about loneliness. Similarly, one probably passes in and out of empty rooms all day without any thought. However, when forced to think about these situations, a judgment is made whether the experience affects one's feelings at all and whether that effect is pleasant or unpleasant.

Since dining alone is an everyday experience, it was surprising to find that people were aware of the situation and did not like it. In fact, it was perceived negatively by more of the sample than any other activity. This is perhaps not surprising, since dining is perceived as a social activity in the first study.

Forty-six percent of the singles and 33 percent of the married respondents indicated that dining alone raised feelings of loneliness. Similarly, in the second study, 46 percent of the singles and 36 percent of the married respondents made this clear. In fact, a number of people reported that when forced to eat alone, they do it standing up and look out the window or distract themselves in other ways. This type of response to an everyday activity that may produce feelings of loneliness is not unusual.

A divorced woman in her forties from the adjuct singles organization sample explained it this way: "I have no trouble now dining by myself in a restaurant, but when I was first divorced, that was a very difficult thing to do. But now I go in by myself and do not think about it." The study question response indicates that this claim by the woman may not be an accurate representation of singles as a whole. Another younger divorced woman from the singles organization confirmed the belief that doing acts alone that are normally done in groups does make you aware that you are alone—and that perhaps you should not display your aloneness in public. With regard to going to a movie, she said: "A lot of times there'd be a movie or something. I wouldn't go alone. One night I said, 'You know, that's really stupid, why shouldn't I go? You go with somebody to a movie, you sit there, you don't talk anyway.' So I went to the movie, and I ran into several couples that I knew, and one of the couples said they were going for pizza and a beer after the movie and I had the best time, just the three of us, and I thought, 'Well, that was really dumb that I hesitated to go alone.'"

Perhaps, the difference between going to a restaurant alone and going to a movie alone lies in the word "participation": At the restaurant you usually have someone to talk to whereas at a movie you don't talk anyway, so it makes no difference that you are alone. So feelings of aloneness, then, are not an all-pervading twenty-four-hour gloom; they are situational, and since singles find themselves more often in situations that are usually done with a companion, it would be expected that more of them would be negative about dining alone (early study: S, 46 percent versus M, 33 percent; current study: S, 46 percent versus M, 36 percent). Add the fact that they were used to a having companion and the relatively high numbers among the divorced are not a surprise; it is a problem that seems to be growing among the divorced (early study: 44 percent; current study: 56 percent).

A seemingly strange question to ask is how one feels when entering an empty room. One would think that one enters or leaves rooms without much thought about whether the room is empty or not. Others may not rationalize the reason, but may intentionally stay out late after work rather than face that empty room, that empty house. The early study seemed to confirm this belief: Most of the components of the sample, except for the divorced, had low numbers claiming feelings of loneliness entering an empty room. Although not high, at 28 percent, the divorced figures were double those of the other sample components.

A divorced person from the singles organization explained this disparity: "Being alone is difficult when newly divorced. It accentuates one's vulnerability. The empty room compounds feelings of loneliness." According to this explanation, the reason for the loneliness feelings are, again, situational and more likely to affect the divorced. This may be so, but then how do we explain the much higher numbers for all the components of the sample in the current study? In the current study, the largest increase in reporting feelings of loneliness in entering an empty room was with the married (early study: 13 percent; current study: 41percent). In fact, their figures are now similar to those of the divorced (42 percent).

With the married components of the sample joining the divorced segment in agreeing that a empty room signifies loneliness, we are left with the surprising discovery that it is the never-married in both studies who were the least likely to perceive entering an empty room as a lonely experience. The explanation for this finding may lie in the word "experience." The never-married in the early study were mostly made up of the baby boomers, and these singles were relatively young and so may have never experienced loneliness. Many were still living at home or with a roommate. In the current study, most of the never-married singles are older, since the reason for their remaining single is generally a delay in getting married. With older age and hence a longer time as singles, their feelings about being alone and loneliness would in all likelihood change. Thus, in the current study the number of never-married respondents who associated entering an empty room with loneliness doubled, from 15 percent to 29 percent. This reasoning, however, does not explain the large increase in negative feelings about this situation by the whole sample in the current study, an increase that meant more of the married than the singles claimed feelings of loneliness in this situation (41 percent versus 35 percent). It is apparently, again, a question of what respondents are normally used to.

A never-married woman from the singles organization summed up her feelings regarding loneliness:

> I hesitate to go places alone—the empty, lonely evenings do me away. I hate not being able to just sit and talk to someone. But at times when I look back on my growth since college I think, *Hey, I'm making it on my own.* Knowing that I can support myself and do for myself without totally depending on someone is a treat.

It would appear that the conditions of a modern society compound feelings of loneliness:

Table 10.2. Feelings of Loneliness

	Early/Current Studies	
	Dining Alone	Enter Empty Room
Never Married	47/38%	15/29%
Divorced	44/56	28/42
Married Once	34/35	12/42
Remarried	33/32	14/36
Singles Total	46/46	18/35
Married Total	33/36	13/41

- Many people now work at home, alone with a computer, instead of at an office filled with people to talk to at the water cooler.
- The assembly line now is supplied by robots and moves so quickly that conversation with any nearby associates is virtually impossible.
- Most people spend free time watching television or reading, and neither of these activities involves others who may be in the room.

In short, group activities that encourage interaction that may dispel feelings of loneliness have been replaced by solo activities.

A QUESTION OF SHARING

One of the most common assumptions about living single is that singles are deprived of emotional attachment: "That central, intimate tie that in our society is most commonly provided by marriage" (Lear 1980). It is believed that at the end of the day the married person has someone to share problems and relieve distress and even share delightful occurrences. On the other hand, it is believed that the single person may have friends, but no one close enough for sharing intimacies. As one divorced person from the singles organization put it, "After the divorce, what I needed most was someone to share things, problems with and conversations with adults." These beliefs about marriage and singleness were seemingly confirmed by a survey by *Playboy* magazine on reasons people marry (Hunt 1974). The survey found only two reasons rated as "very important" by clear majorities of the men: "Having another person to share one's life" (74 percent) and "Having someone to share life experiences with" (62 percent). This emphasis on sharing was also reiterated by the people in this study. Asked "What are the advantages of being married?" both the married and single respondents replied mostly in terms that indicated shared feelings:

- Companionship
- Love and companionship
- Companionship and someone to share decisions with
- Someone to share both the good and the bad of life
- Having someone to share your life with
- The opportunity to converse with someone every day

As can be seen, the terms most used in these responses were "companionship" and "sharing." Previously, these needs might have been met with a network of friends or by living in a community of people who shared common interests. However, changes brought about by the developments of modern society have affected these options. In a sense, modern society has made us into a nation of migrants: We move in large numbers away from our friends, extended family, and close communities to our nuclear nests in the suburbs. Without these attachments, the loneliness of emotional isolation becomes more pronounced (Lear 1980). As noted, both the married and the singles indicated that the advantages of being married were companionship and sharing. Does this mean that on more direct questions dealing with these conditions the singles would surpass the married in being deprived of such? To test this idea, two questions dealing with their experience with these factors of loneliness were asked the sample: "Do you have anyone to share with?" and "Do you have anyone to discuss things with?" Since these factors were supposedly only an issue for singles, only these components were asked these questions.

Apparently, these conditions do present issues, but only for a minority of singles. Only 20 percent of the singles in the early study said that they had no one to share things with, but this increased to 28 percent in the current study. It appears that the anonymity of modern society is making it more difficult to find people to share with. Strangely, the situation is reversed when dealing with the second question: A much larger proportion of the sample found it difficult to find people with whom to discuss matters than share with in the early study (30 percent versus 20 percent), but this was reversed in the current study (15 percent versus 28 percent). Thus, finding people to talk to, being perhaps less intimate, has become easier, whereas sharing—a more intimate encounter—has become more difficult.

In the earlier study, the difficulty of finding someone to discuss things with seemed to be an extreme problem for the divorced, since almost half (49 percent) found it difficult to accomplish, but this condition reversed itself in the current study (15 percent). The result is that on both questions not too many singles claimed these conditions (28 percent on the sharing question and 15 percent on the discussing question).

Table 10.3.   Loneliness Truths (Yes)

| | Early/Current Studies | | | |
| | No One: Share | | No One: Discuss | |
	Rarely	*Mostly*	*Rarely*	*Mostly*
Never Married	82/72%	18/28%	74/85%	26/15%
Divorced	75/73	25/27	51/85	49/15
Total	80/72	20/28	70/85	30/15

Surprisingly, membership in an organization did not affect the responses to these questions. In an organization for singles, it would seem to be easier to find people both to share with and to discuss things with, yet the answers given by the adjunct group were in the same range as the general sample.

Again, what is seen is that feelings of loneliness depend on the individual's situation at the time; it is not a pervasive, constant feeling. As one divorced women from the singles organization noted, "The only time I am really lonely is if I have something really fantastic or really bad to share. Every day, I'm not lonely." Similarly, a divorced man indicated how his feelings with regard to loneliness are situational: "Last night my daughter had a Christmas play and I had to sit by myself in that lousy audience, and I didn't have anybody to share with, and I was disgustedly out of it."

LONELINESS BELIEFS

Considered the great bugaboo for singles, the topic of loneliness required more effort to check on its reality. So two final questions were asked of the single components of the sample: "Do you believe most people are alone and that it's not just a problem for singles?" and "Did you join an organization in order to find companionship and negate loneliness?" Similar responses were found for both questions. Few singles in the early study thought that most people are alone (17 percent) and even fewer did in the current study (7 percent).

Table 10.4.   Loneliness Beliefs (Yes)

	Early/Current Studies Most People Are Alone
Never Married	12/6%
Divorced	31/10
Total	17/7

Table 10.5. Loneliness Deeds (Yes)

	Early/Current Studies *Joined For Companionship*
Never Married	22/15%
Divorced	17/24
Total	21/19

The biggest drop in this belief was shown by the divorced (31 percent versus 10 percent). Similarly, and surprisingly so, few singles in both studies reported joining organizations in order to find companionship (early study; 21 percent; current study: 19 percent). However, this result was skewed by the never-married, who did not finding this a necessary outlet in either study (early study: 22 percent; current study: 15 percent) whereas the divorced found this effort a more necessary outlet in the current study (17 percent versus 24 percent).

CONCLUSION: HELPFUL HINTS

Being alone in a couples' world signifies failure—the failure to have people around. It appears difficult to believe that one could be content with one's own company, so it seems incomprehensible that one might actually choose to be alone—if you are alone, it means that you must be lonely. This belief is magnified for singles on Saturday night, when it is believed everyone else is out having fun. This being the case, it is necessary to do something—anything—in order to avoid the failure of solitude. Perhaps, then, the first question that people suffering from feelings of loneliness ask is: What can I do about it? Not surprisingly, there are a number of diversions from the feeling that people take:

- *Take action.* Call a friend or visit someone. Since loneliness reflects a need for intimacy, actions such as this can resolve this issue,
- *Do something that lessens the loneliness.* Exercise, listen to music, read, work, spend time on a hobby, play a game, learn to play a musical instrument, or take a walk. These activities provide personal accomplishment and benefits that may help overcome feelings of unworthiness.
- *Deal with the symptoms negatively.* Do nothing, cry, get drunk, watch television, take tranquilizers, or go to bed and sleep.
- *Do something that provides a distraction.* Go for a drive or go shopping. Diversions may take your mind off the feeling as those of the negative activities but those types of activities will not work (Rubenstein and Shaver 1982).

Nor does a reliance on married couple friends seem to work, since an unattached person at a couples' gathering is invariably seen as a threat by someone present. In short, it is important to take our pastimes seriously, not only because they will make our lives more fun but because they may also lead to associations with like-minded people. Besides, traveling alone on vacations usually means that you are likely to have pleasant company by meeting like-minded travelers along the way and, perhaps, someone to travel with. An added benefit of traveling in medium-sized groups is that there is someone in charge to make traveling alone easier.

Not surprisingly, the growth in the number of singles and the stereotyped belief that they suffer from loneliness has led to an industry to help deal with the problem—to fill the void left by the older, conventional methods of forming relationships that are no longer operational in modern, urban society. Now, besides bars, there are various activities such as clubs, dances, and hotel weekends; apartment complexes for singles; awareness centers; encounter groups, pseudoreligious and mystical groups; and the Internet. The effort to assuage loneliness usually begins with visits to the local bar scene. Disenchantment here is what leads the lonely single to try the other arenas noted earlier. However, it should be remembered that these programs are offered by an industry for profit and so their efforts may be limited in providing relief. Thus, the singles industry has turned the effort to seek companionship into a commodity to be sold and so is usually a negative means for dealing with the problem.

Despite the fact that being single was always considered to be a more pitiful state for women than for men—think of the terms "spinster" versus "swinging bachelor"—the singles industry has had to court women to participate in their activities by offering reduced or free entrance fees to their clubs and other social events, since women have traditionally been reluctant to admit their status by attending by themselves.

Abetting women's efforts were the development of the birth control pill and the creation in the later part of the twentieth century of a new philosophy, as expressed by Helen Gurley Brown:

> The single woman of the seventies . . . has more sensational options at her fingertips than women have ever had before. The trick is in learning how to use them! Many of the old, rigid rules have broken down, thank goodness, and the woman alone is no longer hemmed in by a handful of no-no's. She can have lovers galore and still be a lady, be envied rather than pitied if she comes unescorted to a party, buy her own summer home or travel alone to Europe. She doesn't need a husband or even a steady beau—to entertain graciously, collect interesting friends or see unusual corners of the world. In short, an unmarried woman can . . . be a complete person without becoming attached to a man.

All of these assertions seem to imply that there are fewer negative effects in being single for women than men, and as God said to Adam, "It is not good for man to be alone" (Gen. 2:18). Therefore, it may be true that the suddenly single man may feel abandoned and desolate, and have difficulty taking care of his needs, but it is also true that a newly solitary woman may feel like a tree falling in an empty forest—no one's wife or lover, with no one to hear her.

Chapter Eleven

Health Dangers

INTRODUCTION:
IS SINGLEHOOD DANGEROUS TO YOUR HEALTH?

The family can act as a buffer against mental and physical illnesses . . . it provides gratification and intimacy to family members. (Cox 2002)

Solitaries eat badly. People alone can fall into vile culinary ruts and, out of sloth and misery, stay there. (Holland 1992)

The family has been called the "shock absorber" of society: It is the place that you turn to for affection and emotional support; a source of security; a place where you can share your dreams, joys, and even negative emotions, where people sympathize with your failures and take care of you when you are ill (Cox 2002).

Considering these benefits of family life, it is, perhaps, not surprising that a survey of 130 studies on a number of well-being indices revealed that singles are generally less happy and more stressed than married people (Coombs 1991). Another example the health benefits of married life is seen when it comes to psychiatric health: An examination of admissions to psychiatric hospitals reveals that for every 100,000 persons, there were 865 divorced/separated people, 701 widowed people, and 685 never-married people, but only 90 married people (Somers 1979). Single men have been found to suffer more nervous breakdowns, to be more socially maladjusted, and to be more subject to depression than married men. What is true for single men is also true for single women: Single women over thirty are also more likely than married women to be depressed, maladjusted, and neurotic (Braito and Anderson 1978;

Libby 1978). If these figures were divided into their respective subcategories, it would reveal that married men and divorced women are the least likely to be exceptionally stressed. In short, marriage is good for one's health—both mental and physical.

The earlier examination of the benefits of marriage had led to the conclusion that such benefits reveal a gender bias—men benefit more than women from marriage. This gender bias also extends to the health benefits of marriage. For example, in various studies on psychiatric treatment, married men had lower rates of treatment than married women. Since it has already been shown that the married are better off than singles in regard to health, it can be safely said that "on almost any index you can name—mental health or whatever—married men are best off" (Bernard 1979). For example, there were higher rates of psychiatric treatment for men among the singles, whereas single women over thirty were found to be healthier than single men over thirty (Bird 1972), and married women were found to be more depressed, more plagued by anxiety, and more under stress than never-married women (Braito and Anderson 1978). These conditions led to an unsurprising finding that never-married women were found to be above average in "personal and social adjustment" (Libby 1978).

Another major reason for this gender bias in marriage is selectivity. As Bernard (1979) notes, our social norms require hypergamous marriages—marriages in which the husband is "above" his wife in terms of age, education, height, occupation, and other important factors. This leads to mixed results in the marriage market: Men at the bottom of the scale with regard to these factors lose out and women lose out if they are at the top of the scale.

A summary of these facts related to health reveals that the unmarried—whether never married, divorced, or widowed—are far more likely to succumb to all causes of death, including automobile accidents, murder, and suicide, and "compared to married people, the non-married . . . have higher rates of mortality than the married: about 50% among women and 250% higher among men" (Ross, Mirosky, and Goldsteen 1990). It appears that "being unmarried is one of the greatest risks that people voluntarily subject themselves to" (Cohen and Lee 1979).

AN EXAMINATION OF COMMON PHYSICAL AND MENTAL HEALTH PROBLEMS

It has been shown that loneliness feelings can lead to a number of physical and psychosomatic problems, such as headaches, insomnia, depression, irrational fears, feelings of guilt, less interest in sex, constant worry, and feelings of unworthiness. In dealing with physical and mental health issues associated with loneliness, a problem arises, since many physical problems may be the result of mental issues; for example, frequent headaches, high blood pressure, and stomach ulcers are often associated with stress. For this reason it was decided to use these three physical systems plus insomnia under the heading "physical problems" and to use feelings of depression, fear, guilt, loneliness, sexual disinterest, worry, and worthlessness under the heading "mental health problems."

Physical Problems

Of the four physical problems, only two were examined, since too few of the sample had high blood pressure or ulcers to record meaningful differences among the four categories involved or between married and singles in general. In examining the physical problem of frequent headaches, a surprise was found in the early study since it was the married, both those married once or remarried, who were more likely to suffer from this malady (27 percent and 21 percent, respectively). The findings from earlier studies had led to the belief that an opposite finding would be found. However, the current study found the expected results: Singles were more likely by a slight margin than their married counterparts to suffer from frequent headaches (15 percent versus 13 percent). This finding was also our first clue that the 1980s were seemingly a more difficult time for both the married and the single than the current period, since for all the physical and mental problems examined, the earlier study resulted in higher figures. This will be examined more fully later.

The figures on insomnia in the early study were also something of a surprise, since there were mixed results—the remarried (25 percent) and the never married (20 percent) were the most likely to suffer from this problem, whereas the divorced were highly unlikely to indicate such a problem (5 percent). It was thought that the many difficulties associated with being divorced would produce the results found in the current study—a complete turnaround, with the divorced reporting this malady in higher numbers, 19 percent, versus 15 percent for the married once, 14 percent for the remarried, and 12 percent for the never-married. Another surprising finding was that the differences between the married and the singles were negligible in both studies—in the earlier study, the ratio was singles at 18 percent versus the married at 17 percent, and in the current study, the ratio was singles at 14 percent versus the married at 15 percent.

Mental Health Problems

Most people would probably define mental health problems as moods that people go through, and so answers on a questionnaire may not be a very accurate reflection of their true impact since memory may not be reliable in this regard. However, mental health problems may also be accompanied by physical ailments that improve the memory of one's mental moods; for example, depression may be accompanied by such symptoms as insomnia or hypertension, loss of energy/fatigue, loss of interest or pleasure in usual activities or a decrease in sexual drive, or feelings of worthlessness or inappropriate guilt. As can be seen, all of the mental heath problems being examined—fears, guilt, loneliness, disinterest in sex, worry, and feelings of worthlessness—may be reflections of depression. It is perhaps for this reason depression has been a rising factor in economically advanced democracies. People born after 1955 in such countries are three times more likely than those in their grandparents' generation to suffer a major depression (Coleman 1993).

Prior studies revealed that the most powerful cause of depression is disruption of family relations. Thus, being divorced, separated, or widowed was associated with higher levels of depression (Lane 2000). Therefore, it was no surprise that all of the findings on mental health were in the expected direction in the earlier study—in each situation singles were more likely than the married to suffer from the problems being examined, and in most cases by more than a two-to-one margin. For both categories, worry was the main problem noted, but the margin was less so for the married—28 percent versus 17 percent. Since the married have greater responsibilities than the singles, it was thought that they would have more worries—and, for that matter, more frequent headaches. The second most common problem for the singles group in the early study—loneliness—comes as no surprise, since loneliness is considered the biggest problem for singles. It is also no surprise that this problem was chosen by the largest margin of difference between the two main categories—25 percent for the singles versus 8 percent for the married. The third most common malady affecting the singles was actually a trio of feelings consisting of guilt, sexual dissatisfaction, and worthlessness. The relatively high number of singles reporting guilt feelings (22 percent) is skewed by the inclusion of the divorced, 30 percent of whom noted this problem. The situation is similar with sexual dissatisfaction (22 percent); the divorced were also the most likely group to make this claim (32 percent), a finding that is not surprising since the discussion in chapter 7 revealed that the divorced also were the most likely to claim being sexually dissatisfied. Finally, the divorced were also the most likely to report feelings of worthlessness (30 percent).

This examination of mental problems reveals that feelings of depression and fear are the least likely to be a problem for singles. Depression was reported at relatively low rates by the married (10 percent) and twice as often by the singles (20 percent), but the results for the singles were not as high as might be expected from the earlier discussion of loneliness. This may be the

result of its complicated definition and a lack of recognition by the respondents: the state of boredom, gloom, inaction, and nonspecific sadness. Fear
apparently is not a problem (S: 9 percent; M: 3 percent).

The 1980 study of physical and mental health problems revealed a confused
finding when comparing possible physical and mental problems. For each of
the mental items examined, the divorced revealed the difficulties of their civil
status, since for each ailment they were the most likely to note such feelings—
but they were also the least likely of the four categories to note the physical
problems of headaches and insomnia, which are physical symptoms often
associated with mental health problems. As noted, a higher number of the
divorced reporting mental health problems comes as no surprise, since studies
have shown that mental issues that lead to divorce are often made worse by
the divorce itself, especially in its early stages. It appears that disappointment
in marriage can lead to mental health problems. The other singles category
also indicate that singleness is second best to marriage by pairing up with the
divorced in being the next likely category to claim these mental feelings
except for feelings of sexual dissatisfaction. This difference with regard to
sexual dissatisfaction may be the result of experience, as it is assumed that the
divorced experienced steady sex lives during their married years.

Turning to the current study, there are some similar findings—but also a
major difference: For all of the problems examined except one, far fewer
respondents in both the singles and married categories noted these problems
than in the earlier study. For the physical problem of frequent headaches, 21
percent of the singles and 27 percent of the married respondents reported this
as a problem in the first study, but only 15 percent of singles and 13 percent of
the married reported it in the current study. Similar are the responses to the
problem of insomnia—17 percent of singles and 18 percent of the married
reported this as an issue in the early study versus 14 percent and 15 percent,
respectively, in the current study.

Mental health problems reveal similarly lower figures for the current study
when compared with the earlier study. Thus, worry was reported as a problem by 28 percent of the singles and 17 percent of the married in the 1980
study, but by only 14 percent and 10 percent, respectively, in the current
study; loneliness was noted by 25 percent of singles and 8 percent of married
respondents in the early study, but by only 11 percent and 6 percent, respectively, in the current study; feelings of guilt were reported by 22 percent of
singles and 11 percent of the married in the early study, versus only 3 percent
of each category in the current study. Dissatisfaction with sex was reported
by 22 percent of singles and 10 percent of the married in the early study, but
only 4 percent of the singles and 7 percent of the married report it in the current study. Feelings of worthlessness and depression also revealed steep

Table 11.1.   Health Problems during the Past Month

	Never Married %	Early/Current Studies Divorced %	Married %	Remarried %	Singles Tot. %	Married Tot. %
Physical Problems						
Headaches	21/15	19/14	27/13	21/12	2/15	27/13
Insomnia	20/12	5/19	16/15	25/14	17/14	18/15
Mental Problems						
Depression	19/5	22/4	10/5	7/6	20/4	10/6
Fears	8/3	11/2	3/3	5/5	9/3	3/4
Guilt	19/2	30/4	9/4	18/3	22/3	11/3
Loneliness	21/12	38/8	8/7	9/2	25/11	8/6
Sexual Dissatisfaction	10/4	32/4	10/6	9/11	22/4	10/7
Worry	29/13	24/16	16/9	23/11	28/14	17/10
Worthless	18/7	30/1	9/4	14/7	22/5	10/5

declines—worthlessness was reported by 22 percent of singles and 10 percent of the married in the early study, but by only 5 percent in each category in the current study; and depression was reported by 20 percent of the singles and 10 percent of the married in the 1980 study, but a mere 4 percent and 6 percent, respectively, in the current study.

It is only with the least frequently claimed mental health problem—feelings of fear—that a change in this pattern is found: Singles reported these feelings at a rate of 9 percent in the early study versus 3 percent in the current study, but 3 percent of married respondents reported these feelings in the early study and this increased to 4 percent in the current study.

The reduction in the numbers reporting these physical and mental health problems seems to indicate that the growth in the number of singles has made it easier to be both single and married: As noted earlier, the growth in the number of singles is mostly the result of a delay in marriage, and the more mature age of both groups seems to be more helpful in dealing with their problems.

ALCOHOL USE

One way to deal with the physical and mental health problems noted earlier would be to drink them into oblivion. This seemed to be true in the early study, since far more singles than married (21 percent versus 7 percent) reported drinking frequently. Unsurprisingly, the group reporting these negative feelings at the highest rates—the divorced—was also the leader in imbibing, at 25 percent. However, this finding is contradicted by the findings on alcohol use in the current study. As noted earlier, the current study reveals a large decline in numbers in all the categories reporting all the problems, but at the same time, there was a very large increase across the categories in the use of alcohol: The number of never-married respondents claiming to drink frequently doubled from 20 percent to 47 percent; for the divorced the increase was less staggering but nonetheless substantial, from 25 percent to 37 percent; the married, who once reported the lowest rate of frequent drinking in both studies, nearly tripled in numbers, from 7 percent to 20 percent; and the remarried also reported drinking frequently at triple the rate of the early study, from 12 percent to 38 percent. The results of the combined subcategories confirm the individual category numbers: The total for singles jumped from 21 percent to 46 percent and for the married from 7 percent to 22 percent.

These mixed results from the two studies would seem to contraindicate a relationship between physical and mental problems and the frequency of alcohol use, or that cultural changes such as eating out more frequently has made drinking with a meal more available.

Table 11.2.   Alcohol Use

| | Early/Current Studies | |
	Rarely/Never	Frequently
Never Married	80/53%	20/47%
Divorced	75/63	25/37
Married Once	93/80	7/20
Remarried	88/63	12/38
Singles Total	79/54	21/46
Married Total	93/78	7/22

The adjunct study of the singles organization sample adds an interesting dimension to the question of why singles drink more than married people: The family situation in a married household serves to restrain drinking. A divorced man put it this way: "I was reluctant to drink in front of my children, but now I can have those drinks after work to 'unwind' and to join the 'crowd' at the local bar." From this remark it appears that this lack of restriction may be a factor in somewhat greater use of alcohol by singles. Another possible reason for the higher rate of alcohol use by the singles lies in their efforts to meet others, usually via the bar scene. The increasing availability of organizations and Internet programs for singles may explain why the increase in frequent use of alcohol by singles in the current study was smaller than the increase in use found in the married portion of the sample.

THE RELATIONSHIP TO SUICIDE

The question of suicide was examined as a means of summarizing the health of singles. Prior studies on this subject had shown that single men are more vulnerable than married men: They die younger and are more likely to commit suicide (Bird 1972; Gove 1973). In his comprehensive early-nineteenth-century study, Emile Durkheim explained this propensity for suicide by single men as a result of the relaxation of the bond that ties him to life—the bond to society. Anticipating the literature that indicated that the lack of married stresses led to greater happiness of single women, Durkheim also found that marriage actually increased suicide among women. Thus, it was a surprise to learn that single women were also more likely than married women to commit suicide (Brody 1979; Somers 1979). However, this greater propensity to commit suicide by single people may be a result of a special group of singles—the widowed, who are ten times more likely to die in the year following the death of a spouse than those surviving spouses who do not die (Brody 1979). Since there are far more surviving widows than widowers, this may also explain the surprising figures on single females versus married females. Unfortunately, an attempt to measure suicide among the samples of the two studies was thwarted by the presence of too few respondents in the current study reporting thoughts of suicide. Considering the large decline in numbers of those noting physical and mental problems in the current study as compared to the earlier study, this finding does not come as a surprise. In the earlier study, it was found that the divorced were far more likely than any other component of the sample to have thought about suicide. Since this earlier study also found that the divorced were more likely to note the physical and mental problems discussed earlier, this is not surprising.

CONCLUSION: CIVIL STATUS AND HEALTH

In sum, the finding on the measurements of health supports the conclusion that marriage is good for one's health. Since this study also included the divorced as part of the singles category, it was important to note whether the biases in civil status and gender noted earlier were any different for this category. Generally, the never-married fare better than the separated and the divorced on health issues. Perhaps not surprisingly, separation and divorce were found to lead to great psychological stress. Studies have found that never-married women are less depressed than either the separated or divorced women. However, the finding is the opposite for the never-married men, who were found to be more depressed than separated and divorced men.

Combining the earlier findings, it can be concluded that marriage is better for one's health than being single; that there is a gender bias in this regard, since married women rather than single women are more likely to have health problems; and that divorce is not healthy for either sex, but, in line with the gender bias shown, it is more unhealthy for men than women. These findings are contradictory to the stereotyped belief of the "swinging bachelor" and the "lonely spinster" since it was found that being single is bad for men and good for women.

Part IV

ASSESSMENTS
AND PROJECTIONS

Chapter Twelve

The Stereotypes Reexamined

INTRODUCTION: AN ASSUMPTION

There is a natural lag between a changing situation and the awareness of that situation. In the early stages in the growth of the singles population, family sociologists "either ignored singles or relegated them to boring out-of-date discussions of dating" (Libby 1978). Since the values of society were so strongly in favor of marriage and the family, singles were not perceived as a distinct social entity "that had its own characteristics, dynamics, and unique features" (Adams 1976). Instead, they were described using stereotypical images, usually negative, that implied that singles were carefree but were also incomplete, lonely, and undesirable. The usual role of stereotypes is to convince an "out" group to become part of the majority—in this case, a means to encourage singles to become part of the cultural norm by getting married.

It was noted in chapter 3 that, like all groups that are not part of the majority, singles use their own stereotypical beliefs trying to explain their "odd" behavior and the benefits of and/or detriments to that behavior. It was assumed, that like most stereotypes, these would turn out to be myths, since that is what the word "stereotype" means—a standardized image of a group based on over-simplified characteristics that do not accurately describe individual members of that group. This does not mean that there were no differences between married and singles, only that these differences were exaggerations of reality and, in this sense, myths. But it is also possible that some of the stereotypes could, over time, become realities.

As a means of examining this possibility, two studies were conducted using a sample of both singles and married respondents to note the ways in which they differed on several factors. As indicated, the first study was done in

1980—when baby boomers were coming of adult age, resulting in a large growth in the singles population. The next study was done in 2005, during another boom in the growth in singles, as these baby boomers did not follow their parents into early marriage. The baby boomers are now middle-aged, and so the current growth in the singles population is due to the baby boomers' children also delaying marriage. The material collected from the first study revealed that some of the common stereotypes about the differences between singles and the married were indeed realities, but also that some were myths. In the later study, some of the numbers had changed, but the original conclusions as to which stereotypes were myths and which were realities held true.

In addition, some of the stereotyped beliefs were supported, but only as they related to one of the two major subcategories of singles. This was an important finding since it meant that, as usual, labels cover up differences in behaviors and, therefore, needs. A somewhat surprising finding was that some of the stereotypes were actually more applicable to one or both of the two major subcategories of the married being examined.

This chapter will present the original findings and reexamine the data in order to determine which of the stereotypes applied to singles are myths, which are realities, and whether there have been any changes in the application of the terms, myths, or realities during this period of large growth for singles. As part of this reexamination, the two major categories will be split into subcategories in order to determine whether the stereotypes apply to all singles or to all the married, or whether they were true only for the never-married, the divorced, the married-once, or the remarried.

Before beginning this endeavor, however, it seems like a good idea to take a look at these stereotypes by asking our sample in the current study what they thought was the public's image of singles. There were no strong beliefs about any of the stereotypes, but this examination will nonetheless give us a clue as to what to expect when examining the stereotypes in detail.

- *Singles are swingers.* The responses from the singles organization support the idea that having more sex partners than the married (12 percent) does not mean having greater sexual pleasure than the married (14 percent). An interesting contrast between the two subgroups is seen with the beliefs concerning sexual satisfaction and satisfaction with life. The never-married are more likely than the divorced to report lower sexual satisfaction (16 percent versus 11 percent), but this does not necessarily mean that they lead less satisfactory lives (8 percent versus 11 percent). Nor does having more sex partners mean that singles are more immoral than the married (5 percent), which seems to support the idea that a revolution in sexual behavior has occurred.

Table 12.1.   Images of Singles (Current Study)

	Never Married	Divorced	Total
They have more sex partners	13%	10%	12%
They are irresponsible	10	14	11
They are happier	14	18	16
They have more fun	19	14	17
They are immoral	5	5	5
They are lonelier	14	15	15
They have less satisfactory lives	8	13	10
They have less sex satisfaction	16	11	14

- *Singles have more fun and are happier.* The idea that singles have more fun (17 percent) and are happier (16 percent) than the married drew the most support. The different response to these impressions by the subcategories indicates that they see a difference between having fun and being happy. It appears that the younger group, the never-married, believe that they do more fun things than the divorced (19 percent versus 14 percent), whereas the divorced were more likely to report being happier than the married (18 percent versus 14 percent). The divorced usually have more responsibilities than the never-married, and this may mean that their perceived happiness is a result of their separation from an unhappy alliance.
- *Singles are lonelier.* As a result of their lifestyle, singles may report being lonelier than the married (15 percent) and that singles are considered more irresponsible than the married (11 percent).

A summary of these stereotypical beliefs reveals that never having been married is a somewhat better position than being divorced, but that neither is really that much worse off than being married.

THE MYTHS

Singles Are Tied to Mother's Apron Strings

An older single indicates his close family ties by noting that he is going to visit his mother. The platitude that follows, however, is not one of praise for showing such devotion but one of ridicule and blame: "Uh, huh—that's the problem. He hasn't been able to let go of those strings." If this same adult is still living at home with a parent, particularly a mother, the ridicule becomes worse. He is a figure of tragedy, one who might have gotten away to marriage if he could have broken the bonds of a possessive mom.

Of course, these beliefs are based on the idea that an unmarried person "must" have made the attempt to seek a mate, whether living at home or not. The stereotype that people remain single because they cannot cut the "silver cord" that binds them to their families finds no support from the data in either study. In both studies, it was the married who were more likely to indicate warm relations with their parents while living at home, but the difference between the two groups was minor in the early study—64 percent of married respondents versus 60 percent of singles—and much larger in the current study—59 percent of married respondents versus 42 percent of singles.

The rejection of the apron strings stereotype gets added confirmation with the figures on those indicating cold or conflicting relations with their parents. Again, in contradiction to the belief, singles were slightly more likely than the married to indicate this type of relationship with their parents in the early study, but the difference was minor—31 percent of singles versus 27 percent of married respondents. This difference in views on those claiming cold or conflicting relations with their parents becomes more dramatic with the current study—the figure for the singles is 42 percent versus only 30 percent for the married.

The rise in the number of singles reporting cold or conflicting relationships with their parents might suggest that the increasing age of those singles is making their parents unhappy with an ongoing decision to flout cultural customs and their parents' wishes by remaining single, but this does not explain why relations with parents are also negative for the married. Nevertheless, both studies show that warm relations with parents are more likely for the married than singles, and so the apron strings stereotype for those remaining single is rejected.

This finding is confirmed when dealing with the factor of current relations between the major categories and their parents. In the early study, married respondents were far more likely than the singles to indicate that their current relations with their parents were warm (70 percent versus 45 percent). Interestingly, these current relationships appear to be changing, but in opposite directions. It appears that singleness is becoming more acceptable to parents, since the number of singles indicating current warm relations with their parents increased from 45 percent to 59 percent. In addition, the number of singles claiming to fight a lot with their parents declined substantially by the time of the current study for both singles (early study: 31 percent; current study: 18 percent) and the married (early study: 13 percent; current study: 1 percent), but singles still report fighting with their parents more than married people do. On the other hand, the married appear to be having more difficulties with their parents, since the number of married claiming current warm relations has declined, from 70 percent to 56 percent. This finding may be the result of a generation gap, since the children are getting married at a much later age than their parents and certainly have different values.

A seeming contradiction to the early findings is indicated when dealing with parental emotions. It might be assumed that warm relations with parents might be an outcome of whether those parents were emotionally open with their children. However, there was little difference between singles and the married in this regard in the early study, regardless of the category studied: both parents (S: 46 percent; M: 46 percent), mother only (S: 24 percent; M: 25 percent), father only (S: 7 percent; M: 7 percent), neither parent (S: 21 percent; M: 21 percent). The current study seems to imply that there is a trend toward parents being less open with their children. Both of the major groupings reported large drops in those claiming that both parents were open with their emotions. However, the decline for singles was minor, to 41 percent, whereas it was much larger for the married, to 36 percent. Apparently, there is no relationship between parents being open with their emotions with their children and whether those current relationships were warm or cool.

The findings from the three questions asking about family relations indicate that there is no relationship between being married or single and family relations either in the past or currently. Thus, the stereotype regarding apron strings was found to be a myth.

Singles Are Happier

Since singles are assumed to be carefree, they should be happier than those with the burdens of marriage and family. Yet when the subcategories of the sample were asked how they compared themselves to single and married acquaintances on happiness, it was found that the married group saw themselves as happier than their single acquaintances by a large margin in both studies, and the margin was increasing (28 percent to 16 percent in the early study; 46 percent to 11 percent in the current study). A similar finding was indicated by the singles component of the sample in the early study: By a small margin, they saw themselves as less happy than their married acquaintances (33 percent to 27 percent). However, this is completely reversed in the current study; now, far more singles see themselves as happier than their married acquaintances (75 percent to 9 percent). This may mean that the growth in the singles population has led to improved lifestyles or that married life is being perceived as becoming more difficult. Either way, it appears that the stereotype itself may be a myth—the married do not think that singles are happier than they are, and in the early study singles did not think they were happier than the married.

Wishing to confirm this finding, respondents were asked how they felt about their own happiness. Maybe the high rating on happiness placed upon others was due to poor ratings placed on their own happiness. In both studies, more of the married than the singles rated themselves as happy, but the difference was small—86 percent versus 76 percent in the early study and 72 percent versus 64 percent in the current study.

It is probably healthy to think of oneself as happy but, at the same time, there may be indicators that contradict this belief. For example, the questions on loneliness discussed in chapter 10 indicate that more of the singles than the married are depressed when alone, feel that they have no one with whom to share activities, and that they have no one with whom to discuss things. Certainly these factors of loneliness are not happiness provoking, so it would appear that the singles are doing some compartmentalizing on the question of happiness. A similar conclusion can be reached by looking at the figures regarding mental health problems in chapter 11. The early study revealed that for every mental health issue examined, more singles than married respondents claimed the problem noted. But these differences largely disappeared in the current study, despite a decline in the numbers in both groups claiming to be happy. Perhaps this means that there is no relationship between happiness and health, or, as noted, compartmentalizing is taking place.

A final glance at the relationship between health and happiness returns us to our previous assumption that singles are not as happy as they proclaim, since far more of them than the married in both studies are likely to drink alcohol frequently (early study: 21 percent for singles versus 7 percent for married respondents; current study: 46 percent for singles versus 22 percent for married respondents). Looking at all the data noted earlier, it can be concluded that the stereotype itself may not be real, but it does exist as a myth.

Singles Are Rich

This stereotype is based in part on the belief that singles must have lots of money since they do not have the expenses of maintaining a family; they seem to have the money required to maintain an affluent lifestyle. Another factor that makes this lifestyle possible is the fact that singles have the freedom to choose how to spend their money, since they are not tied to joint decisions on finances. In addition, without family considerations, singles are able to make professional commitments based on mobility and potential, but employers apparently believe that singles have fewer expenses and less responsibility and therefore do not need or deserve the same salaries as married workers. The Internal Revenue Service also seems to believe this, since singles are taxed higher proportionally to married couples. Supermarkets continue this bias against singles and their supposed wealth, with bargains only for larger, family-size items.

Despite these biases, the facts reveal that married couples, on average, are far more affluent than singles. The current study indicates that the statistics on

Table 12.2. Civil Status and Income (Current Study)

	<$20,000	$20,001–$40, 000	$40,001–$50,000	$50,000+
Never Married	48%	32%	10%	11%
Divorced	32	35	18	14
Married	24	36	14	26
Remarried	2	31	31	36
Singles Total	42	33	13	12
Married Total	19	35	18	28

income do not support the stereotype. When it comes to income, most singles report incomes in the lowest range, less than $20,000 per year, versus for the married (42 percent versus 19 percent). In addition, fewer singles claim to be in the higher income bracket of $40,000 or more: 25 percent versus 46 percent of the married. This result may be due to the fact that the never-married are younger and are thus more likely to be at the bottom of the economic ladder, or held back by divorce. Another reason for this income discrepancy may be the fact that in many, if not most, married households, both parents are working. The result is that the married are better off economically than the singles, and the stereotype of singles as wealthier is not supported by fact.

Being Single Is Now More Acceptable

This is a belief promulgated by singles to explain their large growth in numbers, and it does seem logical. However, two facts indicate that neither singles nor society believe this to be true. The review of titles in the *Readers' Guide to Periodicals Literature* in chapter 5 illustrates that there has been little change throughout the century in the preoccupation of singles with marriage. As indicated, finding a mate remains one of the major subjects listed under the singles heading. In the next chapter, this conclusion will be discussed further. When the singles in our sample were asked what their civil status would be in five years, the overwhelming response was "married." Perhaps regrettably, this belief that being single is more acceptable must be placed among the stereotypes.

THE REALITIES

Singles Are Swingers

Before beginning an examination of the data on sexual behavior found in the two studies, it is important to recognize that the term "swinger" is something of a misnomer when applied to singles since, by definition, one has to be married to be a swinger. At the same time, it is not incorrect to apply the term to singles, since it is now often applied to any person who goes out frequently in order to recruit as many partners as possible for sexual relations. Use of the term reveals a gender bias, since it is believed to be more applicable to men than to women. Since the term can now be applied to both the married and to the single, the question becomes one of whether it is more true for one category than the other. Therefore, the facts will be examined as a means of discovering whether singles are swingers and whether the married should be included in that category.

In order to make the assertion that one is a swinger, it is necessary to determine the basis for that assertion. In short, how many sexual partners make one a "swinger"? After examining the data, it was decided that ten was a good dividing point, so to be labeled a swinger for these studies, one must have had a minimum of eleven sexual partners. Actually, in the early study two or more sexual partners would have qualified one as a swinger because at all but the lowest figure, more singles than married claimed these numbers of partners. If there were no current study, it would be quite easy to claim that the stereotype of singles as swingers would be true since they had had more—albeit only slightly more—sexual partners. In fact, the swinger stereotype would be more true if the claim was applied only to the divorced, since it was that category that reported having more partners by a wide margin over any other subcategory.

The label "swinger" also showed to be true in the current study but only when defining it as one who has had eleven or more sexual partners, since it is only at this level that singles outstripped their married counterparts. What is seen at the other sexual partner levels is confirmation that sexual activity is seemingly more acceptable today for all groups, and this is confirmed with the fact that all subcategories report having had more sexual partners at all levels in the current study than in the early study. This may be true for the married because they are marrying later and so had more partners prior to marriage, but it also could be true as a fact of current married life.

Although the term "swinger" applies to one who has a number of sexual partners, it was believed that number of partners does not tell the complete story of the differences between singles and the married in regard to sexual behavior. For example, it was found that an increased number of sexual partners does not mean increased frequency of sexual intercourse per week and that increased frequency does not correlate with increased sexual satisfaction. Another important factor affecting sexual satisfaction may be the scorecard: How do you compare to others as far as number of sexual partners? The results indicate that those in both categories believe that others have more sexual partners.

Based on the original definition of a swinger, the swinger stereotype as applied to singles is a reality, but it may not be for very much longer since the married are rapidly increasing their numbers of sexual partners.

Singles Have More Fun

It may seem like a contradiction to say that the stereotype regarding singles being happier than the married is a myth while at the same noting that the stereotype claiming that singles have more fun is a reality, but this is so because the relationship between the happiness and fun is tenuous. Happiness, as noted previously, is a feeling that is based on a number of outside factors such as getting a pay raise, seeing your favorite sports team win, or noting that you are better off than your single or married friends. Fun, on the other hand, may give you momentary pleasure, but it may not produce an overall feeling of happiness since it was not done for that purpose. For example, swimming may be fun but not pleasurable since it was done as part of an exercise effort. This means that to answer the question on fun it was necessary to make a list of activities that people enjoy and then make a judgment as to which ones would be more fun to do. Since far more people in both segments of the sample chose visiting friends over visiting relatives, it was assumed to be more fun. In the early study, there was no difference between the two segments in choosing the most popular activity, visiting friends (55 percent). In the current study, the popularity of visiting friends remained high, but declined slightly for both categories: 53 percent for the singles versus 47 percent for the married.

On the other hand, in the early study visiting relatives appeared to be a low priority and was more often selected by the married (42 percent versus 18 percent). Interestingly, the current study reveals a reversal in the popularity of visiting relatives by the two groups: more of the singles now report visiting relatives (27 percent), whereas fewer married respondents chose this option (30 percent)—and the difference between the two categories is now a minuscule 3 percent.

Getting back to the question of fun, visiting friends was a very popular outing and more singles than married respondents chose this option. Visiting relatives was not as popular, so it can be assumed to be less fun to visit relatives; it was chosen more often by married respondents than singles. Going to restaurants or to a movie were both popular options and so assumed to be fun. The married were somewhat more likely than the singles to go out to dine, but the difference was narrow in the current study as going to a restaurant became a more popular outing for more singles. It was believed that singles probably eat out quite often, so this may be as a necessity rather than as a fun activity. The current study shows that going out to movies has become a popular outing for the married, and their percentage is not much different from that of the singles. Visiting nightclubs (bars) reveals the most decisive difference between the groups in both studies: For singles the figures for the two studies are 36 percent and 45 percent, respectively, whereas for the married the figures are 19 percent and 16 percent. Since visiting friends and going to nightclubs (bars) are both assumed to be more fun than visiting relatives, and singles engage in these two activities more often than married people do, the stereotype about singles having more fun can be accepted as a reality.

A backup question in this regard was related to the time spent in a passive activity like watching television versus the time spent visiting friends. Unfortunately, both groups reported watching television in similar numbers and also had similar figures visiting friends for multiple hours. A better picture of fun and watching multiple hours of television would have been revealed if the respondents were asked about their activities while watching television: smoking pot or drinking beer?

Singles Are Lonely

The stereotype of singles as lonely would appear to contradict the one dealing with sexual behavior. On the one hand, because singles do not have mates, they supposedly suffer from loneliness as a result. In fact, it is referred to as their great bugaboo. On the other hand, singles are also stereotyped as being swingers, which implies that while they may not have mates, they have lots of partners to help assuage their supposed loneliness. Therefore, the next section examines the loneliness stereotype in light of the replies regarding sexual partners in order to note whether these two stereotypes are truly contradictory.

Loneliness is such a major stereotype regarding singles that it was believed that no single question could resolve the issue. Thus, four questions were asked regarding reflections of loneliness and two more on beliefs regarding loneliness. The first question was based on the idea that those who are lonely are more likely to be depressed and unhappy. The results of these two expressions of loneliness were mixed: As expected, in both studies singles were more likely than the married respondents to indicate feelings of depression (early study: 23 percent versus 15 percent; current study: 21 percent versus 18 percent), but it is clear that feelings of depression are a larger problem currently for the divorced than for any of the other categories.

One would think that if one is depressed then one would also be unhappy, but that does not seem to be the case since it was the married who were more likely to claim feeling unhappy in both studies (early study: 18 percent versus 12 percent; current study: 11 percent versus 9 percent). Again, among singles feelings of unhappiness were shown to be more of a problem for the divorced than for the never-married. This finding on unhappiness, however, might tie in with another stereotype: that singles, with their carefree lifestyle, are happier than the married—but this part of the stereotype was shown to be untrue.

Since the married were believed to have someone to share good and bad things and to have someone to discuss problems and such with since they have a mate, it was decided that asking this question of the married would produce negligible results. After all, it is supposed to be the singles who do not have a companion with whom to do these things. So only the singles were asked whether the absence of a mate meant that they had no one to share or discuss things with. It appears that this is true, but for only a small minority in each study. Only 20 percent of singles in the first study reported having no one to share with, but this seems to be a growing problem since 28 percent of the singles noted this in the current study. With regard to not having someone to discuss issues with, an opposite is seen: 30 percent of the singles indicated that this was true for them in the first study, but this figure was cut in half, to 15 percent, by the time of the current study. This reduction in the number of those singles claiming to have no one to discuss things with seems to illustrate an improvement for the divorced, who showed a huge drop in the numbers making this claim.

Feelings of loneliness can be accentuated by being alone when dining and/or by entering an one empty room. Dining is a social act, so it would be no surprise to find that the singles were more likely than the married to have experience loneliness when dining alone, but this turned out to produce more feelings of loneliness for both groups in both studies—46 percent of the singles and 33 percent of the married reported these feelings in the early study and 46 percent of the singles and 36 percent of the married reported them in the current study. Again, the divorced were more likely than the never-married to note this problem, probably because it was a sharp change from their prior married lifestyle. But this was the case only in the current study, which indicates that this is becoming a larger problem for the divorced.

The question of entering an empty room revealed mixed results—and indicated a problem that seems to be growing. In the early study, only 18 percent of the singles and 13 percent of the married noted this activity as a problem, while in the second study 35 percent of the singles and 41 percent of the married reported it. Not only was there a large jump in those noting this as a problem, but it was also more of a problem for the married, who, being used to company, apparently do not like the idea of being alone in an empty room.

Two more questions on loneliness were asked of the singles only in order to round out the image of loneliness for them: Did they join organizations in order to escape their loneliness? Only small numbers in both studies took joined organizations in order to find company (early study: 21 percent; current study 19 percent), and again, it was the divorced who were more likely to take this type of action.

The final question dealt with the idea that the problem of loneliness was true of most people, not just singles. This idea also had little support from the singles in both studies (early study: 17 percent; current study: 7 percent). The larger numbers in the first study were mostly a reflection of the divorced—a reflection that disappeared in the current study. This finding, then, was the only loneliness factor that indicated an improvement for the divorced—a recognition that was perhaps true of them was not necessarily true of most people.

It should be noted that these conditions reflecting loneliness were usually noted by a minority of both groups, that when more singles than married noted loneliness it is more accurate to say that it was a problem of the divorced rather than for singles in general, and that in a few instances the married actually noted more of a problem with loneliness factors. Thus, it would appear that the loneliness stereotype is indeed more applicable to singles, but it certainly does not appear to be the great bugaboo.

Singles Are Deviant

Again, there appears to be a contradiction in this summary of the stereotypes examined. On the one hand, it is claimed that the belief that something is wrong with being single is a myth, and on the other hand it is claimed that the belief that singles are deviant is a reality. The reason for this is that the belief that being single is wrong is an application to individuals of a group, but the label "deviant" is applied to the whole group, because that group is a minority and so deviates from the majority. This may seem like nit-picking, so further examples are necessary to illustrate that being single is not necessarily wrong but that as a group singles are, indeed, deviant.

Since the belief that something is wrong is a perception and is a means for explaining that person's deviancy from the norm, then something must be wrong with those who do not conform to the majority belief by becoming married by a certain age:

- They are tied to their parent's apron strings.
- They are selfish and do not want to share their achievements.
- They have put careers ahead of the moral requirement to marry.
- They are sexual playboys or playgirls.
- There is the excuse of a shortage of men.
- That they are limited by geographical location and religious beliefs.

As can be seen, there are numerous reasons people do not marry. These are beliefs about individuals and so cannot be applied to singles as a group. Examine the preceding allegations:

- The belief that singles are tied to their parent's apron strings was shown to be a myth (chapter 6).
- Although not discussed, the responses to the question on volunteer time indicates that singles were somewhat more likely than the married to engage in volunteer activities.
- It was shown that the need for education and getting started on a career may delay marriage, but for the overwhelming majority it does not eliminate marriage altogether.
- The current statistics indicate that having a large number of sexual partners is not limited to singles.
- Shortages of men or women are limited to very specific places and can be easily eliminated with greater efforts with the use of the Internet and many other options now offered to the market of singles.

Since deviancy is defined by a statistical relationship, there are a number of deviant groups in society that may not be perceived as such. Unfortunately, they usually are perceived as such and then they are discriminated against for being different. This situation has been seen throughout history in the case of civil status, race, gender, religious beliefs, and so forth. This cause and effect regarding being deviant raises an interesting question: Since singles are a rapidly growing segment of society and now make up more than 50 percent of the adult population, what happens now that they are the majority? Will parents encourage their children not to marry? Will religious organizations urge people to follow in the steps of Jesus and not marry, or like the Buddha, leave their families? Will the media glorify singlehood while pointing out the negatives of being married? Hardly! Singles are deviant as a group since they have not married, and that is all there is to it.

Life Is Getting Better for Singles

This stereotype has been confirmed as a reality through the examination of a number of factors. Like many minorities of the past and present, efforts by them and their supporters have led to the lessening of perhaps unintended discriminatory acts against them. No one would argue with a history that reveals fewer of these unfavorable conditions for such groups as people of color, senior citizens, and women. The same can be said for singles. These improvements in conditions for singles can be seen in a number of areas. Their growing numbers and perception as market means that there are now apartments, bars and clubs, trips, web sites, and so forth aimed sepecifically at singles. The media confirms this perception with a change in the topics listed in the *Readers' Guide to Periodical Literature* (discussed in chapter 5) and with

Table 12.3.   The Stereotypes

Myths:	Realities:
Singles are tied to their mothers' apron strings.	Singles are swingers.
Singles are happier.	Singles have more fun.
Singles are rich.	Singles are lonely.
Being single is more acceptable.	Singles are deviant.
Something is wrong with singles.	Life is getting better for singles.

more television programs and movies glorifying the benefits of being single rather than the overwhelming emphasis on the benefits of marriage. Although this list of improvements for singles could continue, further change is not necessary since the existing list already shows that the stereotype is a reality. Perhaps in the future, the mythical belief that being single is a normal alternative to being married will also become a reality.

These improvements in the single lifestyle and growth in the singles population do not mean that marriage will fade as the dominant civil status. Married life still has many advantages in many crucial areas: The married are more likely to be more happy (chapter 9), less lonely (chapter 10), and more healthy (chapter 11). Although the alternative to marriage has become more attractive, it has not replaced it as the most desirable civil status—an assertion supported by all the titles about finding a mate listed in the *Readers' Guide* and in the answer by the sample to the question "Where do you see yourself in five years: still single or married?" The overwhelming majority saw themselves as married (chapter 13).

THERE IS SOMETHING WRONG WITH SINGLES

This examination of the stereotypes applied to singles can be summarized by turning to another mythical stereotype that seemingly sums up all the stereotypes: Something must be wrong with them since they are not conforming to the norm of marriage.

This stereotype is illustrated in this description from Anthony Trollope's 1876 novel *The Prime Minister*:

> This was Barrington Erle, a politician of long standing, who was still looked upon by many as a young man, because he had never done anything to compromise his position in that respect. He had not married, or settled himself down in a house of his own, or become subject to gout, or given up being careful about the fitting of his clothes. . . . He was in truth much nearer fifty than forty;—nevertheless he was felt in the House and among Cabinet Ministers, and among the wives of members

and Cabinet Ministers, to be a young man still. And when he was invited to become Secretary of Ireland it was generally felt that he was too young for the place. He declined it, however, and when he went to the post-office, the gentlemen there all felt that they had a boy put over them. Phineas Finn, who had become Secretary of Ireland, was in truth ten years his junior. But Phineas Finn had been twice married, and had gone through other phases of life, such as make a man old.

It seems that what was wrong with Barrington Erle was not that he was old or that he looked old, but that he was not experienced—he had not married, and, having not taken on that responsibility, was considered too inexperienced to take on other responsibilities. The question remains: Has anything changed since 1876? It was noted in the historical examination of marriage that there have been a number of stereotypes about what was supposedly wrong with singles, but apart from a note of defensiveness on the part of the singles, there does not appear to be any inherent problem within singles themselves. The defensiveness, it should be noted, was a response to negative labels—understandable and certainly not indicative of anything wrong. Granted, the measures of loneliness and happiness may indicate that singles do not fare as well as the married on these measures, but there is nothing wrong with being lonely or sad some of the time. In fact, the reverse is true: If a person, married or single, never had these feelings we would wonder what is wrong with him or her. On the other hand, singles do seem to have more freedom to go wherever and do whatever they desire—a freedom that many a married person often wishes they also had, but that does not mean there is something wrong with the married person.

Remaining single might be wrong if by doing so singles were hurting themselves and/or society. But are they hurting themselves by being single? People may wonder what is wrong with an older, never-married person that he or she did not marry. This viewpoint was indicated several times in the review of headings in the *Readers' Guide* (chapter 5), but considering all the topics citing problems with marriage in the *Readers' Guide*, one could easily ask what is wrong with the married that they have so many problems. Granted, the divorced segment of the singles population may be seen as having done something wrong or having caused problems for themselves, but since a good proportion of those who divorce will remarry within a short time, it could also be said that it was right to separate in order to regroup for a better future marriage.

The question of wrongness could also be reversed: What is right about being single? On taxes, society benefits because singles pay a proportionally higher tax rate than the married do; on population control there is the benefit of singles marrying later and so having smaller families; on consumption, because they do not have families to support, they are able to spend more money supporting cultural interests and social causes; and with more free time, they are able to volunteer more often for needed community services.

This review of various things that are supposed to be wrong with being single indicates not only that they are assertions without any backing when applied to singles as a group, but that the belief that there is may be the most wrong and most destructive of all the stereotypes applied to them.

CONCLUSION: WHAT DOES IT MEAN?

Finding that some of the stereotypes are myths and that some are realities does not indicate on its face whether these results were good or bad for singles. Therefore, it is necessary to reexamine the stereotypes in order to note their effect as myths or realities.

First, we will look at the myths. The stringer image was shown to be a myth, and this is positive for the image of the single since it means that they are single of their own volition. That singles are happier than the married is a myth is a negative for the singles image because being happier was supposedly one of the major benefits of being single. The belief that singles are richer than the married was also shown to be a myth. Perhaps this finding would have turned out different if the comparison was done on a one-to-one salary basis because married couples often have two incomes, but the fact remains that singles are not richer than the married, and this has a negative implication for singles. An increasing acceptance of singlehood as a valid alternative to marriage is perhaps one of the strongest and most hoped-for beliefs by singles, but, unfortunately, it just is not so. This is major negative for singles, who would like to feel accepted. On the other hand, the stereotype that there is something wrong with singles is a myth, which is a very positive finding for singles since this belief is widespread.

Turning to the realities brings us face to face with the supposed bugaboo of being single: They are lonelier than the married, and suffering from loneliness is not a positive attribute of being single. The discussion of sexual behavior revealed that limitations on this behavior seem to have been lifted, and singles have taken advantage of this greater acceptance more than the married have—a positive result. That singles have more fun than the married needs no explanation, since having fun is clearly a positive. That singles are still seen as a deviant group cannot be positive, since being deviant usually results in discrimination, a negative consequence. But singles do have something to cheer about—things are getting better for them overall, and that is very positive indeed.

This review of the myths and realities indicates five negative results and five positive results. Considering the fact that singles are seen as deviating from societal mores regarding marriage, a five-to-five standoff may be seen as an overall positive result. In sum, our cultural climate is increasingly accepting both singleness and divorce, but this does not mean that this lifestyle is less stressful than marriage. It also does not mean that marriage is stress free since it cannot live up to all our expectations or be conflict free. This is so because of the unrealistic myths involving marriage and because society provides for few guidelines and little training for this lifelong role.

Chapter Thirteen

The Future

INTRODUCTION: THE DEATH OF THE FAMILY

The loss of many of the functions of the "traditional family" has apparently led to a decline in its moral influence as a civil status to which everyone must aspire. This loss of influence can be seen in various trends:

- A number of those who are now never married, supposedly on a temporary basis due to a delay in marriage, may turn out to be permanent.
- Fifty percent of all marriages will be dissolved by divorce over their lifetime.
- The number of out-of-wedlock births is high.
- The number of single-parent families is increasing.

These factors—plus trends toward the fulfillment of individual needs, greater sexual permissiveness, increasing marital equality, a continuing rise in dual-career families, and the continuing trends toward smaller families, child-free families, and single-parent families—have led to an erosion of many "traditional" family patterns and a belief by many that the death of the family, as we know it, is occurring. It really makes no difference whether information is true or false, if a person believes it to be true, then it is true for that person, who will then act on it accordingly. If people accept the traditional, idealized image of the nuclear family, they will try to limit what they perceive to be a breakdown of this type of family structure by opposing things they believe to be encouraging this breakdown:

- The Equal Rights Amendment, since it challenges the traditional gender division of labor

- Sex education, since sexual activity should be limited to marriage
- Laws that make divorce easier, since marriage is supposed to be a lifetime commitment

What is ignored in all this is that the "traditional family" image is one that has changed with changing conditions and that the current model became the standard model because its structure fitted the needs of society at the time. What this implies is that a return to the "traditional family" of the 1950s requires a return to the conditions of that period. To do this, Alvin Toffler (1980) indicates that we must:

1. Freeze all technology in order to maintain a factory-based, mass-production society. Since it is the computer that is the greatest threat to this desire, they must be smashed!
2. Subsidize manufacturing and block the rise of the service sector in the economy. This is necessary since the blue-collar worker is more tradition-minded than the white-collar professional or technical workers in regard to the family.
3. Apply nuclear and other highly centralized energy processes to deal with the energy crisis, since a centralized society is a better fit for the nuclear family and energy systems affect the degree of centralization.
4. Ban the increasingly fractured media, since nuclear families work best where there is national consensus on information and values.
5. Return women to their former position as housewives by reducing their wages to the absolute minimum. In order for the nuclear family to have a nucleus, there must be adults in the home.
6. Slash the wages of younger workers in order to make them more dependent for longer periods on their families. The family will be more nuclearized as a result.
7. Ban contraception and research into reproductive biology. This will lessen the independence of women and extramarital sex—looseners of nuclear ties.
8. Cut the standard of living to pre-1955 levels. This will lessen the ability of unattached people, such as the divorced and working women, to make it on their own.
9. Reattach our increasingly disjointed society. The nuclear family can remain dominant only in a society where changes in the arts, business, education, and so forth lead toward diversity, and individuality are restrained.

In short, in order to return to the "traditional family," it would be necessary to return to the conditions of 1950s by turning back time and freezing history itself.

Of course, this is not possible—nor would most people desire to return to those conditions. This is shown by the fact that only about 7 percent of the population could be defined as a nuclear family—a working husband, a housekeeping wife, and two children.

The predictors of the death of the family ignore the fact that throughout history there has always been a plurality of family forms. The nuclear family has been idealized since about the Civil War, despite the fact that there were other existing family forms and that most people experience several types of family forms throughout their lifetimes. In examining the current family types, it will be noted that it is probable that most people will move from a nuclear family orientation, to a dyadic relationship family, to a nuclear family with children or a childfree family, and certainly to a childfree family as the children grow up and leave home.

What, then, is the future of the family? Does it even have a future? As the nuclear family becomes less dominant, it will be replaced by an assortment of family structures. In short, the "traditional" form of marriage will not retain its monopolistic control, nor is there much to suggest that it will be more enduring in the next century unless there are real changes in the job market, with better jobs and more flexible work schedules. The family structure will change in the future—as it has throughout history. As a result, the marriage of the future will be one of many options, since different people will want different things from their relationships. Marriage will certainly not die, since many of its functions are irreplaceable, but it may be more risky since more options means greater demands—and this may not mean happier marriages

ELEMENTS OF THE NEW "TRADITIONAL SOCIETY"

An Array of Marriages

We speak as if there exists only one type of marriage and yet our vocabulary indicates a multitude of types: The increasing precursor of marriage is cohabitation—a marriage in all but name; newlyweds usually follow from premarital sex or can be the aftermath of cohabitation; since marriage is seemingly becoming a more risky business, more and more marriages have prenuptial agreements, which may also indicate what type of marriage is preferred—sexually open, commune, group; with both partners now working, there comes what has been called the commuter marriage; the seemingly high rate of divorce leads to an increasing number of remarriages; recent legal battles have also awakened us to the fact that there are now same-sex marriages, in fact if not in law.

An Array of Families

The array of marriage types is reflected in an array of family types: family of orientation, single-parent families, blended families, multi-child or single-child families, post-parental families, and, with longer life spans, extended families.

The Childfree Culture

History indicates that society has been moving from a "child-centered" to an "adult-centered" home lifestyle. In the past, fewer people remained single far into adulthood because survival often depended upon having a mate and children. Additionally, relatively few parents lived very long after their youngest children left home. This meant that most households centered around children. The trend toward a childfree culture is the result of a number of factors, but mainly it is because more women choose to forgo parenthood in order to focus on their careers outside of the home. Add to this the fact that working mothers often receive little help with household or child-rearing tasks from their husbands and you have an extra incentive to remain childfree. Other factors affecting the trend toward childlessness are seen in the demographics of this population:

- Generally, the more highly educated a woman is, the more likely she is to be voluntarily childless.
- Voluntary childlessness is much greater in urban areas than in rural areas, and because more people live in urban areas this has a profound effect on birth rates.
- It appears that for some reason, first-born (25 percent) and only children (37 percent) are more likely to remain childlessness.
- Memories of growing up in a household with negative experiences lead many to the decision not to have children.

  Voluntarily childless couples also have different attitudes and values:

- They have negative attitudes toward pregnancy, childbirth, and childrearing.
- They like the freedom from child-care duties.
- They see childlessness liberating and as providing a greater chance for self-fulfillment.
- Compared to their parents, they are more likely to be egalitarian in decision making and in doing housework.
- They are more likely to profess no religious affiliation. (Rogers and Larson 1988)

There are also financial advantages to being childless. Without the added responsibility and stress of raising children, couples are free to concentrate on their careers. Perhaps these factors explain why marriages with children are less satisfactory than those not so encumbered.

It is estimated that about 5 percent of all women remain child free voluntarily, but this figure is expected to rise due to the increase in older women who are still childless. This will result in a doubling of childless women to about 10 or 12 percent. The relatively large figures on childlessness and potential childlessness have resulted in the rise of pronatalist organizations to help counter this trend, despite the fact that the percentage of childfree couples today is actually only about a quarter of what it was in the 1920s, when only about 33 percent of all adults lived at home with children under the age of eighteen.

The Single-Parent Household

Even in those households with children, there has been an explosive growth in the number of single-parent families. Actually, the number of single-parent families in the past five years has grown eleven times faster than the number of dual-parent families. Nearly 1.5 million babies—a record—were born to unmarried women in the past year, an increase of 24 percent since 1970. In the past, this growth would have been due mostly to teenagers having unplanned pregnancies, but that is no longer the case. Births among unwed teens have been declining since the 1970s, from 50 percent of all such births to a current rate of 24 percent. There is now an increasing trend toward unwed motherhood for adult middle-class women. In the past decade, births among these women have doubled. There has also been an increase in adoptions by both single men and single women. As with the increase in childlessness, there are a number of factors involved in this growth of single parents: the large number of separations, divorce, and delay in remarriage. All these factors mean that about 30 percent of American children are being raised by a single parent—a figure that was about the same in 1910. This return to large numbers of single-parent families has led to government efforts to reduce the so-called negative impact of this type of household situation and to the recognition of single-parent families as a market; for example, there are now support groups for single parents such as Single Parents by Choice and Parents Without Partners.

The Aggregate Family

Of course, most divorced people do remarry, and many even remarry after two or more divorces. This has resulted in what might be termed an aggregate household, since it is combining different families into a single household.

With more than 60 percent of divorced persons remarrying, it is estimated that 25 percent of American children are being raised in such households.

The Future

A glance at history indicates that the family may have changed over time, but that it has always existed in some form as people have always mated, procreated, and provided for the socialization of their children. In this sense, the family is here to stay as individuals move through a number of family experiences.

THE GROWTH OF SINGLES

Another factor in the changing family system has been the growth of singles. As noted, history reveals an explosion in the number of singles—those people living alone, outside a family altogether. Today, more than a fifth of all households consist of a single person living alone. It is, in part, this rapid and continuing growth of the singles population that has led to the desire by many for a return to the "good old days" of the 1950s—the golden age of marriage.

One study of singles indicates that they believe this growth in the number of singles is healthy.

The reasons given to support this growth as healthy are:

- It is a step toward sexual freedom.
- It is replacement for marriage.
- It offers an attractive alternative to marriage.
- It provides freedom of choice.

The reasons given to support it as unhealthy are:

- It is a sign of the breakup of the social structure and family unit.
- It marks the disintegration of norms and values that have kept society intact for centuries. (Simenauer and Carroll 1982)

Table 13.1.   Singles Expansion

	Men	Women
Generally Healthy	30%	18%
Very Healthy	6	2
Healthy	24	27
Unhealthy	15	23
Profoundly Unhealthy	3	6

Table 13.2. The Future of Singles

	Men	Women
It will become a significant alternative to marriage	39%	37%
It will be just one of many new alternatives	15	14
It is just a fad	13	18
It is the beginning of a new trend	7	4
It will probably remain the way it is today	22	24
Don't know	4	3

In addition, an increasing number of formerly married people are finding that living solo is preferable. Also, as noted, the rising number of singles has led to the recognition of singles as a market, which has resulted in more services and products designed for their benefit and which has made it easier to be single and has added to its appeal as a lifestyle. Thus, the singles in the study cited previously believe that the future of singles in modern society is positive.

The reasons given in support of these beliefs include:

- Singlehood will never replace marriage.
- It is an alternative in the next few years.
- Marriage and traditional values will ultimately return.
- It will do away with marriage and become the foundation for a society based on complete sexual freedom.
- It will neither grow nor decline. (Simenauer and Carroll 1982)

In contradiction to most of these beliefs, the stereotypes about singles include that among the benefits of being single is that they have the freedom to do what is pleasurable to them. Without family restrictions, they can do whatever they like, have more sexual freedom, live wherever they like, and even work where they want. However, the modern society has created a more cold and impersonal world—one that separates family and friends from personal contact, and so the ideals of singlehood publicized by *Cosmopolitan* and *Playboy* tend to remain fantasies.

WHAT DOES THE FUTURE HOLD?

Longitudinal studies reveal a pattern of discontent with traditional marriage. This includes "a decline over time in the following areas:

- companionship,
- demonstration of affection, including kissing and intercourse,

- common interests,
- common beliefs and values,
- beliefs in the permanence of marriage, and marital adjustment." (Skolnick 1973)

It would appear that marital stability does not necessarily imply marital satisfaction. This discontent with marriage has led to experiments with alternatives to "traditional family" forms:

- Cohabitating couples
- Communal family living
- Group marriage
- Single-parent families
- Open marriages
- Singleness

On the other hand, greater movement toward remaining single long term rather than as a delay in marrying due to education and career would seem to depend on the development of a positive philosophy as to the benefits of singlehood. These benefits include: greater freedom of choice, greater possibilities for self-development, and greater opportunities. The presence of a much larger number of singles would also require the development of more sources for personal and social development, as well as the elimination of biases and discrimination. Probably the greatest need for singles in maintaining their status is support from other singles. A viable lifestyle for singles, then, includes a sense of relatedness so that they can interact meaningfully, the development of patterns of independence, and social acceptance. However, this has not happened and it does not seem to be happening. The answer to two questions asked of the singles component of the sample in the current study confirms the assertion that marriage is still the preferred type of relationship. When asked "Is marriage the normal status of adults?" an overwhelming majority—64 percent—of the sample replied in the affirmative.

Table 13.3.   Being Married: Normal

	Yes	No
Never Married	68%	32%
Divorced	60	40
Total	64	36

Table 13.4.　Five Years from Now (I Will Be)

	Married (and)	Single (and)
Happy	34%	10%
Unhappy	1	12
Affluent	13	12
Fulfilled	5	2
Successful	7	6
Secure	7	4
Have a family	30	24

This positive reply to the statement that marriage is the normal state for adults is confirmed by the answer to the question of what civil status they saw for themselves in their own futures. Far more saw themselves as married and happy (34 percent) than single and happy (10 percent). Although few saw themselves as unhappy in the future (13 percent), far more were among those who saw singlehood in their future than marriage (12 percent versus 1 percent). Also not checked by many were two other replies that marriage was better: More who saw marriage in their future saw themselves as fulfilled versus unfulfilled (5 percent versus 2 percent), and more saw themselves as secure rather than insecure (7 percent versus 4 percent). Interestingly, both those who saw themselves as married and those who saw themselves as single in the future indicated that they expected to have a family. This indicates that the growth in the single-parent family will likely continue.

Despite these positive beliefs about marriage, the singles population has grown to the point where they have become a majority of the population. Will anything now change as a result?

- Will there be changes in where people live, from suburban enclaves to the central cities?
- Will there be changes in employment conditions and requirements since employers will not have to deal with employees' families?
- Will there be changes in architecture, in advertising, in consumption patterns, in education, in political affairs, and in numerous other areas of human endeavors?

Philip Wiley once wrote a book on a similar theme. In alternate chapters he noted how men would survive without any women in the world and how women would survive without any men in the world. This is not a true picture of a society of singles, but it does give a picture of what conditions might be like if responsibilities for close others were no longer applicable. Wiley saw women adjusting to this possibility much more easily than men. Perhaps the same answer could be applied to the idea of a majority of the population being single. Perhaps there will be some changes in reality and some changes in expectations, but despite a majority in numbers, the results of our sample indicate that singles will probably never be considered to be the majority, regardless of their numbers, when it comes to the desire of the population.

Appendix

The Questionnaire

A. Background

1. Gender:
    1) Female _____
    2) Male _____

2. Age:
    1) 20–29 _____
    2) 30–39 _____
    3) 40–49 _____
    4) 50+ _____

3. Education:
    1) Less than high school diploma _____
    2) High school diploma _____
    3) College degree _____
    4) Post-graduate work _____

4. Civil Status:
    1) Never Married _____
    2) Single but cohabitating _____
    3) Married, first time _____
    4) Separated _____
    5) Divorced _____
    6) Widowed _____
    7) Remarried _____

5. Living Arrangements:
    1) Living in a nuclear family _____
    2) Living in a non-related household _____
    3) Living alone _____

6. Do you have children?
    1) Yes_____
    2) No _____

B. Family Background

7. What is the status of your parents?
    1) They are together _____
    2) They are separated _____
    3) They are divorced _____
    4) One is deceased _____
    5) Both are deceased _____

8. How would you describe your parent's relations when they are/were together?
    1) Very loving and stable _____
    2) Generally warm and stable _____
    3) Stable but emotionally cold _____
    4) Generally cold and conflicting _____
    5) Grew up with only one parent _____

9. Were emotions freely expressed in your childhood home?
    1) Both parents generally expressed their emotions openly _____
    2) My mother usually expressed her emotions _____
    3) My father usually expressed his emotions _____
    4) Neither parent expressed emotions openly _____

10. How would you describe your current relations with your parents?
    1) Warm and stable, few conflicts _____
    2) Cool and stable, few conflicts _____
    3) Periods of closeness alternate with fights _____
    4) We fight a lot _____
    5) Currently we are not speaking with each other _____
    6) I am close to only one parent _____

C. Outlooks

11. How satisfied would you say you are most of the time?
    1) Very satisfied _____
    2) Satisfied _____
    3) Neither satisfied or dissatisfied _____
    4) Dissatisfied _____
    5) Very dissatisfied _____

12. Compared to you, how satisfied are your single acquaintances?
    1) Much more satisfied than I _____
    2) Somewhat more satisfied than I _____
    3) About as satisfied as I _____
    4) Somewhat less satisfied than I _____
    5) Much less satisfied than I _____

13. Compared to you, how satisfied are your married acquaintances?
    1) Much more satisfied than I _____
    2) Somewhat more satisfied than I _____
    3) About as satisfied as I _____
    4) Somewhat less satisfied than I _____
    5) Much less satisfied than I _____

14. How satisfied are you with the kind of person you are?
    1) Very satisfied _____
    2) Moderately satisfied _____
    3) Neither satisfied or dissatisfied _____
    4) Moderately dissatisfied _____
    5) Very dissatisfied _____

For each of the following items, indicate how satisfied you have been with it over the past six months.

15. Recognition/Success
    1) Very satisfied _____
    2) Moderately satisfied _____
    3) Slightly satisfied _____
    4) Not at all satisfied _____

16. Your financial situation
    1) Very satisfied _____
    2) Moderately satisfied _____
    3) Slightly satisfied _____
    4) Not at all satisfied _____

17. Your job or primary activity
    1) Very satisfied _____
    2) Moderately satisfied _____
    3) Slightly satisfied _____
    4) Not at all satisfied _____

18. Personal growth and development
    1) Very satisfied _____
    2) Moderately satisfied _____
    3) Slightly satisfied _____
    4) Not at all satisfied _____

19. Being in love
    1) Very satisfied _____
    2) Moderately satisfied _____
    3) Slightly satisfied _____
    4) Not at all satisfied _____

20. Your sex life
    1) Very satisfied _____
    2) Moderately satisfied _____
    3) Slightly satisfied _____
    4) Not at all satisfied _____

21. Your social life
    1) Very satisfied _____
    2) Moderately satisfied _____
    3) Slightly satisfied _____
    4) Not at all satisfied _____

22. Your friends
    1) Very satisfied _____
    2) Moderately satisfied _____
    3) Slightly satisfied _____
    4) Not at all satisfied _____

D. Lifestyles

23. How often do you go out socially?
    1) Less than once a week _____
    2) Once a week _____
    3) Twice a week _____
    4) Three times a week _____
    5) Four or more times a week _____

24. Where do you go out socially? (rank all those that apply)
    1) Movie _____
    2) Nightclub/bar _____
    3) Restaurant _____
    4) A sporting event _____
    5) Theater/concert _____
    6) Visit friends _____
    7) Visit relatives _____
    8) Other (indicate) _____

On the average, how many hours per week do you spend on the following activities:

25. Doing volunteer activities? 0 1 2 3 4 5 more _____

26. Time spent with friends? 0 1 2 3 4 5 more _____

27. Doing leisure activities? 0 1 2 3 4 5 more _____

28. Time spent with relatives? 0 1 2 3 4 5 more _____

29. Doing religious activities? 0 1 2 3 4 5 more _____

30. Time watching television? 0 1 2 3 4 5 more _____

31. How does your lifestyle make you feel?
    1) Very happy _____
    2) Moderately happy _____
    3) Okay _____
    4) Moderately unhappy _____
    5) Very unhappy _____

32. Do you get a lot of fun out of life?
    1) Yes _____ 2) No _____

33 Do you feel conspicuous dining alone in a restaurant?
    1) Yes_____ 2) No_____

34. Would you hesitate to attend a social event unescorted?
    1) Yes_____ 2) No_____

35. Have you joined social organizations to find companionship?
    1) Yes_____ 2) No_____

36. Do you feel depressed when you are alone?
    1) Yes_____ 2) No_____

37. Do you equate living alone with a state of unhappiness?
    1) Yes_____ 2) No_____

38. Do you think there is something deviant about choosing to live alone?
    1) Yes_____ 2) No_____

Next section for the unmarried only! If married, go to question 54

E. Being Single

39. I have friends that understand me.
    1) Rarely true _____
    2) Sometimes true _____
    3) Often true _____
    4) Mostly true _____

40. I cannot discuss my problems with anyone.
    1) Rarely true _____
    2) Sometimes true _____
    3) Often true _____
    4) Mostly true _____

41. There is no one with whom to share my happy and sad moments.
    1) Rarely true _____
    2) Sometimes true _____
    3) Often true _____
    4) Mostly true _____

42. Most people are alone and friendless.
    1) Rarely true _____
    2) Sometimes true _____
    3) Often true _____
    4) Mostly true _____

43. Rank in importance the places you generally meet the opposite sex.
    1) Bars _____
    2) Blind dates _____
    3) Church _____
    4) Singles' organizations _____
    5) School _____
    6) Web sites _____
    7) Work _____
    8) Other (Please specify) _____

44. Rank in importance the attributes you seek in a companion.
    1) Being healthy _____
    2) Confidence _____
    3) Consideration _____
    4) Financial well-being _____
    5) Humor _____
    6) Looks _____
    7) Sociability _____
    8) Other (Please specify) _____

45. Would you accept a date with someone you are not attracted to?
    1) Yes _____ 2) No _____

46. Would you engage in intimate relations with a date to avoid losing his or her attention?
    1) Yes _____ 2) No _____

47. Do you believe that you have to be "in love" or care for someone deeply before you have sexual relations?
    1) Yes _____ 2) No _____

48. Do you believe that something is wrong with those not married because they are not married?
    1) Yes _____* 2) No _____
    * Why? (Explain why) _____

49. For someone over 30, being married is the normal way to be.
    1) Yes _____ 2) No _____

50. What are society's images of unmarried people as compared to married people? (Check all that apply)
    1) They have more fun _____
    2) They are happier _____
    3) They have had more sexual partners _____
    4) They have greater sexual satisfaction _____
    5) They are more immoral _____
    6) They are more irresponsible _____
    7) They are lonelier _____
    8) They are less satisfied with their life _____
    9) Other (Please specify) _____

51. Why are you not married? (Rank answers that apply)
    1) You are having too much fun _____
    2) You love your freedom and privacy _____
    3) It never seemed like a desirable option _____
    4) You never found the right person _____
    5) You lost the right person _____
    6) Something is wrong with you _____
    7) Other (Please specify) _____

52. Do you think that being unmarried will be a permanent status for you?
    1) Yes _____ 2) No _____

53. Five years from now, I will be: (Check all that applicable)

Married and	Unmarried and
1) Happy _____	2) _____
3) Unhappy _____	4) _____
5) Affluent _____	6) _____
7) Fulfilled _____	8) _____
9) Successful _____	10) _____
11) Secure _____	12) _____
13) Have a Family _____	14) _____
15) Other: Fill in _____	16) _____

F. Myself

54. Which of the following has been true of you in the past month? (Check all that apply)
    1) Constant worry/anxiety _____
    2) Crying spells _____
    3) Feelings of depression _____
    4) Feelings of worthlessness _____
    5) Frequent headaches _____
    6) Insomnia _____
    7) Irrational fears _____
    8) Lack of interest in sex _____
    9) Often feeling guilty _____
    10) Often feeling lonely _____
    11) Other (Please specify) _____

55. How often do you use intoxicating substances?
    1) Every day _____
    2) Several times a week _____
    3) Once a week or so _____
    4) Once or twice a month _____
    5) Rarely _____
    6) Never _____

56. How many sexual partners do you think most people of your age, gender, and marital status have had?
    1) None _____
    2) 1 _____
    3) 2–5 _____
    4) 6–10 _____
    5) 11–20 _____
    6) More than 20 _____

57. With how many partner(s) have you had sexual intercourse?
    1) None _____
    2) 1 _____
    3) 2–5 _____
    4) 6–10 _____
    5) 11–20 _____
    6) More than 20 _____

58. On average, during the last six months, how often have you had
sexual intercourse?
1) Never or almost never _____
2) Once or twice a month _____
3) Once or twice a week _____
4) Several times a week _____
5) Daily or more often _____

59. In general, how satisfied are you with your sex life?
1) Very satisfied _____
2) Satisfied _____
3) Neutral _____
4) Dissatisfied _____
5) Very dissatisfied _____

60. What was your total personal income before taxes?
1) Less than $20,000 _____
2) $20,001-$ 30,000 _____
3) $30,001-$ 40,000 _____
4) $40,001-$ 50,000 _____
5) $50,001 or more _____

61. If you could change lives with another person that you know, would you
do it?
1) Yes _____ 2) No _____
Why? _____
Is that person?
1) Married _____ 2) Unmarried _____

62. Comments you would like to make:

_____
_____
_____

Thank you!

Bibliography

Ackerman, N. (1972). In H. Hart (ed.), *Marriage: For and Against*. New York: Hart.

Adams, M. (1976). *Single Blessedness: Observations on the Single Status in Married Society*. New York: Basic Books.

Bader, R. (1981). *Do Marriage Preparation Programs Really Help?* Milwaukee: National Council on Family Relations.

Bane. M. J. (1976). *Here to Stay: American Families in the Twentieth Century*. New York: Basic Books.

Barkas, J. L. (1980). *Single in America*. New York: Atheneum.

Bell, R. R. (1972). In H. Hart (ed.), *Marriage: For and Against*. New York: Hart, pp. 78–91.

Bernard, J. (1979). "Marriage: His and Hers." In L. Cargan and J. Ballantine (eds.), *Sociological Footprints*. Belmont, CA: Wadsworth.

———. (1982). *The Future of Marriage*. New York: Bantam.

Bird, C. (1972). In H. Hart (ed.), *Marriage: For and Against*. New York: Hart, pp. 168–86.

Braito, R., and D. Anderson. (1978). "Singles and Aging." Paper presented at the Society for the Study of Social Problems Conference, San Francisco.

Brody, J. E. (1979, May 8). "Marriage Is Good for Health and Longevity, Studies Say." *New York Times*.

Brooks, A. (1981, May 24). "Single at Midlife: Divorce Suburban Style." *New York Times Magazine*, 30–31, 66–70.

Brown, H. G. (2003). "The Newest Glamour Girl of Our Times." In H. Sigerman (ed.), *Columbia History of American Women since 1941*. New York: Columbia University Press, pp. 171–74.

Chudacoff, H. P. (1999). *The Age of the Bachelor: Creating an American Subculture*. Princeton, NJ: Princeton University Press.

Clanton, G. (1984). "Social Forces and the Changing Family." In L. A. Kirk-
endall and A. E. Gravatt (eds.), *Marriage and the Family in the Year 2020*.
Amherst, NY: Prometheus Books.

Cohen, B. L., and I-S. Lee. (1979). "A Catalogue of Risks." *Health Physics* 36,
707–22.

Coleman, D. (1993). "Marriage Research Reveals Ingredients of Happiness in
Perspectives." In K. Scotler and M. Warren (eds.), *Marriage: A Reader*. New
York: Oxford University Press.

Coombs, R. (1991, November). "A Healthier Marriage." *American Demographics*,
40–48.

Coontz, S. (1992). *The Way We Never Were: American Families and the Nostalgia
Trap*. New York: BasicBooks.

———. (2006, June 5). "Three 'Rules' That Don't Apply." *Newsweek*, 49.

Cox, F. D. (2002). *Human Intimacy: Marriage, the Family, and Its Meaning*. 9th ed.
Belmont, CA: Thomson.

Deegan, D. Y. (1969). *The Stereotype of the Single Woman in American Novels: A
Social Study with Implications for the Education of Women*. New York: Octagon.

deGrazia, S. (1964). *Of Time, Work, and Leisure*. New York: Twentieth Century
Fund.

Ehrenreich, B. (1983). *The Hearts of Men: American Dreams and the Flight from
Commitment*. Garden City, NY: Anchor Books/Doubleday.

Ehrenreich, B., and D. English. (1978). *For Her Own Good: 150 Years of the
Experts' Advice to Women*. Garden City, NY: Anchor Press.

French, M. (1978). *The Women's Room*. New York: Jove.

Friedan, B. (1963). *The Feminine Mystique*. New York: W. W. Norton.

Gallup, G. (1976, June 22). "Pollster Visits Nation's 'Barometer.'" *Dayton Journal Herald*.

Galston W. A. (1996, Summer). "Divorce American Style." *Public Interest* 124,
12–26.

Glenn, N. D., and C. N. Weaver. (1988). "The Changing Relationship of Marital Status to Reported Happiness." *Journal of Marriage and the Family* 50,
317–24.

Glueck, B. (1949). "Why Are You Single?" 199–200. In H. Holland (ed.), *Are You
Emotionally Mature?* New York: Farrar, Straus.

Gordon, S. (1976). *Lonely in America*. New York: Simon & Schuster.

Gordon, T. (1994). *Single Women: On the Margins?* New York: New York University Press.

Gove, W. R. (1973). "Sex, Marital Status, and Psychiatric Treatment: A
Research Note." *Social Forces* 58, 89–93.

Hetherington, E. M., and J. Kelly. (2002). *For Better or Worse*. New York: W. W.
Norton.

Hiltz, S. R. (1981). "Widowhood: A Roleless Role." In P. Stein, *Singlelife*. New
York: St. Martin's Press.

Hite, S. (1995, March/April). "Bringing Democracy." MS 5, 54–61.

———. (1976). *The Hite Report*. New York: Dell.

Holland, B. (1992). *One's Company: Reflections on Living Alone*. New York: Ballantine Books.

Hunt, H. (1974). *Sexual Behavior in the 1970s*. Chicago: Playboy Press.

Kando, T. M. (1975). *Leisure and Popular Culture in Transition*. St. Louis: Mosby.

Kinsey, A. C., W. B. Pomeroy, and C. E. Martin. (1948). *Sexual Behavior in the Human Male*. Philadelphia: W. B. Saunders.

————. (1953). *Sexual Behavior in the Human Female*. Philadelphia: Saunders.

Langman, S. (1987). "Social Stratification." In M. B. Sussman and S. K. Steinmetz (eds.), *Handbook of Marriage and the Family*. New York: Plenum.

Laumann, E. O., and Y. Youm. (2000). "Sexual Expression in America." In E. O. Laumann and R. T. Michael (eds.), *Sex, Love, and Health in America: Private Choices and Public Policies*. Chicago: University of Chicago Press.

Larson, J. H. (1988, January). "The Marriage Quiz: College Students' Beliefs in Selected Myths about Marriage and Family." *Family Relations* 27, 3–11.

Lear, M. W. (1980, November). "Loneliness: More Common Than the Common Cold." *Redbook*, 33, 202, 204, 206.

Libby, R. (1978). "Creative Singlehood as a Sexual Lifestyle: Beyond Marriage as a Rite of Passage." In B. I. Murstein (ed.), *Exploring Intimate Life Styles*. New York: Springer.

Moneymaker, J., and F. Montanino. (1978). "The New Sexual Morality: A Society Comes of age." In J. M. Henslin and E. Sagarin (eds.), *The Sociology of Sex: An Introductory Reader*. New York: Schocken.

Murstein, B. I. (1974). *Love, Sex, and Marriage through the Ages*. New York: Springer.

Myers, L. (1977). "Marriage, Honesty, and Personal Growth." In R. W. Libby and R. N. Whitehurst (eds.), *Marriage and Alternatives: Exploring Intimate Relationships*. Glenview, IL: Scott, Foresman.

Myers, L., and G. Leggett. (1972, February). "A New View of Adultery," 52–62.

Nass, G. D., R. W. Libby, and M. Fisher. (1981). *Sexual Choices: An Introduction to Human Sexuality*. Belmont, CA: Wadsworth Health Sciences Division.

Newsweek. (1973, July 16). "Games Singles Play," 3.

————. (2006, April 20). "Sex and Love: The New World," 50–54.

New York Times. (2006, July 17). "Who Needs a Husband?" 19.

Nuta, V. R. (1981, September). "Single-Parent Children: What Can You Expect?" *The Single Parent*, 21–25.

O'Brien, P. (1973). *The Woman Alone*. New York: Quadrangle.

Parkes, C. M. (1972). *Bereavement: Studies of Grief in Adult Life*. New York: International Universities Press.

Rawlings, E. (1966). "Family Situations of Married and Never Married Males." *Journal of Marriage and Family* 28:4, 485–90.

Reiss, I. (1972). *Readings on the Family System*. New York: Holt, Rinehart and Winston.

Reiss, I. L. (1976). *Family Systems in America*. Hinsdale, IL: Dryden Press.

Rogers, L. K., and J. H. Larson. (1988). "Voluntary Childlessness: A Review of the Literature and a Model of the Childlessness Decision." *Family Perspective* 22:1, 43–58.

Rosenblatt, R. (1977, March). "The Self as a Sybarite." *Harpers*, 12–14.

Ross, C. E., J. Mirosky, and K. Goldsteen. (1990). "The Impact of the Family on Health: Decade in Review." *Journal of Marriage and Family* 52, 1061.

Ruben, H. L. (1986, August). "Adultery, Infidelity, Cheating." *New Woman*.

Rubenstein, C., and P. Shaver. (1982). *In Search of Intimacy: Surprising Conclusions from a Nationwide Survey on Loneliness & What to Do about It*. New York: Delacorte.

Rubin, Z. (1979, October). "Seeking a Cure for Loneliness." *Psychology Today* 82, 85–86, and 89–90.

Saxton, L. (1977). *The Individual, Marriage, and the Family*. 3rd ed. Belmont, CA: Wadsworth.

Schwartzberg, N., K. Berliner, and D. Jacob. *Single in a Married World*. New York: W.W. Norton, 1995.

Simenauer, J., and D. Carroll. (1982). *Singles: The New Americans*. New York: Simon & Schuster.

Skolnick, A. S., and J. H. Skolnick. (1977). *Family in Transition: Rethinking Marriage, Sexuality, Child Rearing, and Family Organization*. 2nd ed. Boston: Little, Brown.

Smith-Lovin, L. (2006). *Social Psychology*. Malden, MA: Blackwell.

Somers, A. R. (1979, April 27). "Marital Status and Use of Health Services." *Journal of the American Medical Association* 241, 1818–72.

South, S., and K. Lloyd. (1995). "A Longitudinal Study of Marital Problems and Subsequent Divorce." *American Sociological Review* 60, 21–32.

Stein, P. (1976). *Single*. Englewood Cliffs, NJ: Prentice-Hall.

Tavris, C. (1978, February). "40,000 Men Tell about Their Sexual Behavior, Their Fantasies, Their Ideal Women, and Their Wives." *Redbook*, 111–13, 176–81.

Toffler, A. (1980). *The Third Wave*. New York: Morrow.

Trollope, A. (1876, 1996). *The Prime Minister*. New York: Penguin Classics.

U.S. Census Bureau. (1999). Statistical Abstract of the United States. Washington D.C.

U.S. News & World Report. (1977, January 31). "The Way Singles Are Changing Us," 59–60.

Waite, L. J., and M. Gallagher. (2000). *The Case for Marriage: Why Married People Are Happier, Healthier, and Better Off Financially*. New York: Doubleday.

Wallerstein, J. (2000). *Children of Divorce*. New York: Hyperion.

Wallerstein, J., J. Lewis, and S. Blakeslee. (2000). *The Unexpected Legacy of Divorce: A 25-Year Landmark Study*. New York: Hyperion.

Wylie, P. (1951). *The Disappearance*. New York: Rinehart.

Index

About the Author

Leonard Cargan is professor emeritus of sociology at Wright State University in Dayton, Ohio. He is the author of several books, including *Being Single: Myths and Realities* (2007), *Doing Social Research* (2007), *Sociological Footprints* (with Jeanne H. Ballantine, 2006), *Marriages and Families: Changing Relationships* (1991), and *Marriage and Family: Coping with Change* (1985).